ALL YOUR WORD PROBLEMS SOLVED

Crushing Standardized Test Math

for the GMAT®, GRE®, SAT®, PSAT/NMSQT®, and ACT®

All Your Word Problems Solved, 1st edition

13-digit International Standard Book Number: 978-1-7320510-0-3

Copyright © 2017 by Adeptation

Notes:

GMAT® is a registered trademark of the *Graduate Management Admissions Council*, which neither sponsors nor endorses this product.

GRE® is a registered trademark of the *Educational Testing Service*, which neither sponsors nor is affiliated in any way with this product.

SAT® is a trademark registered by the *College Board*, which was not involved in the production of, and does not endorse, this product.

PSAT/NMSQT® is a registered trademark of the *College Board* and the *National Merit Scholarship Corporation*, which are not affiliated with, and do not endorse, this product.

ACT® is a registered trademark of *ACT, Inc.*, which neither sponsors nor endorses this product.

Table of Contents

Chapter 1 Welcome! 1-8

Chapter 2 How to Use These Materials 2-10

Pick up a pencil and follow along with the examples.........................2-10

Learn principles & techniques, not step-by-step instructions 2-10

Use a structured-but-flexible approach..2-11

Use words, units, etc. to give numbers meaning...............................2-12

Learn equations in words, not letters 2-13

Chapter 3 Approaching Math Differently 3-16

Chapter 4 The Short List of Things You Should Memorize 4-19

The times tables, up to 15 by 15 4-19

Perfect squares & perfect cubes 4-19

Instantly recognize the powers of 2 4-20

Fractions, decimals, and percents..4-21

Chapter 5 Divisibility Rules 5-23

Group 1: Divisibility rules for 2, 4, and 8 (powers of 2) 5-23

Group 2: Divisibility Rules for 5 and 10 5-24

Group 3: Divisibility rules for 7 and 11 5-24

Group 4: Divisibility rules for 3 and 9 (powers of 3).........................5-24

Group 5: Rules for 6, 12, and 24 (powers of 2 times a 3) 5-25

Chapter 6 Mental Math Techniques 6-26

Principles of mental math for standardized tests..............................6-26

Tips for calculating an exact answer, more efficiently 6-27

Tips for estimating the answer, efficiently & decisively 6-31

Other mental math tricks...6-33

Chapter 7 Number Properties.. 7-34

Key terminology to master about number properties.........................7-34

Choosing test cases for number properties questions 7-35

Approach to answering number properties questions 7-36

Other terminology you need to know 7-36

Number properties: odds & evens..7-40

Number properties: positives & negatives.......................................7-41

Skill builder: how to test if a number is prime 7-42

How to succeed on number properties questions 7-43

Chapter 8 Translating Words to Math 8-45

Rules & tips for translating words to math 8-46

Math clue words and what they mean 8-47

Constraint clue words and what they mean.. 8-48

Geometry clue words and what they mean 8-49

Chapter 9 Linear Equations.. 9-55

Practical applications of linear equations & functions 9-55

Graphing a linear equation in standard form 9-56

The slope of a line represents the rate 9-56

The Y-Intercept represents the beginning value 9-56

The value of X represents the quantity or time used 9-57

The value of Y represents the ending value or total 9-57

Relating linear equations & functions to real life 9-58

Chapter 10 Exponential Equations 10-64

Practical applications of exponential equations 10-64

Graphing an exponential equation in standard form 10-65

Relating exponential equations & functions to real life............................ 10-65

Special cases: doubling & half-life formulas 10-66

The doubling formula.. 10-66

The half-life formula 10-67

Special cases: future value & the rule of 70 (or 72) 10-67

The future value formula (for a one-time payment) 10-67

The rule of 70 (alternative = rule of 72)... 10-68

Chapter 11 Dimensional Analysis.. 11-69

What is dimensional analysis?... 11-69

Refresher: metric units of measure.. 11-69

Refresher: metric prefixes 11-70

Rules & tips for dealing with units... 11-71

Chapter 12 Ratios & Proportions.. 12-76

Ratios & proportions 12-76

Translating words to math in ratio problems 12-76

Part-to-part vs. part-to-whole ratios 12-77

Adjusting ratios... 12-78

Solving multi-part ratios... 12-80

Chapter 13 Word Problems with Systems of Equations................................ 13-82

Some word problems require a system of equations 13-82

Types of word problems w/ systems of equations 13-82

Chapter 14 Intro to the Tables & Labels Strategy 14-87

Chapter 15 Work-Rate Word Problems 15-88

    Practical applications of work-rate problems 15-88

    How to approach work-rate problems: tables & labels 15-88

        Use tables to organize information 15-88

        Use labels to add meaning to numbers 15-89

Chapter 16 Distance-Rate Word Problems 16-98

    How to approach distance-rate problems: 2 methods................................... 16-98

        Diagramming: draw diagrams to visualize information 16-98

        Use tables to organize information 16-101

        Use labels to add meaning to numbers 16-102

Chapter 17 Mixture & Dilution Word Problems.. 17-107

    Recognizing a mixture vs. a dilution problem 17-107

    Using tables & labels for mixture & dilution problems.................................. 17-108

        Use tables to organize information 17-108

        Use labels to add meaning to numbers 17-108

    Alternative approaches... 17-116

Chapter 18 Retail Math – Percent Of vs. Percent Change 18-117

    Essential formulas & relationships for retail math 18-117

    Handling successive percent changes 18-120

Chapter 19 Interest Problems 19-128

    Essential formulas & relationships for interest 19-128

Chapter 20 Profit, Revenue, & Cost Problems... 20-134

    Essential terms & formulas for profit, revenue & cost 20-134

Chapter 21 Coordinate Geometry 21-140

    What is coordinate geometry?.. 21-140

    Coordinate geometry basics: plotting points in the XY-plane 21-140

    Finding the distance between two points in the XY-plane 21-143

    Linear equations in the XY-plane 21-145

Chapter 22 Geometry Shapes & Solids 22-148

    Lines & angles... 22-148

    Polygons 22-149

    Circles.. 22-158

    Solids 22-162

Chapter 23 Geometry Complex Figures 23-164

    Displacement method from science class 23-164

Displacement method applied to Geometry questions 23-165

Chapter 24 Parabolas.. 24-172

    Parabolas: multiple forms of the same equation 24-172

        Parabolas: intercept form... 24-173

        Parabolas: vertex form 24-174

Chapter 25 Probability 25-178

    Thinking through the logic: words first, math second 25-181

    Examples: coin flips... 25-183

    Examples: number cubes (dice) 25-185

    Examples: mutually exclusive events 25-188

    Examples: casino games & lotteries 25-190

Chapter 26 Permutations & Combinations.. 26-193

    Which approach do I use, when? 26-193

    What is the formula for permutations? For combinations?.................. 26-194

    Comparing permutations & combinations.................................... 26-195

    Things to watch out for with permutations & combinations problems........ 26-196

    Exploring variations of combinations questions........................... 26-197

    Thinking through the logic: words first, math second 26-197

    Pizza menu – use for all problems in this sub-section.................... 26-199

Chapter 27 Statistics & Weighted Averages 27-206

    What are the measures of centrality?..................................... 27-207

    What is the normal distribution? What do I need to know?............... 27-208

    Weighted averages 27-210

    Percentiles, deciles, quintiles, and quartiles 27-211

    Box-and-whisker plots 27-213

Chapter 28 Functions & Symbol Problems 28-217

    Functions & symbol problems are just equations 28-217

    Functions 28-217

        Understanding the domain & range of a function 28-218

        Identifying the domain of a function 28-218

        Identifying the range of a function 28-221

        Multiple functions, nested functions & PEMDAS 28-222

    Symbol problems 28-224

        Multiple Symbol Problems, nested symbol problems & PEMDAS.......... 28-225

Chapter 29 Sequences & Series Part 1 29-226

    General sequence & series notation 29-226

All Your Word Problems Solved

What kind of sequence is it? 29-227

Finding the sum of an arithmetic sequence 29-230

Word problems related to sequences & series 29-236

Chapter 30 Patterns, Logic & Reasoning 30-242

Clues to use patterns, logic, and reasoning 30-242

How can you approach these questions?..................................... 30-242

Chapter 31 Triple Venn Diagrams 31-251

Understanding the triple venn diagram.. 31-251

Visualizing the triple venn diagram 31-252

Solving the triple venn diagram.. 31-253

Chapter 32 Closing 32-256

Word Problems. Does even thinking about solving word problems in math make you feel tense, anxious, confused, or frustrated? You're not alone. Few topics in school cause as much cold-blooded panic as the dreaded word problem.

Most **high school students** – even ones who excel in their math classes – find word problems on the **PSAT/NMSQT, SAT, and ACT** tough to solve consistently and efficiently.

Adult students preparing for the **GMAT or GRE** find word problems just as daunting as they were in high school. These students find it challenging to quickly re-learn what feels like the entirety of the 6th through 11th/12th grade math curriculum.

Most major publishers only **briefly** explain word problems and demonstrate **simple** examples in their study guides, then challenge students to make the leap to solving **very difficult** **practice problems**. Even students in test prep courses offered by these major publishers remain confused and lacking confidence about how to approach word problems.

How do I know this?

Because I have **extensive** teaching, tutoring, and academic coaching experience, developed in parallel with my corporate experience.

The author's teaching, tutoring, and academic coaching experience includes not only standardized test prep, but also a vast array of math-intensive courses at the college, graduate, and MBA levels.

In other words, **this author has seen a lot of people do a lot of math** over the years and has accumulated deep insight about **why some students struggle with understanding and retaining concepts, why good students make mistakes,** and how to help you **get the right answer on the first try**.

My teaching, tutoring, and academic coaching experience spans all these subjects:

- College Admissions Test Prep for: PSAT/NMSQT, SAT, and ACT
- Graduate Admissions Test Prep for: GMAT and GRE
- Math: Algebra 1, Algebra 2, Geometry, Trigonometry, Precalculus, Quantitative Reasoning
- Economics: AP, IB, College, Graduate & MBA Microeconomics and Macroeconomics, with algebra and with calculus
- Finance: College & MBA finance courses
- Accounting: College & MBA Financial Accounting, Managerial Accounting
- Statistics & Related Courses: College, Graduate & MBA Statistics, Market Research Methods, Research Methods for Psychology
- Business & Marketing: Decision Models, Consumer Behavior, Microsoft Excel

What makes this book dramatically more useful than most other books out on the market?

- The **accumulated insight** from teaching both classes and individuals such a broad range of subjects to hundreds of students of varying ages and ability levels. The methods presented in this book are the ones which work the most consistently for the broadest range of students. Every section of this book has been tested with students aged 15 to 40+ preparing for the most common standardized college and graduate admissions tests, including the PSAT/NMSQT, SAT, ACT, GMAT and GRE.

- The **simplification** of approaches and formulas, plus intentional communication in ways which make things **sticky and memorable**, so you recall it on test day. Most authors of math books explain things in a very academic way, which can be both frustrating and not particularly memorable. I want you to gain an appreciation for math and understand how it relates to your everyday life, so that you learn that **word problems are much more intuitive than they seem at first**. Occasionally you will find some parts of this book are repetitive; that's intentional to reinforce the connections you should be making across topics and/or approaches. Other parts are highly detailed, and feel dense; that's also intentional, so you can prepare yourself for the seemingly infinite variations and complexities a good test question can introduce into an otherwise familiar topic.

- The **depth of explanation** and **progressive build-up of example difficulty** so there's no big jump from examples to practice problems found in your test's Official Guide. Enough variations in the wording to get you prepared for your test.

- **Written entirely by a single author**, with strategies which are cross-referenced throughout the book, so you can easily refer to a topic previously covered.

All Your Word Problems Solved serves as a valuable supplement to whichever test-specific study guide you prefer. This book will help you learn to systematically decode math word problems, set up the correct equations, organize your scratch work to "error-proof" yourself, and efficiently arrive at the right answer, every time.

In this book, you will learn a set of **structured-but-flexible approaches** which can be **combined in different ways** to solve even the hardest questions on your standardized tests.

You'll also find **refresher content** and a **variety of examples for word problems related to concepts in Algebra 1, Algebra 2 and Geometry**.

You'll find out how to recognize, approach, and solve word problems of many types: linear increase & decrease, exponential growth & decay, ratios, proportions, age problems, work-rate, distance-rate, systems of equations, mixtures, dilutions, interest, profit, percent change, complex geometric figures, probability, permutations & combinations, weighted averages, sequences, patterns, functions and symbol problems.

Whether you are using these materials to learn certain math concepts for the first time or to relearn them for success on one of the major standardized tests, you will benefit from understanding a core set of principles which will accelerate your learning.

PICK UP A PENCIL AND FOLLOW ALONG WITH THE EXAMPLES

You do not learn to ride a bike by reading about it.

You do not learn to swim by reading about it.

How will you learn to solve word problems? Certainly not by reading about it.

The way to get good at math is to pick up a pencil and do math.

So, grab a graph paper notebook and a pencil, and follow along with the examples throughout this book. Resist the temptation to read ahead. Push yourself to stop and think through each step, one step at a time.

Re-read sections as needed, to ensure you understand the concepts, formulas, and relationships presented.

LEARN PRINCIPLES & TECHNIQUES, NOT STEP-BY-STEP INSTRUCTIONS

Being good at math is a lot like being good at cooking.

- With cooking:
  - If you learn a new <u>recipe</u>, then you will be familiar with those ingredients, those tools, and those ingredients. You have learned how to be successful with making <u>one thing</u> but probably will <u>need a new recipe to make something different</u>. Result? You know 1 recipe.

  - If you learn a new <u>principle or technique</u>, then you can apply this principle or technique flexibly to similar ingredients and similar tools. You have learned how to be successful doing <u>one thing</u> and can probably <u>figure out how to apply this principle or technique to make something different</u>. Result? You know 1 recipe, with a bunch of possible variations.

  - If you learn a <u>set of principles or techniques</u>, which you can <u>combine with one another in different ways</u>, then you can cook just about anything!

  - The best chefs start with an idea for the ingredients and techniques, but quickly adjust as needed based on what ingredients and tools are on hand in the kitchen and the time allowed.

  - For example, you could learn one specific recipe to make pot roast in the slow cooker. Or, if you learn principles and use a template which requires a 3-pound piece of boneless meat, 1 cup of liquid, 1 pound of vegetables, plus seasonings, all slow-cooked for 8-9 hours, then you can make **endless variations** by mixing-and-matching:

All Your Word Problems Solved

- Meat = beef, pork, turkey, etc.
- Liquid = red wine, white wine, stock, broth, apple cider, etc.
- Vegetables = any combination of carrots, celery, potatoes, parsnips, onions, leeks, etc.
- Seasonings = sage, thyme, rosemary, garlic, a premade mix, etc.

- With math:
  - If you put your effort into learning a specific step-by-step way to solve a problem, then you can probably solve the same problem, stated in the same way, with new numbers. Result? A modest improvement in your math success.
  - If you put your effort into learning a **structured-but-flexible approach** to solve one problem, then you can probably figure out how to apply this disciplined but flexible approach to solve a wider variety of problems. Result? A step-change improvement in your math success.
  - If you then realize that everything in these materials is intended to convey a **set** of structured-but-flexible approaches, which can be **combined with one another in different ways**, then you can solve just about <u>any</u> problem! Result? A mindset shift and a dramatic improvement in your math success.
  - The best problem solvers start by choosing an approach and applying efficient techniques, but quickly adjust as needed based on what information is given in the problem and the time allowed.

There are always **multiple paths to an answer**. Sometimes several approaches could work. The recommended approaches you'll find in these materials have been designed and tested to work for a wide variety of people with varying abilities, including:

- Students who love math, those who hate it, and those who fear it
- Students with learning disabilities, such as dyslexia and dyscalculia, or attention and/or processing disorders, such as ADHD or weak spatial-reasoning abilities

*So, **you** are highly likely to succeed if you practice using the strategies in these materials!*

USE A STRUCTURED-BUT-FLEXIBLE APPROACH

When it comes to Problem Solving, <u>**your job**</u> **is to decompose the hard problems into a set of simpler, solvable parts**. How do you learn to become consistently successful with Problem Solving?

- The **organization of your scratch work matters**, more than you might realize. Countless careless errors are made due to poor organization, mis-copied equations, accidental changes of positive or negative signs, and/or poor handwriting.
  - **Use graph paper**. The gridlines help you line up the different components of each equation, and to visually distinguish numerators from denominators, numbers from exponents, and so on.

o Write formulas using the **Words First, Math Second approach**, and allow **breathing room between the terms.** A bit of white space between each term helps your brain process the distinct components of the formula instead of seeing it as one big blob. The **Tables and Labels approach** combines the approaches above with a structure for organizing the all the pieces of info.

o Place each value (number) from the problem underneath the word it represents, using the gridlines to maintain vertical alignment.

o **Stack fractions to facilitate cancelling** out common factors. Write them:

Like this: $\frac{1}{4}$ Not like this: ¼

- **Practice Translating Words to Math.**

  o The section **Translating Words to Math** serves as the foundation of the overall approach covered in all these materials, so start there.

  o Then, the other sections build upon this foundation and add concept-specific information for specific types of problems, such as Ratios & Proportions, Work-Rate problems, Distance-Rate problems, Probability, Geometry, etc.

- **Learn the keywords, clues, and signal phrases** which help you recognize which concept(s) a word problem is testing.

USE WORDS, UNITS, ETC. TO GIVE NUMBERS MEANING

Numbers, when detached from meaning, will do whatever you tell them to do. A computer or calculator will only calculate the right output if you give it the right inputs.

Your value, as a current or future college-educated professional, comes from knowing how to correctly input numeric information into the computer or calculator. It does not come from being told exactly what to do and how to do it.

- This skill, called Problem Solving, applies to so much more than just math.

- The maximum height of your career "ceiling" will be, in large part, determined by the extent to which you are willing to learn how to problem solve and figure out how to do things you do not already know how to do.

- Would you like to have high earning potential and get frequent promotions? Then you must learn to think flexibly and efficiently to solve problems others cannot solve.

Thus, you should view your calculator as the last step or last resort, not the first.

Also, many of the wrong answer choices on multiple-choice tests are the result of errors in logic, not calculation. Therefore, your success on standardized tests is much more dependent on finding a good approach and knowing how to put the right pieces of information in the right place, and much less dependent on your ability to calculate something precisely.

The following strategies are designed to help you **attach meaning to numbers**:

- **Translating Words to Math**
- **Learning Equations in Words**, **Not Letters**
- **Choosing Meaningful Variables**
- **Tables & Labels Approach** (for Work-Rate, Distance-Rate, Mixtures, etc.)
- **No Naked Numbers** (always write the units)
- **Dimensional Analysis** (how to convert the units)

Even better, if your approach and set up of the problem is correct, then the calculations will generally be straightforward.

Sometimes, you will not even need to calculate – you will be able to use another technique called **Estimate-and-Eliminate**.

LEARN EQUATIONS IN WORDS, NOT LETTERS

Why should you learn, study, and practice equations in **Words**, **Not Letters**?

- Words are **easier to learn**, **retain**, **and recall** than variables.
- Words make it **easier to understand what information goes where** in the formula.
  - Different knowledge domains or course subjects use different variations of the same essential formulas.
  - For example, the **exponential growth formula** appears in biology, chemistry, physics, finance & time value of money, and economics. But, each subject uses a different set of letters to represent the subject-specific concepts.
  - That's a lot of effort! Instead, learn the master formulas <u>once</u> and then understand how to **use and modify** them for subject-specific applications.
- The same letters get repeated (x, y, h, k, n, m, r, etc.) in many different formulas, which means these are too easy to get mixed up. The scope of the college and graduate admissions tests requires mastery over concepts you learned over several years in your middle school and high school math courses. There is a lot of material to re-learn.
  - Words help you remember formulas <u>correctly</u>.
  - Learning equations in words also improves your grasp of the underlying concepts and relationships among variables.

Some examples are shown on the following pages.

Core Concept	Related Equations & Formulas	Learn This, Not That
Linear Increase or Decrease	Linear equation Total cost (economics)	Use: $$Ending = Beginning + (Rate * Quantity)$$ Instead of these: $$y = mx + b$$ $$TC = VC \text{ per unit} * \#Units + FC$$
Exponential Growth or Decay	Exponential growth/decay (sciences) Future value of 1-time payment (finance) Doubling formula (biology, finance) Half-life formula (nuclear physics)	Use: $$Ending = Beginning * (1 + Change)^{Time}$$ Instead of these: $$FV = PV * (1 + r)^n$$ $$D = D_0 * \left(\frac{1}{2}\right)^{\frac{t}{h}}$$
Interest	Simple Interest	Use: $$Principal * Int.Rate * \# Periods = Int.Amount$$ Instead of this: $$p * r * n = i$$
	Compound Interest	Use: *The exponential growth formula, with modifications* If you want the future value of the investment, which is the **total of the original investment plus interest earned**, you make a modification based on the number of compounding periods per year. $$Ending = Beginning * \left(1 + \frac{Change}{\# \text{ of Periods}}\right)^{Time * \# \text{ of Periods}}$$ If you want **only the interest earned**, use the formula above, <u>then</u> calculate the difference between the ending and beginning amounts. $$Interest\ Earned = Ending - Beginning$$

Core Concept	Related Equations & Formulas	Learn This, Not That
Percent Change	Percent Change of a Number Percent Change of a Percent Percent Change of a Ratio	Use: $$Percent\ Change = \frac{New - Original}{Original}$$ If you want to find the percent change <u>of a percent</u>, you make a modification as follows: $$Percent\ Change = \frac{New\ Pct - Original\ Pct}{Original\ Pct}$$ If you want to find the percent change <u>of a ratio</u>, you make a modification as follows: $$Percent\ Change = \frac{New\ Ratio - Original\ Ratio}{Original\ Ratio}$$

You can greatly improve your ability to solve math questions with confidence if you start to **think about math differently** than you ever have before.

Consider, for a moment, that every action you can undertake in math has an opposite action. There's a pair of operations for "**building up**" and "**breaking down**."

- One set of actions will involve taking parts and building them up to produce a whole

- The opposites of these actions will involve taking a whole and breaking it down to identify its parts

The **building up** actions are usually easier to remember. Throughout your education, you probably spent a little more of your time practicing these actions. You'll have a lot more muscle memory for these **building up** actions.

The **breaking down** actions are generally a little harder to remember. Throughout your education, you probably spent a little less of your time practicing these actions. You'll likely find that these **breaking down** actions are the skills which require more effort to recall, relearn, and practice.

Often, you will just "know" how to build up from the parts to a whole. But you must "figure out" how to break down from the whole to its parts. Why then are there so many questions which require **figuring things out**?

> The ability to take a whole and **figure out the process** of
> **breaking it down** into its component parts is essential,
> not only for success in math problems, but also for
> personal and professional goals.

- **How do you break down a big project, like writing a 12-page research paper, into a series of smaller, more achievable parts**? Perhaps your teachers did this breaking down process for you and provided a list of the smaller parts and their deadlines. But as you advanced to higher grades, you started receiving projects for which you needed to determine how to break them down into smaller, more doable parts and determine your own timeline for completing each part. Those smaller project parts – such as identifying sources, creating notes, creating an outline, writing a draft, editing the draft, writing the works cited page, etc. – are individually so much less daunting than the big task. Smaller = more doable.

- **How do you break down a big project, like "earn an extra $6,000" this year, into a series of smaller, more achievable goals**? Perhaps you reframed this and asked yourself how you could earn an extra $500 each month, or $100-150 per week. Smaller goals are more motivating. Smaller = more doable.

- **How do you approach a math word problem**? Break it down. Use any of the strategies and approaches found in these materials, including:
  - Words to Math
  - Words First, Math Second

o   Tables & Labels

o   Taking a simple equation in Words and drilling down to a more detailed form of the equation

o   Etc.

Now, let's take a closer look at some of the various **building up** actions in math and their corresponding **breaking down** actions.

Building Up Actions	Breaking Down Actions
Adding	Subtracting (primary) Adding a Negative
Multiplying	Dividing (primary) Multiplying by the Reciprocal Factoring Simplifying / Reducing Fractions
Squaring a Number	Taking the Square Root
Cubing a Number	Taking the Cube Root
Distributing	Factoring Out
FOILing	Factoring a Quadratic Equation (primary) Using the Sum of Squares rule* Using the Difference of Squares rule* *if applicable
Raising a base to an exponent to find a number	Taking the logarithm, in a certain base, of a number, to find an exponent

The table shows some **building up** actions have multiple related **breaking down** actions.

More students have trouble with subtraction than with addition.

- If you find the rules for subtracting difficult to recall, <u>reframe</u> subtracting a positive number as adding a negative number.

- <u>Why</u> can this help? You can add numbers in any order, so instead of worrying about the correct order of operations for subtraction, you can add all the positives together, add all the negatives together, and then do the final calculation.

More students have trouble with division than with multiplication – <u>especially</u> when asked to divide by a fraction.

- If you find it hard to divide by a fraction, <u>reframe</u> this as **multiplying by the reciprocal**.

- <u>Why</u> can this help? You can multiply numbers in any order. Also, you can look for ways to use cancelling to your advantage to make the numbers as small as possible before you start to multiply them, which is helpful when no calculators are allowed.

- Instead of dividing one number by another, you could use factoring to break down both numbers, then cancel out the common factors. Smaller numbers are easier to handle.

More students have trouble with factoring equations than with either distributing or FOILing.

- Check your work – if you factored a certain equation, you can check that you factored it correctly by FOILing or Distributing. If the result matches what you started with, then you have correctly factored the equation.

Thus, if you can think about each of the **breaking down** actions as the opposite of their corresponding **building up** actions, you will strengthen your understanding of the breaking down actions and your ability to use them correctly... and have a way to check your work.

CHAPTER 4 THE SHORT LIST OF THINGS YOU SHOULD MEMORIZE

THE TIMES TABLES, UP TO 15 BY 15

If you do not already have these memorized, practice with a set of flashcards.

PERFECT SQUARES & PERFECT CUBES

You should know all of the perfect squares for N = 1 through 15, and all the perfect cubes for N = 1 through 10.

N =	N^2 =	N^3 =
1	1	1
2	4	8
3	9	27
4	16	64
5	25	125
6	36	216
7	49	343
8	64	512
9	81	729
10	100	1000
11	121	
12	144	
13	169	
14	196	
15	225	

INSTANTLY RECOGNIZE THE POWERS OF 2

Here's a tip to instantly recognize all the powers of 2 that you might see on your test.

Think about the evolution of technology and the 'upgrades', which all happen in powers of 2 thanks to the binary nature of computers. Depending upon your age, you can use different technology references to make this 'sticky'.

Let N =	Then 2^N =	Children of the 80s: Video Game Consoles & the memory in your early PCs	Children of the 90s: Apple® Products
1	2		
2	4		Original iPhone® / 4GB
3	8	Original NES® / 8-bit Nintendo	iPhone / 8GB
4	16	Sega Genesis® / 16-bit	iPhone / 16GB
5	32	Super Nintendo® / 32-bit	iPhone / 32GB
6	64	Nintendo 64® (1996)	iPhone / 64GB
7	128	128 MB RAM	iPhone / 128GB
8	256	256 MB RAM	
9	512	512 MB RAM *(remember what an upgrade this felt like?)*	*Now you can predict the future – you know what memory sizes future iPhone models will have.*
10	1024	1 GB (technically 1024 MB)	
11	2048	2 GB (technically 2048 MB)	
12	4096	4 GB (technically 4096 MB) *Also, UHD "4K" TVs*	

Original NES, Super Nintendo, and Nintendo 64 are trademarks of Nintendo Co. Ltd., registered in the U.S. and other countries.

Sega Genesis is a trademark of Sega Games Co. Ltd., registered in the U.S. and other countries.

Apple and iPhone are trademarks of Apple Inc., registered in the U.S. and other countries.

All Your Word Problems Solved

FRACTIONS, DECIMALS, AND PERCENTS

Memorize these equivalencies, along with the tips to recognize the decimal & its fraction.

Fractions of	Fraction	Decimal	Percent	Pattern to Recognize _Assumes fraction is simplified_
N/2	1/2	0.50	50%	
N/3	1/3	0.3333	33.33%	Single, repeating digit that's a 3 or 6
	2/3	0.6666	66.66%	
N/4	1/4	0.25	25%	2-digit decimal or percent, ending in a 5
	2/4 = 1/2			
	3/4	0.75	75%	
N/5	1/5	0.20	20%	Multiple of 10%, led by an even digit
	2/5	0.40	40%	
	3/5	0.60	60%	
	4/5	0.80	80%	
N/6	1/6	0.1666	16.66%	The first digit is unique, after which a different digit repeats that's either 3 or 6
	2/6 = 1/3			
	3/6 = 1/2			
	4/6 = 2/3			
	5/6	0.8333	83.33%	
N/8	1/8	0.125	12.5%	3-digit decimal or percent, ending in a 5 _Note: this is similar to the pattern for divisibility, shown in the next section. The decimal is 3-digits because 8 is 2 to the 3rd_
	2/8 = 1/4			
	3/8	0.375	37.5%	
	4/8 = 1/2			
	5/8	0.625	62.5%	
	6/8 = 3/4			
	7/8	0.875	87.5%	

Fractions of	Fraction	Decimal	Percent	Pattern to Recognize *Assumes fraction is simplified*
N/9	1/9	0.1111	11.11%	Single, repeating digit, which is equal to N from the numerator
	2/9	0.2222	22.22%	
	3/9 = 1/3			
	4/9	0.4444	44.44%	
	5/9	0.5555	55.55%	
	6/9 = 2/3			
	7/9	0.7777	77.77%	
	8/9	0.8888	88.88%	
N/11	1/11	0.090909	9.09%	Two repeating digits, which are equal to the N from the numerator times 9
	2/11	0.181818	18.18%	
	3/11	0.272727	27.27%	
	4/11	0.363636	36.36%	
	5/11	0.454545	45.45%	
	6/11	0.545454	54.54%	
	7/11	0.636363	63.63%	
	8/11	0.727272	72.72%	
	9/11	0.818181	81.81%	
	10/11	0.909090	90.90%	

Most standardized test prep books will provide you with a list of divisibility rules for the numbers 2 through 10, written in order from smallest to largest. That's good, but not great, because it's inefficient to learn them sequentially.

There are **patterns** to the divisibility rules which makes it <u>easier to learn and retain</u> the rules which are similar by groups.

These are important! When you encounter values with 6 or more digits, the test does <u>not</u> expect you to calculate the old-fashioned way, and instead rewards you for finding shortcuts to confirm whether X is divisible by certain numbers. *Note: The GMAT does not allow the use of a calculator. Other standardized tests may allow use of a calculator, but most of the time you can still solve the questions using mental math shortcuts.*

GROUP 1: DIVISIBILITY RULES FOR 2, 4, AND 8 (POWERS OF 2)

Is X divisible by...	Rule	Example	Example Explanation
2	Look at the last digit. See if that is divisible by two.	2,568,31<u>8</u> Yes!	The last digit = 8. 8 is divisible by 2. Therefore, this big number <u>is</u> divisible by 2.
4	Look at the last 2 digits. See if that is divisible by four.	45,6<u>38</u> No!	The last two digits = 38. 38 is <u>not</u> divisible by 4. Therefore, this big number is <u>not</u> divisible by 4.
8	Look at the last 3 digits. See if that is divisible by eight.	37,<u>246</u> No!	The last three digits = 246. 246 is <u>not</u> divisible by 8. Therefore, this big number is <u>not</u> divisible by 8.

TIP: If needed, the logic would continue for all powers of 2. What's the pattern? Well, for all powers of 2, the number of digits you need to look at is equal to the exponent of 2.

Since 8 is 2 cubed, you'd need to look at the last 3 digits. If you wanted to test divisibility by 32, which is 2 to the fifth power, then you'd need to look at the last 5 digits. Thankfully, though, the actual computation required for standardized test math usually isn't that tough on sections where calculator usage is not allowed.

GROUP 2: DIVISIBILITY RULES FOR 5 AND 10

Look at the last digit. These are probably the only divisibility rules you learned in school!

GROUP 3: DIVISIBILITY RULES FOR 7 AND 11

These numbers do <u>not</u> have rules or follow patterns. Sorry!

GROUP 4: DIVISIBILITY RULES FOR 3 AND 9 (POWERS OF 3)

Is X divisible by...	Rule	Example	Example Explanation
3	Add up the digits. The sum must be divisible by 3.	52,902 Yes!	5+2+9+0+2 = 18. 18 is divisible by 3. Therefore, this big number <u>is</u> divisible by 3.
9	Add up the digits. The sum must be divisible by 9.	4,368,217 No!	4+3+6+8+2+1+7 = 31 31 is <u>not</u> divisible by 9. Therefore, this big number is <u>not</u> divisible by 9.

All Your Word Problems Solved

GROUP 5: RULES FOR 6, 12, AND 24 (POWERS OF 2 TIMES A 3)

Is X divisible by...	Rule	Example	Example Explanation
6	6 = 2 * 3 <u>Both</u> the rule for divisibility by 2 and the rule for divisibility by 3 must be true.	1704	Rule for 2: Last digit is 4, which is divisible by 2. Rule for 3: Sum of digits is 12, which is divisible by 3. Therefore, this big number <u>is</u> divisible by 6.
12	12 = 4 * 3 <u>Both</u> the rule for divisibility by 4 and the rule for divisibility by 3 must be true.	2556	Rule for 4: Last two digits are 56, which is divisible by 4. Rule for 3: Sum of digits is 18, which is divisible by 3. Therefore, this big number <u>is</u> divisible by 12.
24	24 = 8 * 3 <u>Both</u> the rule for divisibility by 8 and the rule for divisibility by 3 must be true.	2872	Rule for 8: Last three digits are 872, which is divisible by 8. Rule for 3: Sum of digits is 19, which is <u>not</u> divisible by 3. Therefore, this big number is <u>not</u> divisible by 24.

PRINCIPLES OF MENTAL MATH FOR STANDARDIZED TESTS

Scan the available answer choices to determine if you need to <u>calculate</u> an exact answer to a standardized test math problem, or if you can <u>estimate</u> a good-enough answer.

- Are the answers clustered close together? You should <u>calculate</u>.

- Are the answers spread far apart? You can probably <u>estimate-and-eliminate</u>.

Your ability to use the estimate-and-eliminate approach is contingent upon ensuring your scratch work is set up correctly. Why is this technique so effective? Because, in the process of creating tempting-but-wrong answer choices for standardized tests, the test maker identifies the handful of mistakes students are likely to make in their approach, and provides the result of these specific mistakes as available answer choices.

Common mistakes the test maker anticipates students will make:

- **Mistakes in translating words to math**
  - **Converting units**: e.g., from meters per second to kilometers per hour. Should you use 1/60 or 60/1 as a conversion factor? *This error is so common, and is why you should remember "no naked numbers" and "let the units lead you" to set up your approach correctly. Cross-reference the section on Dimensional Analysis.*

  - **Ratio questions**: Did you put the right part in the right place in the fraction? Did the question give you the ratio of A to B, and the ratio of B to C, but then turn around and ask you to find the ratio of C to A? The ratio of A to C will, assuredly, be one of the tempting-but-wrong answer choices available to you.

  - **Percent questions**: If you were given a percent and a number, is that number logically the <u>part</u> or the <u>whole</u>?

  - **Word problems**:
    - Did you mix up related-but-different terms? e.g., median vs. mean
    - Did you fail to notice and adapt your approach for small word changes?
      - "of the amount" vs. "of the *remaining* amount..."
      - Be very careful about <u>what follows the phrase "of the..."</u> in any question involving percents or percent change!
      - "a positive integer" vs. "an integer"
    - Did you put a piece of information (number, variable, or percent) into the equation in the wrong place? *Remember to build your logic in words first, math second.*

- **Losing track of positive and negative signs**, especially in Arithmetic and Algebraic Expressions

- **Not answering the right question**. You may have correctly solved for a *different* piece of information than the test maker asked you to find. This is especially common in complex word problems. It's so satisfying to arrive at an answer that we often forget what we just calculated, and that there might be another step. *Remember to use meaningful variables, and plan your work so you don't lose sight of the question, even when there are many steps required to arrive at that answer.*

- **Mishandling "tens and tenths"**, also called place value
  - **Scientific notation**: How many zeroes should there be in the final answer?
  - **Percent questions**: Where should you place the decimal?
  - **Decimal questions**: Where should you place the decimal?

TIPS FOR CALCULATING AN EXACT ANSWER, MORE EFFICIENTLY

Calculation Technique	Example
Re-partnering Using more academic math terminology, this means "take advantage of the associative property of multiplication and/or the associative property of addition."	**What is 45 * 14?** This question could be made easier if you see that there's a factor of 2 inside the 14, which could be "re-partnered" with the 45 to produce a multiple of 10. You would then multiply that new multiple of 10 by what remains after you factor the 2 out of the 14. Factor out the 2 from the 14, then "re-partner" the 2 with the 45. $\quad$ 45 * (2 * 7) $\quad$ (45 * 2) * 7 $\quad$ 90 * 7 = 630 **What is (127 + 42) + (73 + 18)?** This question is easier if you "re-partner" the terms so they add up to different multiples of tens (look at the units digits). $\quad$ (127 + 73) + (42 + 18) $\quad$ 200 + 60 = 260

Calculation Technique	Example
Multiplying any 2-digit number by 11	Separate the digits with a placeholder in the middle • $35 * 11 = 3\_5$ Add the digits of the original number, and put the result in the placeholder • $3+5 = 8$ • 3$\underline{8}$5
Multiplying any number by five	Multiplying by 5 is mathematically equivalent to dividing by 2, then multiplying by 10. So as a shortcut, you can: Divide by 2, then tack on a zero at the end. • $36 * 5 = \frac{36}{2} * 10 = 18 * 10 = 180$ • $840 * 5 = \frac{840}{2} * 10 = 420 * 10 = 4200$
Dividing any number by five	Dividing by 5 is mathematically equivalent to dividing by 10, then multiplying by 2. So as a shortcut, you can: Drop the last zero and double the result. • $\frac{460}{5} = \frac{460}{10} * 2 = 46 * 2 = 92$ • $\frac{3700}{5} = \frac{3700}{10} * 2 = 370 * 2 = 740$

Calculation Technique	Example
Recognize when you should switch among fractions, decimals, and percents, to make a problem easier to solve using mental math.	**What is 37.5% of 560?** This is a 3-digit number times another 3-digit number. *Can* you do it by hand? Yes. *Should* you do it? No. It is more efficient to substitute a fraction for the percent. $$37.5\% = \frac{3}{8}$$ Then, substituting in the fraction, we get: $$What\ is\ \frac{3}{8}\ of\ 560?$$ $$Q = \frac{3}{8} * 560$$ Now you may see that 560 is divisible by 8. Cancel out the 8's, and you're left with 3 * 70. $$Q = \frac{3}{8} * 560$$ $$Q = 3 * 70 = 210$$

Ignore the tens-and-tenths until the end.
 	
In other words, ignore <u>place value</u> until the last step.
	What is $\sqrt{\sqrt[3]{0.000064}}$?
	
	Ignore the decimals for now. What's the square root, of the cube root, of 64?
	
	What's the cube root of 64?
	
	    4
	
	What's the square root of that?
	
	    2
	
	The correct answer needs a 2 in it. Eliminate any answers with digits other than 2 (and one or more zeros).
	
	Now, deal with place value (the tens-and-tenths, or how many zeroes there will be tacked on the end of numbers greater than one, or how many digits there will be after the decimal for numbers less than one).
	
	The square root of the cube root of a number is equal to the sixth root of that number. What's the sixth root of 0.000001?
	
	    That would be 0.1.
	
	Your answer needs a single digit after the decimal.
	
	Put the logic together, and your answer = 0.2

Calculation Technique	Example
Always be cancelling. You should reduce fractions as much as possible before you multiply.	**What is three-fifths of one-sixth of 47,500?** $$\frac{3}{5} * \frac{1}{6} * 47500 = ?$$ Since all 3 terms are linked by multiplication, and all are on the same side of the equation, look for common factors in any of the numerators and any of the denominators. The 3 in the numerator and the 6 in the denominator are both divisible by 3. Cancel out the 3. $$\left(\frac{1}{5} * \frac{1}{2}\right) * 47500 = ?$$ Then, the 5 and 2 in the denominators combined will produce a 10 in the overall denominator. You can cancel both the 5 and the 2 with one of the zeroes in the 47,500. $$\frac{1}{10} * 47500 = ?$$ $$= 4750$$ *You always want to cancel out as many common factors as possible, <u>before</u> you multiply. Why? Because it's so much easier to deal with finding common factors of a set of small-to-medium numbers rather than trying to figure out how on Earth to divide one medium-to-large number by another medium-to-large number.*

TIPS FOR ESTIMATING THE ANSWER, EFFICIENTLY & DECISIVELY

Estimation strategies will not work if the problem is not set up correctly. Make sure that you've accurately translated words-to-math, organized your work so it's easy to follow, and written down labels and units as needed to make sure you've set up your approach correctly.

You will likely need a combination of 2-3 of these techniques to arrive at the correct answer.

Estimation Technique	Example
Rounding down & rounding up terms for multiplication of large numbers	**What is 23 * 67?** If you're multiplying 2 numbers together, round one of them <u>down</u> to the nearest multiple of 10 and round the other <u>up</u> to the nearest multiple of 10. So, 23 * 67 is approximately 20 * 70 Because 20 * 70 = 1400, you can safely eliminate any answer choices less than 1000 and any answer choices more than 2000. *If needed, use another technique to decide between the remaining answer choices.*
Last digit strategy for multiplication of large numbers	**What is 296 * 43?** We could do this one longhand, but it would be time consuming. We can look at the last digit of each number, 6 and 3, and multiply these together. 6 * 3 = 18 So, the result of 296 * 43 must end in an 8. Eliminate any answer choices that do not end in an 8 (have a units digit of 8). *If needed, use another technique to decide between the remaining answer choices.*

Estimation Technique	Example
Estimate using *calculated* upper & lower boundaries. Eliminate answers below the lower bound or above the upper bound.	**What is 32^2?** Select 30 & 35 as boundaries because there are shortcuts for squaring 2-digit numbers ending in either zero or five. 32 falls between 30 & 35, so 32^2 must fall between 30^2 & 35^2. $30^2 = 900$ and $35^2 = 1225$ So, 32^2 must be between 900 & 1225. Eliminate any answer choices less than 900. Eliminate any answer choices greater than 1225. *If needed, use another technique to decide between the remaining answer choices.* *See subsequent pages for the shortcuts to finding the perfect squares of 2-digit numbers ending in 0 or 5.*
Estimate using *logical* upper & lower boundaries. This applies to weighted average and mixture problems. Then, find the simple average. Will the resulting mixture (or combined average) **logically** be the same as the simple average? If not, should it be more than, or less than, the simple average?	**Sarah has 3 liters of a solution of bleach which is 10% concentrated, and 5 liters of a solution of bleach which is 20% concentrated. If she pours both bleach solutions into a single container, what is the concentration of the combined bleach solution?** Determine *logical* boundaries: • The combined solution cannot be weaker (less concentrated) than the weaker of the two solutions. • The combined solution cannot be stronger (more concentrated) than the stronger of the two solutions. • So, the combined solution must be between 10% and 20% concentrated. Eliminate any answer choices less than 10%. Eliminate any answer choices greater than 20%. Find the simple average. If we had equal amounts of 10% concentrated and 20% concentrated bleach solutions, our combined mixture would be (10% + 20%) / 2 = 15% concentrated. But, we do <u>not</u> have equal amounts. We have <u>more</u> of the <u>stronger</u> bleach solution. That means our combined solution must be <u>more</u> concentrated than the simple average suggests. Eliminate any answer choices equal to, or less than, the simple average. *Often, only one choice will remain!*

All Your Word Problems Solved

OTHER MENTAL MATH TRICKS

Calculation Technique	Example
Squaring large numbers for any 2-digit number that <u>ends in a zero</u>.	Square the tens digit and tack on 2 zeros on the end. • $30 * 30 = (3^2) * 100 = \underline{9}00$ • $40 * 40 = (4^2) * 100 = \underline{16}00$ • $80 * 80 = (8^2) * 100 = \underline{64}00$
Squaring large numbers for any 2-digit number that <u>ends in a five</u>.	Write down "25" with a placeholder in front of it like this: _____25 Take the tens digit of your original number, and multiply by that digit+1. Put the result in the placeholder you created. • $35 * 35 = (3*4)$ ___ $25 = \underline{12}25$ • $65 * 65 = (6*7)$ ___ $25 = \underline{42}25$ • $75 * 75 = (7*8)$ ___ $25 = \underline{56}25$
Squaring large numbers with two <u>consecutive numbers</u>	The squares of two consecutive numbers, N and N+1, are related using this equation: • $(N + 1)^2 = N^2 + N + (N + 1)$ To find 46^2, plug in 46 as the (N+1) in the equation above and 45 as the (N), then use the shortcut for 45^2 to quickly calculate what 46^2 equals. • $(46)^2 = 45^2 + 45 + (46)$ • $(46)^2 = 2025 + 91$ • $(46)^2 = 2116$ To find 39^2, plug in 39 as the (N) in the equation above and 40 as the (N+1), then use the shortcut for 40^2 to quickly calculate what 39^2 equals. • $(40)^2 = 39^2 + 39 + (40)$ • $1600 = 39^2 + 79$ • $1600 - 79 = 39^2$ • $1521 = 39^2$

KEY TERMINOLOGY TO MASTER ABOUT NUMBER PROPERTIES

Be sure you understand the differences among key terms related to number properties. Know with certainty which kinds of numbers are included or excluded from the set.

Term	Definition & Additional Info	Set Includes	Set Excludes
Whole Numbers	The set of Whole Numbers may also be called the Counting Numbers	{1, 2, 3, 4...999...}	• Negatives • Zero • Decimals • Fractions • Radicals (roots) such as √2 or √3 • Pi • Square roots of negative numbers
Integers	The set of Integers includes all whole numbers, plus: • Negatives • Zero	{-999...-3, -2, -1, 0, 1, 2, 3...999...}	• Decimals • Fractions • Radicals (roots) such as √2 or √3 • Pi • Square roots of negative numbers
Rational Numbers	The set of Rational Numbers includes all integers, plus: • Decimals which are either terminating or repeating, and can thus be re-expressed as fractions • Fractions	{-999...-3, -2.5, -2, -1, 0, 1/3, 5/8, 1, 2, 3...999...}	• Radicals (roots) such as √2 or √3 • Pi • Square roots of negative numbers *A number is considered irrational when the decimal equivalent is both non-terminating and non-repeating, and cannot be re-expressed as a fraction.*

Term	Definition & Additional Info	Set Includes	Set Excludes
Real Numbers	The set of Real Numbers includes all Rational Numbers, plus: • Radicals (roots) such as $\sqrt{2}$ or $\sqrt{3}$ • Pi	$\{-999...-3, -2\sqrt{2}, -2.5, -2, -1, 0, 1/3, 5/8, 1, \sqrt{3}, 2, 3, \sqrt{10}...999...\}$	• Square roots of negative numbers

CHOOSING TEST CASES FOR NUMBER PROPERTIES QUESTIONS

On standardized tests, it is imperative that you make sure to consider and evaluate test cases from all seven parts of the number line. Those seven parts of the number line are:

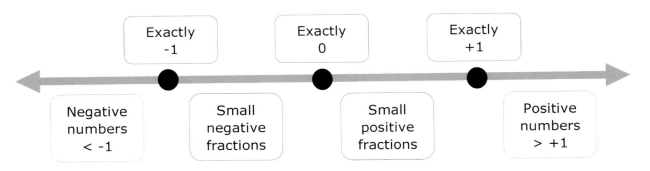

When you read any Number Properties question, **do not make assumptions** – consciously ask yourself what different kind(s) of numbers you need to test with the relationships or equations given in the question. Examples of different kinds of numbers include:

- Positive vs. negative
- Integer vs. fraction or decimal
- Odd vs. even
- Consecutive vs. non-consecutive numbers such as {4, 5, 6} vs. {4, 11, 99}

APPROACH TO ANSWERING NUMBER PROPERTIES QUESTIONS

Question Wording	Approach
Must be true	• Find any reason to **rule out** answers. • If any test case makes the statement untrue, then eliminate that answer choice.
Could be true	• Find any reason to **rule in** answers. • If any test case makes the statement true, then choose that answer choice.
Cannot be true All of these **must** be true **except**...	• Find any reason to **rule in** answers. • If any test case makes the statement true, then eliminate that answer choice.

OTHER TERMINOLOGY YOU NEED TO KNOW

Term	Definition & Additional Info

Prime Number vs. Composite Number	• A **prime number** is any number which is not divisible by any numbers other than 1 and itself.
	    ○ Equivalently, a <u>prime number</u> is any number whose only <u>factors</u> are 1 and itself.
	    ○ These numbers are prime: 2, 3, 5, 7, 11, 13, 17, 19, 23, 29, 31, 37, 41, 43, 47, 53, 59, 61, 67, 71, 73, 79, 83, 89, 91, 97, et al.
	    ○ You should also memorize these facts:
	        • 1 is not prime.
	        • 2 is the smallest prime number, and the only even prime number.
	        • Negative numbers are never prime.
	• A **composite number** is any number which is not prime.

Term	Definition & Additional Info

Factor vs. Multiple	• A **factor** is a number which divides evenly into another, larger number. **Divisor** is another word for **factor**.
	
	   ○ Each number has a <u>finite</u> quantity of factors.
	
	   ○ The smallest positive factor of a number is 1.
	
	   ○ The largest positive factor of a number is itself.
	
	   ○ The _factors_ of 65 include 1, 5, 13, and 65.
	
	• A **multiple** is a number which is a smaller number times another number.
	
	   ○ Each number has an <u>infinite</u> quantity of multiples.
	
	   ○ The smallest positive multiple of a number is itself.
	
	   ○ The _multiples_ of 65 include 65, 130, 195, 260, and more.

Greatest Common Factor vs. Least Common Multiple	• The **greatest common factor** of two numbers is equal to or less than the smaller of the two numbers. • The **least common multiple** of two numbers is equal to or greater than the larger of the two numbers. ○ Conceptually, the **least common denominator** of two fractions is <u>the same thing</u> as the least common multiple of the two denominators.
Prime Factors vs. All Factors of a Number	• To find the **prime factors** of a number, you'll need to create a <u>factor tree</u>. • To find **all the factors** of a number, you'll need to create a <u>factor table</u>.

"How Many Prime Factors"
 	
vs.
 	
"How Many Distinct Prime Factors"
	• If a test question asks you to count how many prime factors a number has, make sure you know whether it specifies <u>distinct</u> prime factors.
	
	• <u>Distinct</u> means different or unique. _Do not double-count the ones which are repeated._
	
	• For example:
	
	   ○ The prime factorization of the number 120 = 2*2*2*3*5
	
	   ○ 120 has 5 **prime factors** (2, 2, 2, 3, & 5)
	
	   ○ 120 has 3 **distinct prime factors** (2, 3, & 5)

Term	Definition & Additional Info
Perfect Square	• A **perfect square** is a number which is the square of another number. • Perfect squares can be the squares of **integers**. For example: ○ $3^2 = 9$, so 9 is a perfect square ○ $11^2 = 121$, so 121 is a perfect square. ○ These numbers are perfect squares: 1, 4, 9, 16, 25, 36, 49, 64, 81, 100, 121, 144, 169, 196, 225, et al. • Perfect squares can also be the squares of **fractions**. For example: ○ $\left(\frac{1}{2}\right)^2 = \frac{1}{4}$, so 1/4 is a perfect square ○ $\left(\frac{2}{3}\right)^2 = \frac{4}{9}$, so 4/9 is a perfect square ○ These fractions are perfect squares: ¼, 1/9, 1/16, 1/25, 4/9, 16/25, et al. ○ A fraction is a perfect square if <u>both</u> the numerator and the denominator are perfect squares. • A number raised to **any even exponent** is a perfect square. ○ $5^{12} = (5^6)^2$, so 5^{12} is a perfect square. ○ $4^{-8} = (4^{-4})^2$, so 4^{-8} is a perfect square.

Term	Definition & Additional Info
Consecutive Numbers	• A set of numbers is considered **consecutive** if they are <u>in order from least to greatest</u>. • Most sets of consecutive numbers can be represented as an **arithmetic sequence**, if the terms are <u>evenly spaced</u> *(i.e., to go from one number to the next, we add a consistent amount). See the section on **Sequences & Series**.* • **Consecutive integers**: o Example: {1, 2, 3, 4, 5, 6…} o Example: {28, 29, 30, 31, 32…} o Example: {-5, -4, -3, -2, -1, 0, 1, 2, 3…} o **Consecutive integers** can be represented algebraically as {N, N+1, N+2, N+3, N+4…} • **Consecutive even integers**: o Example: {2, 4, 6, 8, 10…} o Example: {28, 30, 32, 34, 36…} o Example: {-8, -6, -4, -2, 0, 2, 4…} o **Consecutive even integers** can be represented algebraically as {N, N+2, N+4, N+6…} • **Consecutive odd integers**: o Example: {1, 3, 5, 7, 9…} o Example: {23, 25, 27, 29, 31…} o Example: {-45, -43, -41, -39…} o **Consecutive odd integers** can be represented algebraically as {N, N+2, N+4, N+6…} • **Consecutive positive multiples of 7**: o Example: {7, 14, 21, 28, 35…} o **Consecutive positive multiples of 7** can be represented algebraically as {N, N+7, N+14, N+21…}

When answering Number Properties questions about **Odds** and **Evens**, it can be helpful to think about things that normally come in pairs – such as shoes, dance partners, or salt & pepper shakers (whatever makes you laugh). **Evens** then are complete pairs, whereas **Odds** imply that there's one unpaired item in the group.

Here's a recap of the rules for **Odds** and **Evens**:

Operation	Rules for Odds & Evens
Addition	• Even + Even = Even • Odd + Odd = Even • Even + Odd = Odd • Odd + Even = Odd
Subtraction	• Even – Even = Even • Odd – Odd = Even • Even – Odd = Odd • Odd – Even = Odd
Multiplication	• Even * Even = Even • Odd * Odd = Odd • Even * Odd = Even • Odd * Even = Even • *Anything times an even will be even*
Exponents	• $Even^2 = Even$ • $Odd^2 = Odd$ • $Even^{any\ power} = Even$ • $Odd^{any\ power} = Odd$

NUMBER PROPERTIES: POSITIVES & NEGATIVES

Here's a recap of the rules for **Positives** and **Negatives**:

Operation	Rules for Positives & Negatives
Addition	• Positive + Positive = *always* Positive • Negative + Negative = *always* Negative • Positive + Negative = it depends on the magnitude of the numbers *(i.e., which has a larger absolute value).*
Subtraction	• Positive – Positive = it <u>depends</u> on the relative magnitude of the numbers *(i.e., which has a larger absolute value).* • Negative – Negative= it <u>depends</u> on the relative magnitude of the numbers *(i.e., which has a larger absolute value).* • Positive – Negative = becomes more Positive *(i.e., a positive number with a larger absolute value).* • Negative – Positive = becomes more Negative *(i.e., a positive number with a larger absolute value).*
Multiplication	• Positive * Positive = Positive • Negative * Negative = Positive • Positive * Negative = Negative • Negative * Positive = Negative
Division	• Positive ÷ Positive = Positive • Negative ÷ Negative = Positive • Positive ÷ Negative = Negative • Negative ÷ Positive = Negative

How can you test if a number is prime?

- First, you must estimate the square root of the number. If a number is a composite number (i.e., not prime), it must have at least one factor less than its square root.

- Next, use a combination of logic and divisibility rules to test whether the number is divisible by any factors less than its square root.

Example: Is 209 Prime?

- **Estimate the square root**
  - We know that 225 is a perfect square (15^2), which is very close to 209.
  - Because 209 < 225, then $\sqrt{209}$ must be < $\sqrt{225}$.
  - So $\sqrt{209}$ < 15

- **Using logic and divisibility rules, systematically test whether 209 is divisible by any prime factors less than our estimated square root of ~15.**
  - Narrow down whether you need to test even factors at all.
  - 209 is odd, so we can rule out all even factors.
  - Visual inspection reveals 209 is not divisible by 5.
  - Test the remaining odd prime factors less than 15. Check whether 209 is divisible by 3, 7, 11, or 13. *We do not need to test for divisibility by 9, because anything divisible by 9 will already be determined to be either prime or not prime when we test if the number is divisible by 3.*
  - 2+0+9 = 11. Thus, 209 is not divisible by 3.
  - There are no handy rules for testing divisibility by 7, 11, or 13, so you'll want to use either the **anchor number strategy** or **long division** to test if 209 is divisible by 7, 11, or 13.
  - What's the **anchor number strategy**? Well, most people are materially better at multiplication and addition than they are at division. So, do "easy multiplication" to get to an anchor number close to the number in the question, then count forward or backward from that anchor number.
  - 7 * 30 = 210. Our anchor number is 210. Because 209 is only 1 less than 210, there would be a remainder, and we know that 209 is not divisible by 7.
  - 11 * 20 = 220. Our anchor number is 220. Then, 220 – 209 = 11. Thus, because we know 209 is a full 11 less than 220, we conclude that 11 * 19 = 209 and that **209 is not prime**.

HOW TO SUCCEED ON NUMBER PROPERTIES QUESTIONS

Questions about number properties require a **careful reading** of the question and attention to detail. **Be mindful of your own tendencies to make assumptions** and choose test cases to deliberately overcome (or "break") these tendencies.

Many students tend to make these assumptions:

- That "a number" is a positive integer. Overcome your assumptions by testing a fraction and/or a negative.

- That "three numbers A, B, and C" or "A < B < C" are positive, consecutive integers. Overcome your assumptions by testing non-consecutives, fractions, and/or negatives.

- That "X > 0" means X is a positive integer. All we know is that X is positive. But it could be a positive fraction. Overcome your assumptions by testing a small positive fraction such as $\frac{1}{2}$ *or* $\frac{1}{4}$

Some other wording which is commonly misinterpreted:

- Greater than vs. greater than or equal to. When a question says...

    o "More than 3" means X > 3, but

    o "At least 3" means X ≥ 3

- Less than vs. less than or equal to. When a question says...

    o "Less than 15" means X < 15, but

    o "At most 15" means X ≤ 15

Example: Equations Using Consecutive Even Numbers

There are two consecutive even integers. The difference between five times the smaller and three times the larger number is 22. What is the smaller number?

- You can represent "two consecutive even integers" as N and N+2, or the words Small and Large, or two different variables of your choosing.
    - Smaller number = Small or N
    - Larger number = Large or N+2
- Work carefully through the next statement. You'll learn more about the Words to Math approach in the next section.
- Difference between means "subtract"

$$5 * Small - 3 * Large = 22$$

- We also know that:

$$Large = Small + 2$$

- Solve as a system of equations, by substituting Small+2 into the original equation.

$$5 * Small - 3 * (Small + 2) = 22$$

- Now, follow the order of operations to solve for the value of the smaller number.

$$5\,Small - 3\,Small - 6 = 22$$

$$2\,Small - 6 = 22$$

$$2\,Small = 28$$

$$Small = \mathbf{14}$$

- Plug this value back into either of the original equations to solve for the value of the larger number.

$$Large = Small + 2$$

$$Large = 14 + 2 = \mathbf{16}$$

Your **ability to translate words to math is considered a core skill** in all math courses and in the math or quantitative section of all the major standardized tests. For word problems, the real "work" involved in the question is figuring out how to set up the equation based upon the information presented – if you do that correctly, the computation is straightforward.

You actually will **use this skill in real life**. When? Any time you are buying a product or service with variable pricing. Companies price their products and services in different ways which can make comparing prices difficult, such as:

- *Buying groceries.* Let's say you can buy a bag of 6 apples for $6.00. You can buy loose apples from one store for 89 cents each. Another store sells apples at $2.00 per pound. Assume the apples are equally sized, and there are 5 apples for every two pounds of apples. Where should you buy apples?

- *Renting a limo for prom.* One company might charge a pickup fee plus a cost per hour. Another company might charge a price per person for up to 6 hours, plus a price per extra hour above 6. A third company might charge a base price plus a cost per mile. Which one is the best deal?

- *Choosing a gym or fitness studio membership.* One gym charges a $200 one-time membership fee plus $60 per month with unlimited classes at no extra charge. The yoga studio near you doesn't charge a membership fee, but costs $100 per month if you pay month-to-month. This yoga studio also offers a 25% discount if you prepay for one year in full. Which one is the better deal, assuming you'll go to the same place for the entire year? Which one is the better deal, if you expect to move within 6 months?

- *Choosing an event venue for a wedding, bar or bat mitzvah, or holiday party.* One venue, a hotel, charges $5,000 plus $50 per person for dinner for an event on a Saturday night. This venue charges a 20% gratuity on the cost of the food, and a 10% sales tax on the entire bill. Another venue, a restaurant, does not charge a fee for their space, but the food is more expensive per person. Let's say this one costs $80 per person, plus the same 20% automatic gratuity and 10% sales tax. Which one is the better deal?

If you're willing to put in just a little bit of effort to translate words to math, you can find better deals and save yourself money on practically anything you might like to buy now or in the future.

RULES & TIPS FOR TRANSLATING WORDS TO MATH

When you're handling word problems, either for classes or for one of the standardized college & graduate admissions tests (PSAT/NMSQT, SAT, ACT, GRE, GMAT, etc.), there are a few techniques you can use which will make it easier to translate words to math:

1. **Read the first sentence or so of the problem, <u>just enough</u> to determine the type of problem it is, and then set up a structure to capture the information**.

   - Some problems are best solved using the **Tables & Labels approach** to organize your work, including: Work-Rate, Distance-Rate, and Venn Diagrams. *You'll learn about the Tables & Labels approach in later sections.*

   - If that's the case, set up your table before proceeding. If not, start at #2.

2. **Read the word problem up until a punctuation mark**.

3. **Stop and translate what you just read from words to math**.

4. **Write it down <u>before</u> you read the next part of the word problem**.

   - **Organize your work**. In your scratch work, have an area set aside to organize each of the following:

     i. **The formula(s) you need to solve the problem.**

        1. **Look for the word "is" which means "equals" and write down the equals sign**.

        2. **Tackle the statement in two parts**. Any words that come before the word "is" in a single statement go on the left of the equals sign. Any words that come after the word "is" go on the right of the equals sign. See the next page for a list of words & phrases and what they mean.

        3. **Try to write the equation in words first, math second**. Most students are better at remembering or figuring out formulas by writing them in words, then placing the values from the question <u>underneath</u> the corresponding words.

     ii. **Always write down the units**. No "naked numbers."

   - **Choose meaningful variables.** For example, if an equation has you solve for the population of a city after 3 years of 20% growth, use **P** for population, **J** for Joe's age, **V** for the value, etc. (instead of the generic X) so you remember what you've just solved for. *Why is this so important? Well, if a problem has lots of steps, you might forget what you were actually solving for; picking a letter for your variable which has meaning in the context of the problem can help you remember what you just solved for, and to know if you're done with the problem.*

5. **Now, read up until the next punctuation mark**. Repeat the steps above as needed. A new sentence requires a new equation. *Commas and periods are used for a reason – so use those grammatical pauses to stop and process what you've just read, and translate it into a written formula, constraints on the possible values of a number, etc.*

All Your Word Problems Solved

MATH CLUE WORDS AND WHAT THEY MEAN

Math Operation	Clue Words & Phrases in a Word Problem
Equals	• Is / are / will be *(any form of the verb "to be")* • Equals • Results in • Yields
Variable	• What / what number / how many *(any question words)* • A variable, a number
P percent, C cents	• What percent • You <u>must</u> express P percent as P/100. D dollars and C cents <u>must</u> be expressed as D + C/100. *If you're used to solving percent questions using decimals, this will take some getting used to on the GMAT or GRE.*
Parentheses	• The quantity of • The result is then
Multiply	• Times • By • Of • Product
Divide	• Divided • Split • Per • Out of • Ratio of
Add	• Added to • Plus • More than • Increased by • Sum of

Math Operation	Clue Words & Phrases in a Word Problem
Subtract	• Subtracted from • Minus • Less* - "17 less X" means "17 – X" • Less than* - "Five less than Q" means "Q-5" • Difference of / difference between • Decreased by
Exponents	• Raised to the power of • To the nth
Set two things equal to each other	• Two points <u>are</u> (or will be) <u>equidistant</u>. Because $D_1 = D_2$, then $R_1 * T_1 = R_2 * T_2$. The area of one shape <u>is the same as</u> the area of another shape • Returned home by the <u>same</u> route
What is [variable] in terms of [other variables]	• This wording simply means "rearrange the equation to isolate this other variable on one side of the equation." • *Example: If Y = MX+B, what is M in terms of Y, X, and B?*

CONSTRAINT CLUE WORDS AND WHAT THEY MEAN

Math Constraint	What This Means
Such that	• *Introduces some constraints on one of the variables, e.g., "for all integers X <u>such that</u> X^2 is a three-digit number."*
If X > 0	• X can be any positive number
For all X such that X≠3	• X can be any number other than 3 • The denominator of the fraction cannot equal zero • Usually, you'll see a statement like this one prior to being given an equation or function which involves fractions. Most often, whichever term is disallowed (given as a constraint) is the one that would make the denominator equal zero, and thus the whole equation becomes undefined.

GEOMETRY CLUE WORDS AND WHAT THEY MEAN

Geometry Clue	What This Means
(A border or frame) of uniform width	<ul><li>*Uniform* is a synonym for constant, consistent, same, and equivalent.</li><li>Uniform width means that the top, bottom, left, and right borders are all the <u>same</u> unknown value. You would need to assign a variable to represent the width of the border.</li><li>Choose a meaningful variable, such as B, to represent the width of the border.</li><li>Let's say both the inner and outer shapes are rectangles.<ul><li>If the inner shape has a length of L and a width of W, then the outer shape has a <u>length of L + 2B</u> and a <u>width of W + 2B</u>.</li><li>If the inner shape has a length of 12 and a width of 5, then the outer shape has a <u>length of 12 + 2B</u> and a <u>width of 5 + 2B</u>.</li></ul></li></ul>

Example #1: A Simple Percentage

What is 65% of 200?

Let's take this down together.

- First, find the word **is**. This means **equals**.
- Tackle what comes before the word **is**. This one's simple: **what** means **a variable**.
- Tackle what comes after the word **is**. 65% of 200.
    - 65% can be represented in any of three ways: 65%, 0.65, or 65/100.
    - **Of** means **multiply**.
    - 200 is simply itself.
    - Putting these together, on the right side of the equation, write **0.65 * 200**.

What is 65% of 200?				
What	Is	65%	Of	200
Y	=	$\dfrac{65}{100}$	*	200

Example #2: A Slightly More Complicated Percentage

42 is what percent of 350?

Let's take this down together.

- First, find the word **is**. This means **equals**.
- Tackle what comes before the word **is**. This one's simple: **42**.
- Tackle what comes after the word **is**. What percent of 350.
    - **What percent** should be represented as P/100
    - **Of** means **multiply**.
    - 350 is simply itself.
    - Putting these together, on the right side of the equation, write **P/100 * 350**.

42 is what percent of 350?				
42	Is	What percent	Of	350
42	=	$\dfrac{P}{100}$	*	350

Example #3: Multiple Percentages

32 percent of 20 percent of what number is 24?

Let's take this down together.

- First, find the word **is**. This means **equals**.
- Tackle what comes before the word **is**. 32 percent of 20 percent of what number.
  - *Careful here – you have two percents in a row!*
  - 32 percent is itself
  - **Of** means **multiply**
  - 20 percent is itself
  - **What number** means a variable. Let's choose Q this time.
  - Putting these together, on the left side of the equation, write:
    - 0.32 * 0.20 * Q
    - 32/100 * 20/100 * Q
- Tackle what comes after the word **is**. This one's simple: **24**.

32 percent of 20 percent of what number is 24?						
32 percent	Of	20 percent	Of	What number	Is	24
0.32	*	0.20	*	Q	=	24
$\frac{32}{100}$	*	$\frac{20}{100}$	*	Q	=	24

Example #4: Aging is a Problem!

Bob is four times as old as his cousin Clara. Six years from now, he will be 2 years less than 3 times as old as Clara. How old is Bob today?

Let's take this down together. Remember, read only up until the punctuation, so you'll work one statement at a time.

Bob is four times as old as his cousin Clara.

- Choose meaningful variables. Let's let B = Bob's age today, and C = Clara's age today.
- Find the word **is**. This means **equals**.
- Tackle what comes before the word **is**. Bob. We'll represent that as B.
- Tackle what comes after the word **is**. Four times as old as his cousin Clara. 4*C.

Bob is four times as old as his cousin Clara.				
Bob	Is	Four	Times (as old as)	Clara
B	=	4	*	C

Now tackle the next statement. Often, a new sentence means a new equation.

Six years from now, he will be 2 years less than 3 times as old as Clara.

- Find the phrase **will be**. This means **equals**.
- Tackle what comes before the phrase **will be**. Six years from now, he…
  - Bob's age today = B, so
  - Bob's age in six years means: **B+6**
- Tackle what comes after the phrase **will be**. 2 years less than 3 times as old as Clara. *Here, though it is not stated explicitly in the word problem, you would compare Bob's current age with Clara's current age and compare Bob's future age with Clara's <u>future</u> age.*
  - Clara's age today = C, so
  - Clara's age in six years means: **C+6**
  - **3 times as old** as Clara's future age: **3*(C+6)**
  - **2 years less than** that means you must subtract 2: **3*(C+6) − 2.**
  - *Notice the tricky wording here. **2 years less than** means "minus 2", not "2 minus." Be on the lookout for inverted word order, especially related to subtraction.*

Six years from now, Bob will be 2 years less than 3 times as old as Clara.					
Six years from now, Bob	Will be	3	times as old	As Clara	2 years less than
B + 6	=	3	*	(C+6)	-2

Now you have a system of two equations with two variables:

$$B = 4 * C$$

$$B + 6 = 3 * (C + 6) - 2$$

You can use either substitution or combination to **solve for B, Bob's age today**. Here, substitution will be easier than combination.

Substitute 4C underneath B, then work through the order of operations and solve.

$$B + 6 = 3 * (C + 6) - 2$$

$$4C + 6 = 3 * (C + 6) - 2$$

$$4C + 6 = 3C + 18 - 2$$

$$C + 6 = 16$$

$$C = 10$$

Plug C = 10 back into either of the original equations to solve for B, Bob's age today.

$$B = 4 * (10) = 40$$

PRACTICAL APPLICATIONS OF LINEAR EQUATIONS & FUNCTIONS

Many things we see in our daily lives, in science, and/or in business, can be described as a relationship between two variables using a linear equation (or function) to represent the relationship. For example:

- A <u>salesperson's total income</u> is comprised of a base salary plus a percentage commission times the revenue from all products sold

$$\text{Total Income } = \text{ Base Salary } + \text{ Commission Rate } * \text{ (Sales Revenue Generated)}$$

- Your <u>total cost</u> to attend the state fair is the sum of the entry fee plus the cost per ride, times the number of rides you go on

$$\text{Total Cost } = \text{ Entry Fee } + \text{ Cost per Ride } * \text{ (\# of Rides)}$$

- The <u>current value of your car</u> is what you paid for it, minus the annual depreciation times the number of years old the car is

$$\text{Current Value } = \text{ Purchase Price } - \text{ Depreciation Rate } * \text{ (Time Elapsed)}$$

- The <u>total cost of a ride in a taxi</u> can be calculated by taking the cost of the flag pull (getting in) plus a rate per mile times the number of miles you ride in the taxi

$$\text{Total Cost } = \text{ Flag Pull Price } + \text{ Price per Mile } * \text{ (\# of Miles)}$$

GRAPHING A LINEAR EQUATION IN STANDARD FORM

The standard form of the equation (or function) for a line is: **y = mx + b**

- Y = the Y-value
- M = the slope of the line, which you may remember equals the "rise over run"
- X = the X-value
- B = the Y-intercept, which you may remember as where the line crosses the Y-axis at X=0

Let's graph a simple equation, Y = 3X + 10. You'll see the equation crosses the Y-axis at an X-value of 0 and a Y-value of 10. This is the same as saying the Y-intercept is 10.

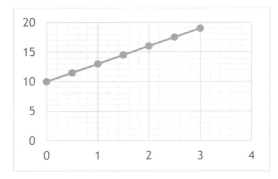

THE SLOPE OF A LINE REPRESENTS THE RATE

You'll notice that all of these equations contain some sort of rate. A **rate** is any "something per something" such as:

- Cents per mile
- Dollars per year
- Commission $ per item
- Price per person

The **rate**, when entered into a linear equation is represented by the **slope** of the line.

THE Y-INTERCEPT REPRESENTS THE BEGINNING VALUE

All of these equations also contain some sort of a **flat fee, or base price, or beginning value**. These are your "cost of showing up" or "the value of something if you do nothing."

Thus, these are represented graphically as the **y-intercept** of a line.

All Your Word Problems Solved

THE VALUE OF X REPRESENTS THE QUANTITY OR TIME USED

In a linear equation, the value of X represents the amount (how many) of a thing which is used, consumed, created, purchased, sold, etc. or the number of units of time elapsed.

THE VALUE OF Y REPRESENTS THE ENDING VALUE OR TOTAL

In a linear equation, the value of Y represents the total price, the final value, the ending population, etc.

RELATING LINEAR EQUATIONS & FUNCTIONS TO REAL LIFE

Use the following table to understand terminology which is related, and where to place each piece of information into the formula for the linear equation in standard form. Knowing how to put the right piece of info into the right place in an equation is more than half the battle with math word problems.

Study this table to understand how to build up your equations. You'll note that I put most of the info in words first: **think through your equation in words first**, **then put the numbers into the equation for each of those parts**.

Y	=	M	*	X	+	B
Value of Y	=	Slope	*	Value of X	+	Y-Intercept
Dependent Variable	=	Rate	*	Independent Variable	+	Initial Value
Ending	=	Rate	*	Quantity	+	Beginning
Total $ spent at State Fair	=	Cost per ride	*	# of rides	+	Entry fee
Current value of your car	=	Depreciation per year *input as a negative value*	*	# of years elapsed	+	Purchase price
What you'll spend on a gym membership	=	Price per month	*	# of months	+	Sign-up fee
Profit from hosting a keg party	=	Price charged per cup	*	# of cups sold	+	Up-front cost of buying the kegs *input as a negative value*
Ending inventory	=	Units produced per labor hour	*	# of labor hours	+	Beginning inventory on-hand

Example #1: Ride-Share Earnings

Sarah just signed up as a ride-share driver. She expects to earn about $15 per hour and will earn a new driver bonus of $200. How many hours does she need to work in order to earn $350 this week?

Step 1: Write an equation which expresses Sarah's income for the current week, in the standard linear form.

Y	=	M	*	X	+	B
Value of Y	**=**	**Slope**	*****	**Value of X**	**+**	**Y-Intercept**
Ending	=	Rate	*	Quantity	+	Beginning
Ride-share income	=	Earnings per hour	*	# of Hours	+	Bonus

Step 2: Insert the values provided in the word problem into the right place.

Ride-share income	=	Earnings per hour	*	# of Hours	+	Bonus
$350	=	$15 per hour	*	H	+	$200

Step 3: Solve the problem using standard algebra to find the value of H, the number of hours Sarah must work to make $350 this week. Work through the order of operations and solve.

$$\$350 = (\$15 * H) + \$200$$
$$\$150 = (\$15 * H)$$
$$\mathbf{10 = H}$$

Example #2: Creating Inventory for Your Own Business

Maria owns her own custom jewelry business. She has 15 necklaces of a certain design left over from a recent craft fair, and she wants to have a total of 60 of this design ready before next weekend's big craft fair. If she has 5 hours available to produce additional necklaces, how many does she need to make per hour?

Step 1: Write an equation which expresses Maria's product inventory, in the standard linear form.

Y	=	M	*	X	+	B
Value of Y	=	Slope	*	Value of X	+	Y-Intercept
Ending	=	Rate	*	Quantity	+	Beginning
Ending inventory of necklaces	=	Necklaces produced per hour	*	# of hours	+	Initial inventory of necklaces

Step 2: Insert the values provided in the word problem into the right place.

Ending inventory of necklaces	=	Necklaces produced per hour	*	# of hours	+	Initial inventory of necklaces
60 necklaces	=	R	*	5 hours	+	15 necklaces

Step 3: Solve the problem using standard algebra to find the value of R, the rate of necklaces produced per hour. Follow the order of operations until you arrive at the final answer.

$$60 = R * 5 + 15$$

$$45 = R * 5$$

$$\mathbf{9 = R}$$

She needs to make **9 necklaces per hour**.

Example #3: Planning a Holiday Party

Frank is planning his company's holiday party. He has received proposals from 3 different venues, but he isn't sure which of them is the best deal. Venue A, a hotel, charges $4000 to rent the space and $80 per person. Venue B, a country club, charges a flat fee of $1500 for the first 10 guests, and $120 for each additional guest. Venue C, a restaurant, charges $150 per person. Assume he does not know how many guests will attend the party, except that the number of guests attending will be at least 10.

Step 1: Write a set of equations to express each venue's total cost in the standard linear form. Use the variable G for the number of guests who will attend the party.

Y	=	M	*	X	+	B
Ending	=	Rate	*	Quantity	+	Beginning
Total Cost, Venue A	=	Cost per Person	*	# of Guests	+	Rental Fee
Total Cost, Venue B	=	Cost per Additional Guest	*	# of Additional Guests	+	Flat Fee
Total Cost, Venue C	=	Cost per Person	*	# of Guests	+	(no charge)

Step 2: Insert the values provided in the word problem into the right place, for each of the 3 equations.

Total Cost, Venue A	=	Cost per Person	*	# of Guests	+	Rental Fee
Total Cost, Venue A	=	$80 per person	*	G	+	$4000

Total Cost, Venue B	=	Cost per Additional Guest	*	# of Additional Guests	+	Flat Fee
Total Cost, Venue B	=	$120	*	(G – 10)	+	$1500

Total Cost, Venue C	=	Cost per Person	*	# of Guests	+	(no charge)
Total Cost, Venue C	=	$150 per person	*	G	+	0

If you got all three equations correct on the first try, congratulations! If not, where did you get tripped up? Probably on figuring out how to translate **additional guests** from words to math for Venue B.

Here's a tip: Most of the time when you get hung up, reading and re-reading a short phrase repeatedly, you should adjust the variable by a constant inside parentheses. In this case, that means the (G - 10) in the equation for the total cost for Venue B.

Step 3: Plug in the number of people (guests) which Frank expects to attend the holiday party. Let's say that he expects 110 guests.

Total Cost, Venue A	=	$80 per person	*	G	+	$4000
Total Cost, Venue A	=	$80 per person	*	110	+	$4000

Total Cost, Venue B	=	$120 per person	*	(G – 10)	+	$1500
Total Cost, Venue B	=	$120 per person	*	(110 – 10) additional guests	+	$1500

Total Cost, Venue C	=	$150 per person	*	G	+	0
Total Cost, Venue C	=	$150 per person	*	110	+	0

Step 4: Solve each of the 3 equations for the Total Cost.

$Total\ Cost, Venue\ A = (\$80 * 110) + \$4000 = \mathbf{\$12,800}$

$Total\ Cost, Venue\ B = (\$120 * (110 - 10)) + \$1500 = \mathbf{\$13,500}$

$Total\ Cost, Venue\ C = (\$150 * 110) + \$0 = \mathbf{\$16,500}$

Venue A is the cheapest option.

Does your answer change if only 70 people RSVP? Change the # of people in each equation.

$$Total\ Cost, Venue\ A\ =\ (\$80 * 70) + \$4000\ =\ \$9{,}600$$

$$Total\ Cost, Venue\ B\ =\ (\$120 * (70 - 10)) + \$1500\ =\ \$8{,}700$$

$$Total\ Cost, Venue\ C\ =\ (\$150 * 70) + \$0\ =\ \$10{,}500$$

Venue B is now the cheapest option.

PRACTICAL APPLICATIONS OF EXPONENTIAL EQUATIONS

Many things we see in our daily lives, in science, and/or in business, can be described as a relationship between two or more variables using an exponential equation (or function) to represent the relationship. Exponential equations express either **growth** or **decay** relationships, often as a function of time. For example:

> *Note 1: When we refer to time, use the elapsed time in years, not the calendar year.*

> *Note 2: These formulas have had some complexities removed to show their commonalities. You may need to modify the general formula for specific conditions or situations stated in a word problem. One of the most frequently used modifications is adjusting time for a growth or decay that happens more than once per year – for example, if the population of bacteria doubles every 3 months, then there are four periods per year.*

Exponential Growth (Increase) relationships:

- The expected future population in a certain city is a function of the current population, its growth rate, and time.
  - *Future Population = Initial Population * (1 + Growth Rate)^{Time}*

- The expected future value of an investment is a function of the initial value (original principal), its rate of return, and time.
  - *Future Value = Present Value * (1 + Rate of Return)^{Time}*

- The expected future cost of college tuition for your child is a function of today's tuition, the rate of inflation, and time.
  - *Future Tuition = Current Tuition * (1 + Rate of Inflation)^{Time}*

Exponential Decay (Decrease) relationships:

- The expected future population of an endangered species is a function of the current population, its rate of decline, and time.
  - *Future Population = Initial Population * (1 – Rate of Decrease)^{Time}*

- The expected amount of nuclear material remaining is a function of the current amount, its rate of decay (or half-life)*, and time.
  - *Remaining Amount = Initial Amount * (1 – Rate of Decay)^{Time}*

*Note: The special half-life formula is covered later in this document.

GRAPHING AN EXPONENTIAL EQUATION IN STANDARD FORM

The standard form of the exponential equation (or function) is: **y = a (k)^x**

- Y = the Y-value
- A = the initial value
- X = the X-value, which most often represents time elapsed
- K = a constant multiplier. K is calculated by solving for (**1 + percent change**)
- Remember too, **change** can be either positive or negative. Change is <u>positive</u> if it's an increase, and <u>negative</u> if it's a decrease.
- Also, **change** can be any type of **relative number**, such as a **percentage** or a **fraction**.

The graph of any exponential function is <u>**curved**</u>.

It's much easier to recall the exponential formula this way:

$$\text{Ending} = \text{Beginning} * (1 + \text{Change})^{\text{Time}}$$

In addition, this variation of the exponential formula makes it more flexible, and therefore much easier, to figure out what piece of information goes where, regardless of what type of word problem we have.

Why bother learning all the distinct variations of it for biology, chemistry, physics, economics, and finance? You shouldn't!

You will, however, need to be aware of how to modify the formula when you encounter questions where the time periods are not consistent throughout the problem.

RELATING EXPONENTIAL EQUATIONS & FUNCTIONS TO REAL LIFE

Use the following table to understand terminology which is related, and where to place each piece of information into the formula for the exponential equation in standard form. Knowing how to put the right piece of info into the right place in an equation is more than half the battle with math word problems. If the question gives you an <u>annual rate</u>, you will need to <u>divide by the number of periods per year</u>. If the question gives you a rate that's already adjusted for the number of periods (e.g., 2% per quarter) then you don't do this.

Study this table to understand how to build up your equations. You'll note that I put most of the info in words first; **think through your equation in words first, then put the numbers into the equation for each of those parts**.

Y	=	A	*	K	^	X
Ending	**=**	**Beginning**	*****	**(1 + Change)**	**^**	**Time**
Final Population	=	Beginning Population	*	$(1 + Annual\ Growth\ Rate)$	^	$Years$
# of Bacteria Cells in the locker room	=	Initial # of Bacteria Cells	*	$\left(1 + \dfrac{Growth\ Rate}{Periods\ per\ Year}\right)$	^	$(Periods\ per\ Year * Years)$
Future Value of Investment	=	Principal Invested	*	$\left(1 + \dfrac{Rate\ of\ Return}{Periods\ per\ Year}\right)$	^	$(Periods\ per\ Year * Years)$
Remaining # of Animals	=	Beginning # of Animals	*	$\left(1 - \dfrac{Rate\ of\ Decline}{Periods\ per\ Year}\right)$	^	$(Periods\ per\ Year * Years)$

SPECIAL CASES: DOUBLING & HALF-LIFE FORMULAS

THE DOUBLING FORMULA

By definition, doubling something means increasing its amount by 100%. So, instead of calculating the constant multiplier as (1+100%) or (1.0 + 1.0), we use the shortcut of letting the **constant k=2**.

$$\text{Ending} = \text{Beginning} * (1 + \text{Change})^{\text{Time}}$$

$$\text{Ending} = \text{Beginning} * 2^{\text{Years}*\text{Doubling Periods per Year}}$$

Using the **doubling formula**: If, for example, the population of a certain insect is currently 250, and doubles once every six months, and we want to find out what the population of that insect will be in 3 years, our variables will be:

Beginning Population = 250

Doubling Period = 6 months

Doubling Periods per Year = 2 periods (12 months / 6 months)

Years = 3

$$\text{Ending} = 250 * 2^{3*2} = 250 * 2^6 = 250 * 64 = \mathbf{16000}$$

All Your Word Problems Solved

THE HALF-LIFE FORMULA

By definition, halving something means decreasing its amount by 50%. So, instead of calculating the constant multiplier as (1-50%) or (1.0 - 0.5), we use the shortcut of letting the **constant k = 1/2**.

$$Ending = Beginning * (1 + Change)^{Time}$$

$$Ending = Beginning * \left(\frac{1}{2}\right)^{Years*Half-Life\ Periods\ per\ Year}$$

Using the **half-life formula**: If, for example, we have five kilograms of a certain radioactive material, which has a half-life of 20 years, and we want to know how much of it will remain after 60 years. Our variables will be:

Beginning Amount = 5 kilograms

Half-Life Period = 20 years

Half-Life Periods per Year = 1/20 of a period (1 year / 20 years)

Years = 60

$$Ending = 5.0 * \left(\frac{1}{2}\right)^{60*\frac{1}{20}} = 5.0 * \left(\frac{1}{2}\right)^{3} = 5.0 * \frac{1}{8} = \frac{5}{8} \textbf{ kilograms}$$

SPECIAL CASES: FUTURE VALUE & THE RULE OF 70 (OR 72)

THE FUTURE VALUE FORMULA (FOR A ONE-TIME PAYMENT)

With interest, and its other financial counterpart, inflation, we usually express the rate of growth as a percentage. When the interest compounds (meaning, the investor earns interest on both the original principal and interest earned in prior years), the value of the investment increases at an increasing rate.

In this formula, you'll find it <u>easiest to re-express that percentage as a decimal</u>.

$$Ending = Beginning * (1 + Change)^{Time}$$

$$Future\ Value = Principal * \left(1 + \frac{Annual\ Rate\ of\ Return}{\#\ Compounding\ Periods\ Per\ Year}\right)^{Years*Compounding\ Pds.\ per\ Year}$$

Using the **future value formula**: If, for example, the original investment is $10,000, the interest rate is 8%, compounded quarterly, and the investor holds this for 5 years, our variables will be:

Beginning Principal = $10,000

Compounding Period = Quarterly = 3 months

Compounding Periods per Year = **4 periods** (12 months / 3 months)

Years = 5

$$\text{Future Value} = \$10000 * \left(1 + \frac{.08}{4}\right)^{5*4} = \$10000 * (1.02)^{20} = \mathbf{\$14859.47}$$

THE RULE OF 70 (ALTERNATIVE = RULE OF 72)

Anyone who has taken an introductory finance course is probably familiar with one of two variations of the same principle. These are **rules of thumb** that help us **estimate how long it will take to double our investment**:

- The Rule of 70
- The Rule of 72

The rule here, is that you take either 70 or 72, divide that number by the interest rate expressed as an integer, and the result will tell you approximately how many years it will take to double your investment. *Use whichever variation makes mental math easier*.

Example #1: Using the Rule of 70

If an investment offers a 5% return, you will double your investment in approximately 70 / 5 = 14 years.

Example #2: Using the Rule of 72

If an investment offers a 6% return, you will double your investment in approximately 72 / 6 = 12 years.

All Your Word Problems Solved

WHAT IS DIMENSIONAL ANALYSIS?

Whenever you have a Math word problem, or an applied math problem in areas as diverse as Chemistry, Economics, or Business, you'll need to **pay careful attention to the units given** in the problem.

On a multiple-choice test, *especially* the standardized college & graduate admissions tests (SAT, ACT, GRE, GMAT, etc.), you might not find an answer you've calculated correctly, if the question asked you to change the units and you overlooked that step.

REFRESHER: METRIC UNITS OF MEASURE

TO MEASURE THIS,	USE THIS BASE UNIT:
mass	gram
distance	meter
volume	liter OR m^3 (cubic meter)
computer memory	byte
temperature	degrees Celsius or Kelvin
frequency (physics)	hertz (Hz)
energy	joule (J)
power	watt (W)
pressure	pascal (Pa)

REFRESHER: METRIC PREFIXES

Here's a list of the standard metric prefixes you are expected to know. The cells highlighted in light purple are the most commonly tested prefixes and units.

Start from the row labeled **base unit**. Here, for example, you'll see that the base unit of distance is the meter, and the base unit of mass is the gram.

- As you move up the table, the units represent larger amounts. *For example, 1 kilogram is bigger than 1 gram, and there are 1,000 grams in 1 kilogram.*

- As you move down the table, the units represent smaller amounts. *For example, 1 centimeter is smaller than 1 meter, and there are 100 centimeters in 1 meter.*

PREFIX	NUMBER	POWER OF 10	DISTANCE	MASS	VOLUME	COMPUTER MEMORY
mega- (M)	1 million	10^6				**megabyte (Mb)**
kilo- (k)	1,000	10^3	**kilometer (km)**	**kilogram (kg)**	kiloliter (kL)	**kilobyte (kb)**
hecto- (h)	100	10^2	hectometer (hm)	hectogram (hm)	hectoliter (hL)	
deca- (da)	10	10^1	decameter (dam)	decagram (dag)	decaliter (daL)	
BASE UNIT	1	10^0	**meter (m)**	**gram (g)**	**liter (L)**	**byte (b)**
deci- (d)	0.1	10^{-1}	decimeter (dm)	decigram (dg)	deciliter (dL)	
centi- (c)	0.01	10^{-2}	**centimeter (cm)**	centigram (cg)	centiliter (cL)	
milli- (m)	0.001	10^{-3}	**millimeter (mm)**	**milligram (mg)**	**milliliter (mL)**	
micro- (μ)	1 millionth	10^{-6}	micrometer (μm)	microgram (μg)	microliter (μL)	

1. **No "naked numbers."** Always write down the units.

2. **Let the units lead you.** When you need to take some value or rate which is given and convert it to a different set of units using one or more conversion factors, you can use the principle of <u>cancelling units</u> to help you make sure you set up the conversion factors correctly. For example, if you're deciding whether to set up a conversion factor as 1 foot per 12 inches or 12 inches per 1 foot, you let the units lead you to put the numbers in the correct place.

    *   **Start with what you're given.** Put this on the left side of your scratch paper.

    *   **Write down the units you need as a result** (what you want to end up with). Put this on the far-right side of your scratch paper.

    *   **Add the necessary conversion factor(s) to the right, one at a time, and cancel units as you go.** If you end up with nonsense units, like dollars squared, then you probably need to flip one or more of your conversion factors.

    *   **When you have the same units on both the left and right side of the equals sign, <u>then</u> you are ready to calculate an answer.**

    *   <u>**Never**</u> place conversion factors <u>underneath</u> the given info. You should only place conversion factors <u>to the right</u> of the given info.

3. **"Sanity check" your work.** Does an answer this large (or this small) seem reasonable?

    *   For example, if you're asked to convert degrees Fahrenheit to degrees Celsius, you might recall from science classes that 0°C is the freezing point of water and 100°C is the boiling point of water. If you converted 86°F to Celsius and got a number close to 100°C, that would be almost boiling hot - but you know 86°F is the temperature of a summer day, but nowhere near hot enough to boil water – so re-check your work.

Example #1: Converting a Single Unit of Measure

Convert 85 inches into feet.

A. Start with what you're given on the left, then write down the desired units on the right.

GIVEN	CONVERSION FACTOR		DESIRED UNITS
85 inches			= ???? feet

B. You have inches, and you want feet. To get rid of inches in the numerator, you write that unit in the denominator of the conversion factor. That means feet must go in the numerator.

GIVEN	CONVERSION FACTOR		DESIRED UNITS
85 inches	Feet		= ???? feet
	inches		

C. Now, enter the values (numbers) which show the relationship between feet & inches.

GIVEN	CONVERSION FACTOR		DESIRED UNITS
85 inches	1 Feet		= ???? feet
	12 inches		

D. Cancel out units and make sure you've got the same units on both the left and right sides of the equation. Here, you can cancel out inches. You see feet in the numerator on the left, and feet in the numerator on the right, so you've got your work set up correctly.

GIVEN	CONVERSION FACTOR		DESIRED UNITS
85 ~~inches~~	1 Feet		= ???? feet
	12 ~~inches~~		

E. Now you can calculate an answer. (85*1)/12 = **7.08**

Example #2: Converting Multiple Units of Measure

Convert 45 meters per second into kilometers per hour.

A. Start with what you're given on the left. Write down the desired units on the right.

GIVEN	CONVERSION FACTOR		DESIRED UNITS
45 meters			= ?? kilometers
second			hour

B. Because this problem has a rate, you have to handle the units in the numerator <u>and</u> units in the denominator. You work the problem in the same manner as in Example #1, but you will need more than one conversion factor. Otherwise the process is the same!

You have meters in the numerator, and you want kilometers in the numerator. So to get rid of meters in the numerator, you write that unit in the denominator of the conversion factor. Then the kilometers unit must go in the numerator.

GIVEN	CONVERSION FACTOR		DESIRED UNITS
45 meters	kilometers		= ?? kilometers
second	meters		hour

C. Now, enter the values (numbers) which show the relationship between kilometers and meters.

GIVEN	CONVERSION FACTOR		DESIRED UNITS
45 meters	1 kilometers		= ?? kilometers
second	1000 meters		hour

D. Cancel out units and make sure you've got the same units in the numerators on both the left and right sides of the equation. Here, you can cancel out meters. You see kilometers in the numerator on the left, and kilometers in the numerator on the right, so you've got your work set up correctly.

GIVEN	CONVERSION FACTOR		DESIRED UNITS
45 ~~meters~~	1 kilometers		= ?? kilometers
second	1000 ~~meters~~		hour

E. Now you're ready to work with the denominators. You have seconds in the denominator, and you want hours in the denominator. Hmm… you may not know how many seconds are in an hour, but you know how many seconds are a minute, and how many minutes are in an hour, so you'll <u>use 2 conversion factors</u> to switch from seconds to hours.

To get rid of seconds in the denominator, you write that unit in the numerator of the conversion factor. That means minutes must go in the denominator. (This is shown in purple).

But, you'll need an additional conversion factor to go from minutes to hours. To get rid of minutes in the denominator, you write that unit in the numerator of the extra conversion factor. That means hours must go in the denominator. (This is shown in blue).

GIVEN	CONVERSION FACTOR	CONVERSION FACTOR	CONVERSION FACTOR	DESIRED UNITS
45 ~~meters~~	1 kilometers	seconds	minutes	= ?? kilometers
second	1000 ~~meters~~	minutes	hours	hour

F. Now, enter the values (numbers) which show the relationship between seconds and minutes (in purple), and the relationship between minutes and hours (in blue).

GIVEN	CONVERSION FACTOR	CONVERSION FACTOR	CONVERSION FACTOR	DESIRED UNITS
45 ~~meters~~	1 kilometers	60 seconds	60 minutes	= ?? kilometers
Second	1000 ~~meters~~	1 minutes	1 hour	hour

G. Cancel out units and make sure you've got the same units in the denominators on both the left and right sides of the equation. Here, you can cancel out seconds and minutes. You see hours in the denominator on the left, and hours in the denominator on the right, so you've got your work set up correctly.

GIVEN	CONVERSION FACTOR	CONVERSION FACTOR	CONVERSION FACTOR	DESIRED UNITS
45 ~~meters~~	1 kilometers	60 ~~seconds~~	60 ~~minutes~~	= ?? kilometers
~~second~~	1000 ~~meters~~	1 ~~minutes~~	1 hour	hour

H. Now you can calculate an answer. (45*60*60)/(1000*1*1) = 162. If you are taking the GMAT, use the **always be cancelling** approach to simplify the calculation for mental math.

GIVEN	CONVERSION FACTOR	CONVERSION FACTOR	CONVERSION FACTOR	DESIRED UNITS
45 ~~meters~~	1 kilometers	60 ~~seconds~~	60 ~~minutes~~	= 162 kilometers
~~second~~	1000 ~~meters~~	1 ~~minutes~~	1 hour	hour

RATIOS & PROPORTIONS

A **ratio** is like a rate: it's a "something per something" which expresses the relationship of two quantities relative to one another.

There are multiple ways to express ratios in words and in math form. All of these phrases are equivalent:

- There are 20 students for every 3 teachers
- The school has a student-teacher ratio of 20:3
- The ratio of students to teachers is 20 to 3
- $\dfrac{20 \; students}{3 \; teachers}$

A **proportion** is two ratios set equal to each other. You can use a variable as a placeholder for whichever value is missing, and solve for the value of the variable by cross-multiplying.

TRANSLATING WORDS TO MATH IN RATIO PROBLEMS

A **ratio** is always presented in simplified (reduced) form. The actual value of each of the two numbers could be <u>any multiple</u> of this ratio.

For example, if we know the ratio of boys to girls in a certain class is 3 to 2:

- There are 3 boys for every 2 girls
- The reverse is also true***: There are 2 girls for every 3 boys
- There <u>could be</u> 15 boys and 10 girls (because 15:10 reduces to 3:2)
- There <u>could be</u> 42 boys and 28 girls (because 42:28 reduces to 3:2)
- There <u>could be</u> 66 boys and 44 girls (because 66:44 reduces to 3:2)
- There <u>could be</u> any number of boys and girls such that we have the ratio of 3M:2M, where M is that constant multiple.

***It is critical that you **pay attention to which way you're asked to present a ratio**. The ratio of boys to girls is 3 to 2, but the ratio of girls to boys is the reciprocal, 2 to 3. It's a common test maker trap to offer choices that switch around which part goes where.

- The ratio of A to B means "A:B" or "A over B"
- The ratio of B to A means "B:A" or "B over A"

PART-TO-PART VS. PART-TO-WHOLE RATIOS

Whenever you're presented with a ratio, you'll want to understand whether the ratio is a **part-to-part ratio**, or a **part-to-whole ratio**. Sometimes, you'll be able to logically infer from a part-to-part ratio what the part-to-whole ratio must be…usually, because there's some **binary condition** (either/or) which logically means that each item is either in one group or the other, but not both. *Progressive sociopolitical values aside, assume anything traditionally accepted as binary, like gender, should be treated as such for the purpose of solving ratio questions on standardized tests.*

For example, if we have: 3 boys for every 2 girls in our class

- This is a **part-to-part ratio** of 3 boys to 2 girls

- We can infer that the whole would equal the total number of boys + girls, so the whole = 5

- Then we have a **part-to-whole ratio** of 3 boys to 5 students

- We have another **part-to-whole ratio** of 2 girls to 5 students

- Therefore, if we're asked "which of the following could be the number of students in the class," we <u>look for numbers which are multiples of the whole</u>, which is 5. The number of students in the class could be any multiple of 5, such as 15, 30, 65, 185, etc., but cannot be 14 or 22 or 36 because these are not multiples of 5.

For example, if we have: 2 store managers for every 15 store associates

- This is a **part-to-part ratio** of 2 managers to 15 store associates

- Absent any info in the problem to suggest otherwise, we can infer that the whole would equal the total number of store managers + store associates, so the whole = 17

- Then we have a **part-to-whole ratio** of 2 managers to 17 store employees

- We have another **part-to-whole ratio** of 15 store associates to 17 store employees

- Therefore, if we're asked "which of the following could be the number of store employees," we <u>look for numbers which are multiples of the whole</u>, which is 17. The number of store employees could be 34, or 85, or 170, or any other multiple of 17, but cannot be 100 or 75 or anything that's not a multiple of 17.

ADJUSTING RATIOS

When you're presented with word problems (like the one shown below) which ask you to adjust ratios, it is very important that you understand the original ratio as a "<u>some unknown multiple of those numbers</u>", and the new ratio as "some <u>*different*</u> unknown multiple of those numbers." Why? Because you're adding a specific value to some unknown number, and you need to represent this algebraically.

Example: Employee-Manager Ratio Changes After Hiring & Firing

In 2015, the ratio of engineers to supervisors was 5 to 2. If, in 2016, the firm hires 30 engineers and lays off 3 supervisors, the ratio of engineers to supervisors will be 3 to 1. How many engineers will the company have in 2016?

Here, we don't know <u>which multiple</u> of 5 and 2 would let us calculate the original number of engineers and the original number of supervisors. Call this the **Mth multiple** to remind yourself that it's some unknown multiple of each of these numbers. You'll see that the variable M is written <u>before</u> the 5 and the 2...to remind you not to add them only to turn around and cancel them out!

$$Original\ 2015\ Ratio = \frac{5\ engineers}{2\ supervisors} = \frac{the\ Mth\ multiple\ of\ 5\ engineers}{the\ Mth\ multiple\ of\ 2\ supervisors} = \frac{\boldsymbol{m5}}{\boldsymbol{m2}}$$

Great. Now let's adjust this ratio. We're going to add 30 engineers and take away 3 supervisors.

$$Adjusted\ Ratio = \frac{(m5 + 30)\ engineers}{(m2 - 3)\ supervisors}$$

The question tells us that, after these adjustments, the new ratio "is 3 to 1." That means, set our adjusted ratio equal to the 3 to 1 ratio. But, remember we do not know <u>which multiple</u> of 3 and 1 would let us calculate the new number of engineers and the new number of supervisors. It's a different multiple than in the original ratio, so let's call this the Kth multiple to remember that it's some unknown multiple of each of these numbers.

We'll set up a proportion.

$$\frac{(m5 + 30)\ engineers}{(m2 - 3)\ supervisors} = \frac{k3\ engineers}{k1\ supervisor}$$

Now, cross-multiply and proceed through the order of operations to solve.

$$k1 * (m5 + 30) = k3 * (m2 - 3)$$

$$5mk + 30k = 6mk - 9k$$

$$39k = mk$$

$$39 = m$$

Plug **m = 39** back into the original ratio to solve for the number of engineers and number of supervisors the company had in 2015.

$$Original\ 2015\ Ratio = \frac{m5\ engineers}{m2\ supervisors} = \frac{39 * 5\ engineers}{39 * 2\ supervisors} = \frac{\textbf{195 engineers}}{\textbf{78 supervisors}}$$

Plug **m = 39** back into the adjusted ratio to solve for the number of engineers and number of supervisors the company had in 2016.

$$Adj.\ Ratio\ 2016 = \frac{(m5 + 30)\ engineers}{(m2 - 3)\ supervisors} = \frac{(195 + 30)\ engineers}{(78 - 3)\ supervisors} = \frac{\textbf{225 engineers}}{\textbf{75 supervisors}}$$

SOLVING MULTI-PART RATIOS

Some test questions will give you a series of ratios which are interrelated, but you need to do some calculations to figure out the ratio of two of the items, based upon the other ratios you were provided.

How to solve multi-part ratios efficiently:

- Set up a table, with the labels for each part across the top (perhaps, A, B, C & D)
- Put each ratio you're given in a separate row, leaving blanks where you do not have information.
- Look for columns with 2 different values in them. Find the least common multiple of this pair of values.
- Multiply up both of the partial ratios to get the common component into its common multiple.
- Repeat steps 3 and 4 until all of the partial ratios are in common terms.
- Now you know the ratio of A to B to C to D.
- Choose the parts asked for in the question, and reduce the ratio of these two parts, if needed. *Beware of questions that ask you for the parts in reverse order, such as C to A. The ratio of C to A is the reciprocal of the ratio of A to C!*

Example: Bakery Production Ratios

A bakery sells four products: biscuits, cupcakes, donuts, and pastries. Each morning, the baker makes cupcakes and pastries in a ratio of 5 to 2. The assistant makes biscuits and donuts in a ratio of 3 to 7. The production plan dictates that biscuits and cupcakes are produced in a 2 to 3 ratio. What is the ratio of biscuits to pastries produced?

- Set up a table, with the labels for each part across the top (perhaps, A, B, C & D)
- Put each ratio you're given in a separate row, leaving blanks where you do not have information.

	Biscuits	Cupcakes	Donuts	Pastries
5 C to 2 P		5		2
3 B to 7 D	3		7	
2 B to 3 C	2	3		

- Look for columns with 2 different values in them. Find the least common multiple of this pair of values.
- Multiply up both of the partial ratios to get the common component into its common multiple. In the <u>Biscuits</u> column, the least common multiple of 3 and 2 is 6. That means we need to:

- ○ Take the 2nd row and multiply each term by 2
- ○ Take the 3rd row and multiply each term by 3

	Biscuits	Cupcakes	Donuts	Pastries
5 C to 2 P		5		2
3 B to 7 D	~~3~~ 6		~~7~~ 14	
2 B to 3 C	~~2~~ 6	~~3~~ 9		

- We repeat the process for the <u>Cupcakes</u> column. Find the least common multiple of this pair of values. In the <u>Cupcakes</u> column, the least common multiple of 5 and 9 is 45. That means we need to:
  - ○ Take the 1st row and multiply each term by 9
  - ○ Take the 3rd row and multiply each term by 5

	Biscuits	Cupcakes	Donuts	Pastries
5 C to 2 P		~~5~~ 45		~~2~~ 18
3 B to 7 D	~~3~~ 6		~~7~~ 14	
2 B to 3 C	~~2~~~~6~~ 30	~~3~~~~9~~ 45		

- Now we see that the <u>Biscuits</u> column is off again. Find the least common multiple of this pair of values. The least common multiple of 6 and 30 is 30. That means we need to:
  - ○ Take the 2nd row and multiply each term by 5.

	Biscuits	Cupcakes	Donuts	Pastries
5 C to 2 P		~~5~~ 45		~~2~~ 18
3 B to 7 D	~~3~~~~6~~ 30		~~7~~ 14 70	
2 B to 3 C	~~2~~~~6~~ 30	3 ~~9~~ 45		

- All of the partial ratios are in common terms, so we're done. Now you know the ratio of Biscuits to Cupcakes to Donuts to Pastries:
  - ○ 30 : 45 : 70 : 18
- Choose the parts asked for in the question, and reduce the ratio of these two parts, if needed. The question asks for the ratio of biscuits to pastries, which is
  - ○ 30 biscuits : 18 pastries
- We can simplify this by dividing each term by 6. **5 biscuits : 3 pastries**

CHAPTER 13 WORD PROBLEMS WITH SYSTEMS OF EQUATIONS

SOME WORD PROBLEMS REQUIRE A SYSTEM OF EQUATIONS

Any time you have two or more variables (unknowns) in a question, you need a **system of equations** to solve for the values of each of the variables individually.

- If you have 2 variables, you will need 2 equations.
- If you have 3 variables, you will need 3 equations.

To solve a word problem with two variables, you should first write out each equation using the **Words to Math** approach. *See section on Translating Words to Math.*

Once you have correctly written each of the required equations, now you can use either of these methods to solve the system of equations and find the values of each variable.

- **Substitution Method**
- **Combination Method** (also called **Elimination Method**)

TYPES OF WORD PROBLEMS W/ SYSTEMS OF EQUATIONS

Read the examples below, all of which are common ways that the major standardized tests ask questions which require students to create two or more equations and solve for the variables in the system of equations.

- **A company makes 2 products, which are sold at 2 different prices**. A company makes two kinds of products. The company makes (some total number) of units. If each unit of Product A sells for (a price) and each unit of Product B sells for (a different price), and the company generates (some total revenue amount) from sales of these products, how many units of Product A are sold?

- **A person has 2 kinds of coins, which come in 2 different denominations**. You have a certain total number of coins in your pocket. All the coins are either quarters or dimes. These coins are worth (some total number of dollars and cents). How many dimes do you have?

- **A business sells 2 types of gift cards, which come in 2 different denominations**. A store sold (a number) of gift cards yesterday, all of which were either worth $25 or $100. If the store earned (some total number of dollars) from sales of the gift cards yesterday, how many of these gift cards were the $25 denomination?

- **A theater, amusement park, or other ticket-selling venue sells 2 types of tickets, which are sold at 2 different prices**. A movie theater earned (some total number of dollars) from ticket sales yesterday. The 210 tickets sold yesterday were all either Matinee or Evening tickets. If a Matinee ticket sells for (one price) and an Evening ticket sells for (a different price), how many Evening tickets were sold yesterday?

All Your Word Problems Solved

What do the examples shown above have in common? Though the information is presented in a different way each time, these are <u>all variations of the same thing</u>.

- You have two variables and thus need two equations to solve.

- One of the required equations must express the **quantity of the two items**.

- One of the required equations must express the **value of the two items**.

Example #1: Joe's Pocket Change

Joe has 17 coins in his pocket, each of which is either a quarter or a dime. If the total value of these coins is $3.65, how many of the coins are dimes?

- **First**, **set up the Quantity equation.** It is helpful to choose variables which are meaningful in the context of the question, so you can keep straight which is which. You could accidentally mix up X and Y, so let's use Q and D for the number of quarters and the number of dimes, respectively.

$$Total\ \#\ of\ Coins\ =\ \#\ of\ Quarters\ +\ \#\ of\ Dimes$$
$$17\ =\ Q\ +\ D$$

- **Second**, **set up the Value equation.** For this equation, the total value of the coins is the sum of the value of the quarters and the value of the dimes. You're expected to know that the value of a quarter equals 25 cents or $0.25, and that the value of a dime equals 10 cents or $0.10. Thus, the value of all the quarters in his pocket could be translated into math as $0.25*Q and the value of all the dimes in his pocket could be translated into math as $0.10*D, where Q and D represent the number of quarters and the number of dimes, respectively (as you used them in the first equation).

$$Total\ Value\ =\ Value\ of\ His\ Quarters\ +\ Value\ of\ His\ Dimes$$
$$Total\ Value\ =\ Value\ of\ Quarter\ *\ \#\ of\ Quarters\ +\ Value\ of\ Dime\ *\ \#\ of\ Dimes$$
$$\$3.65\ =\ \$0.25\ *\ Q\ +\ \$0.10\ *\ D$$

- Now that you have both the Quantity equation and the Value equation written correctly, use <u>either</u> the **Substitution Method** or the **Combination (Elimination) Method** to solve for the value of D, the number of dimes.

Example #2: Amusement Park Ticket Sales

An amusement park generated $52,250 in ticket sales yesterday. The amusement park charges different prices for adults and for children. The total number of tickets sold was 1300. If the price of an Adult ticket is $50 and Child tickets are discounted 30% off the adult price, how many of each type of ticket were sold?

- **First, set up the Quantity equation.** It is helpful to choose variables which are meaningful in the context of the question, so you can keep straight which is which. You could accidentally mix up X and Y, so let's use A and C for the number of adult tickets and the number of child tickets, respectively.

$$Total \ \# \ of \ Tickets \ = \ \# \ of \ Adult \ + \ \# \ of \ Child$$
$$1300 \ = \ A \ + \ C$$

- **Second, set up the Value equation.** For this equation, the total value (revenue) of the tickets sold is the sum of the value of the adult tickets and the value of the child tickets. The question tells you the price of an adult ticket is $50, but does not directly tell you the price of a child ticket. Here, the test maker has included a little extra wrinkle which you must deal with. A <u>discount of 30% **off**</u> the adult price is equivalent to paying <u>70% **of** the adult price</u>, so each child ticket = $50*0.7 = $35. Thus, the value of all the adult tickets sold could be translated into math as $50*A, and the value of all the child tickets sold could be translated into math as $35*C, where A and C represent the number of adult tickets and the number of child tickets, respectively (as you used them in the first equation).

$$Total \ Ticket \ Sales \ = \ Value \ of \ Adult \ Tickets \ + \ Value \ of \ Child \ Tickets$$

$$Total \ Ticket \ Sales$$
$$= \ Value \ of \ 1 \ Adult \ * \ \# \ of \ Adult \ + \ Value \ of \ 1 \ Child \ * \ \# \ of \ Child$$
$$\$52{,}250 \ = \ \$50 \ * \ A \ + \ \$35 \ * \ C$$

- Now that you have both the Quantity equation and the Value equation written correctly, use <u>either</u> the **Substitution Method** or the **Combination (Elimination) Method** to solve for the number of each type of ticket sold.

Example #3: Concert Venue Beer Sales

A local concert venue offers beers for sale in two sizes, regular and large. Each regular-sized beer costs $8 and each large-sized beer costs $12. If the venue sold a total of 1500 beers during a recent concert, and the total revenue from beer sales was $16,400, how many large-sized beers were sold?

- **First**, **set up the Quantity equation**. It is helpful to choose variables which are meaningful in the context of the question, so you can keep straight which is which. You could accidentally mix up X and Y, so let's use R and L for the number of regular beers and the number of large beers, respectively.

$$Total \ \# \ of \ Beers \ = \ \# \ of \ Regular + \ \# \ of \ Large$$
$$1500 \ = \ R \ + \ L$$

- **Second**, **set up the Value equation**. For this equation, the total value (revenue) of the beers sold is the sum of the value of the regular beers and the value of the large beers. The value of all the regular beers sold could be translated into math as $8*R and the value of all the large beers sold could be translated into math as $12*L, where R and L represent the number of regular beers and the number of large beers sold, respectively (as you used them in the first equation).

$$Total \ Beer \ Revenue \ = \ Value \ of \ Regular \ Beers \ + \ Value \ of \ Large \ Beers$$
$$Total \ Beer \ Rev. = \ Value \ of \ 1 \ Reg.* \ \# \ of \ Reg. + Value \ of \ 1 \ Large \ * \ \# \ of \ Large$$
$$\$16,400 \ = \ \$8 * R + \$12 * L$$

- Now that you have both the Quantity equation and the Value equation written correctly, use <u>either</u> the **Substitution Method** or the **Combination (Elimination) Method** to solve for the number of large beers sold.

Example #4: Carnival Games

Melissa likes to play a certain carnival game where she tosses a small metal ring toward a set of targets which are blue or red. If the ring lands on a blue target, she scores three points. If the ring lands on a red target, she scores ten points. If she succeeded in landing a ring on a total of thirteen targets and scored a total of 74 points, how many of the rings landed on red targets?

- **First, set up the Quantity equation.** It is helpful to choose variables which are meaningful in the context of the question, so you can keep straight which is which. You could accidentally mix up X and Y, so let's use B and R for the number of blue targets and the number of red targets, respectively.

$$Total \: \# \: of \: Targets \: Hit \: = \: \# \: of \: Blue \: + \: \# \: of \: Red$$
$$13 \: = \: B + R$$

- **Second, set up the Value equation.** For this equation, the total value (points scored) of the rings landed on any targets is the sum of the value (points scored) of the rings landed on blue targets and the value (points scored) of the rings landed on red targets. The value of all the rings landed on blue targets sold could be translated into math as 3*B and the value of all the rings landed on red targets could be translated into math as 10*R, where B and R represent the number of rings landed on blue targets and the number of rings landed on red targets, respectively (as you used them in the first equation).

$$Total \: Points \: Scored \: = \: Score \: from \: Blue \: Targets \: + \: Score \: from \: Red \: Targets$$
$$Total \: Points \: Scored = \: Value \: of \: 1 \: Blue \: * \: \# \: of \: Blue \: + \: Value \: of \: 1 \: Red \: * \: \# \: of \: Red$$
$$74 \: points = \: 3B \: + \: 10R$$

- Now that you have both the Quantity equation and the Value equation written correctly, use <u>either</u> the **Substitution Method** or the **Combination (Elimination) Method** to solve for the number of rings landed on red targets.

All Your Word Problems Solved

You'll learn about the tables & labels strategy for approaching word problems which require both of the following:

- A **simple three-part formula**, such as:
    - $Rate * Time = Work$
    - $Rate * Time = Distance$
    - $Interest\ Rate * Principal = Interest\ Amount$
- **Two parts that combine to form a whole**, such as:
    - Two individuals each doing the work separately, then the pair working together
    - Driving to work, driving home from work, then the round-trip
    - The first segment of a trip, the second segment of a trip, then the total trip
    - The first type of investment, the second type of investment, then the total investment

The material in the following pages is intentionally repetitive, to drive home how flexible the **tables & labels approach** is and so you **focus on what is slightly different** in how you apply and execute the tables & labels approach for different types of questions.

PRACTICAL APPLICATIONS OF WORK-RATE PROBLEMS

When we see work-rate problems on a standardized test, they seem disconnected from reality – after all, how often are we filling an empty tank or painting houses together with a friend? But, work-rate problems are actually quite relevant when we think about business operations and project management. The ability of a machine or a person to produce goods or deliver services can be described by the rate, or the amount of work done per unit of time. We also know that many machines, and definitely all people, work at different rates. For example:

- **Production and scheduling decisions**. How many machines are needed to produce a particular job in a certain amount of time? If we want to shorten the timeline needed to ship products to a customer, how many more machines do we need to add?

- **Project management** and **resource allocation**. If two or more people are working on the same project, but produce work at different rates, what is the combined rate for the group? If one person is reallocated to a different project, how much more time will the remaining team members need to complete the assignment?

HOW TO APPROACH WORK-RATE PROBLEMS: TABLES & LABELS

USE TABLES TO ORGANIZE INFORMATION

For all work-rate problems, you should use tables for two purposes:
- To organize the information presented in the problem, and
- To help you figure out how to build any necessary formulas

How should you lay out your table?

- Row labels: Add meaningful labels to the rows, and skip a couple rows between each row label.

- Column labels: Use **rate * time = work** across the top of the page as your column headers. Be sure to leave a space at the left to add your row labels, and to make each space wide enough to allow you to fill in the values and units for each part of the table.

- Rates: Most rates are presented as **fractions**, which must be written on 2 lines (not crammed onto a single line) so you can more easily work with the fractions (e.g., finding a least common denominator and/or simplifying the fraction by cancelling out common terms).

USE LABELS TO ADD MEANING TO NUMBERS

Label your units in the table and in any equations related to this information. *Watch out for questions which provide given information in one unit, but present answers in terms of different units.*

Combined rates: You can add (or subtract) rates, as needed, based upon what the question asks you to do.

- <u>Working together</u>: Add the rates. If you have machines M and N, their combined rate is equal to the sum of their individual rates.

$$R_{M+N} = R_M + R_N$$

Here's an example of what the basic table layout might look like for this problem:

	Rate	*	Time	=	Work
Machine M					
Machine N					
M+N together					

- <u>Working against each other</u>: Subtract the rates. Watch out for wording that suggests two people, or two processes, are working in opposite directions. *Think of this as the "leaky bathtub" problem. If you're trying to fill a tub from the faucet, but there's a slow leak, the tub will not fill up as fast as you might otherwise expect it to. You need to subtract off the rate of the leak to find the net rate at which the tub will fill up with water.*

$$R_{F-L} = R_F - R_L$$

Here's an example of what the basic table layout might look like for this problem:

	Rate	*	Time	=	Work
Faucet					
Leak					
Faucet-Leak					

Next, **systematically transfer info** from the word problem into the table you laid out. You can start transferring the pieces of information in any order, but make sure you enter each piece into the correct place in the table.

Work	Might be any kind of units of production, such as: • Widgets made • Houses painted • Jobs completed
Time	May be given in seconds, minutes or hours. If time is given in mixed units, you <u>must</u> convert these mixed units to <u>one</u> of the two units, and You <u>must</u> also <u>use improper fractions</u> or <u>decimals</u> instead of mixed numerals. For example: <table><tr><td><u>Instead of this</u></td><td><u>Use one of these</u></td></tr><tr><td>1 hour 20 minutes</td><td>$\frac{4}{3}$ *hours* 80 minutes</td></tr><tr><td>5 minutes 30 seconds</td><td>5.5 minutes 330 seconds</td></tr></table>
Rate	A rate is any "something per something" such as: • Widgets per hour • Miles per hour • Beats per second • Houses painted per week You'll note that, in all your work problems, the rate is an <u>amount of work</u> per a <u>unit of time</u>. **To find the rate, create a fraction which places the amount of work over the amount of time.** For example, if it takes 3 hours to complete 2 jobs, then: $$\text{Rate} = \frac{2 \text{ jobs}}{3 \text{ hours}}$$

Leave fractions in their factored and unsimplified form until you get to the very last step – solving for the specific piece of information that you need.

- Most of the time, you'll be able to cancel out some terms in the final equation to reduce the fractions and enable easy mental math.

- **Leave proportional rates in factored form** as well. For example, let's say 3 identical machines can produce 5 widgets in 2 hours. You want to add one more machine that's identical to the original 3 machines. What will be the combined rate of all 4 of these machines?

3 machines can produce	$\dfrac{5\ widgets}{2\ hours}$
Add 1 more machine, which works at 1/3 of the rate that 3 of them do.	$\dfrac{1}{3} * \dfrac{5\ widgets}{2\ hours}$
Combined rate of 4 machines. Add the two fractions. *In this case, you have 3/3 in the first one and 1/3 in the second one, and a common factor of 5/2.* *Another way to look at it is that 4 machines work at 4/3 the rate of 3 machines.*	$\dfrac{4}{3} * \dfrac{5\ widgets}{2\ hours}$

Simplify away any unnecessary complexities that make the mental math harder than it needs to be.

For example, if the work produced is the same for each of the 3 rows in your table, such as 20 houses or 65 widgets, **just call that '1 job' or '1 batch'** in each of the 3 rows. This is especially useful in:

- Problem Solving questions which use <u>variables</u>, instead of numbers, in the rate or the time

- GMAT Data Sufficiency questions or GRE Quantity Comparison questions

Last, **fill in other blank spots in the table**, working up, down, left and/or right, based upon what information you have, and what information you need to find.

- **TIP**: Efficiently filling in the table should be more of a <u>Sudoku-like sequence of movements</u>

- If you try to always apply a linear, left-to-right, top-to-bottom approach, you're much more likely to get stumped on how to fill in portions of the table.

Example #1: Painting Houses With A Friend

Bob can paint a house in 12 days. Margo can paint three houses in 28 days. How long will it take the two of them, working together, to paint six houses?

Step 1: Start by setting up your table.

	Rate	*	Time	=	Work
Bob					
Margo					
Bob+Margo together					

Step 2: Systematically transfer info from the word problem into the table, putting each piece into the right place.

	Rate	*	Time	=	Work
Bob			12 days		1 house
Margo			28 days		3 houses
Bob+Margo together					6 houses

Step 3: Fill in other cells in the table, based on what you have and what you need to find. Work backwards from the goal, so you see what you need to fill in.

- Your goal: Solve for <u>Time, Bob+Margo</u> working together
- To find that, you need to find the <u>Rate, Bob+Margo</u> working together
- To find that, you need to find the <u>Rate for Bob alone</u> and the <u>Rate for Margo alone</u>.

You can find the individual rates by creating a fraction, with the amount of work in the numerator and the amount of time in the denominator.

	Rate	*	Time	=	Work
Bob	$\dfrac{1\ house}{12\ days}$		12 days		1 house
Margo	$\dfrac{3\ houses}{28\ days}$		28 days		3 houses
Bob+Margo together					6 houses

To find the <u>Rate of Bob+Margo together</u>, add the fractions for their two individual rates. You'll need to find the least common denominator, which is 84.

$$\frac{\mathbf{7}*1\ house}{\mathbf{7}*12\ days}+\frac{\mathbf{3}*3\ houses}{\mathbf{3}*28\ days}\ =\ \frac{7\ houses}{84\ days}+\frac{9\ houses}{84\ days}\ =\ \frac{16\ houses}{84\ days}$$

	Rate	*	Time	=	Work
Bob	$\dfrac{1\ house}{12\ days}$		12 days		1 house
Margo	$\dfrac{3\ houses}{28\ days}$		28 days		3 houses
Bob+Margo together	$\dfrac{16\ houses}{84\ days}$				6 houses

Now, find the Time for Bob+Margo together, fill in the remaining cell using the equation **Rate * Time = Work**.

$$\frac{16\ houses}{84\ days}*T\ =\ 6\ houses$$

Here, you can multiply both sides by the reciprocal of the rate, to isolate Time on one side of the equation.

$$\frac{84\ days}{16\ houses}*\frac{16\ houses}{84\ days}*T\ =\ 6\ houses*\frac{84\ days}{16\ houses}$$

Then, cancel out units and terms.

$$T\ =\ 6\ \cancel{houses}*\frac{\overset{21}{\cancel{84}}\ days}{4\ \cancel{16\ houses}}\ =\ \overset{3}{\cancel{6}}\ \cancel{houses}*\frac{\overset{21}{\cancel{84}}\ days}{\underset{2}{\cancel{4}}\ \cancel{16\ houses}}\ =\ \frac{63\ days}{2}$$

All Your Word Problems Solved

	Rate	*	Time	=	Work
Bob	$\dfrac{1 \text{ house}}{12 \text{ days}}$		12 days		1 house
Margo	$\dfrac{3 \text{ houses}}{28 \text{ days}}$		28 days		3 houses
Bob+Margo together	$\dfrac{16 \text{ houses}}{84 \text{ days}}$		$\dfrac{63 \text{ days}}{2}$		6 houses

You'll need **31.5 days** to paint the 6 houses.

Example #2: The Leaky Bathtub

A faucet can fill a bathtub at a rate of 16 gallons per minute. John notices that it took seven minutes to fill his 80 gallon bathtub. He suspects there might be a leak. How quickly does this leak flow?

Step 1: Start by setting up your table. Logically, the faucet & leak work against each other, so you'll subtract the two rates.

	Rate	*	Time	=	Work
Faucet					
Leak					
Faucet-Leak					

Step 2: Systematically transfer info from the word problem into the table, putting each piece into the right place.

	Rate	*	Time	=	Work
Faucet	$\dfrac{16 \text{ gallons}}{\text{minute}}$				
Leak					
Faucet-Leak			7 minutes		80 gallons

Step 3: Fill in other cells in the table, based on what you have and what you need to find. Work backwards from the goal, so you see what you need to fill in.

- Your goal: Solve for <u>Rate of Leak alone</u>

- To find that, you need to find the <u>Rate, Faucet-Leak</u> working against each other

	Rate	*	Time	=	Work
Faucet	$\dfrac{16 \text{ gallons}}{1 \text{ minute}}$				
Leak					
Faucet-Leak	$\dfrac{80 \text{ gallons}}{7 \text{ minutes}}$		7 minutes		80 gallons

To find the <u>Rate of Leak alone</u>, set up the equation so that the Rate of Faucet minus the Rate of Leak equals the Rate of Faucet-Leak.

$$\frac{16 \text{ gallons}}{1 \text{ minute}} - \textbf{Rate of Leak} = \frac{80 \text{ gallons}}{7 \text{ minutes}}$$

Isolate the Rate of Leak on one side of the equation.

$$\frac{16 \text{ gallons}}{1 \text{ minute}} - \frac{80 \text{ gallons}}{7 \text{ minutes}} = \textbf{Rate of Leak}$$

You'll need to find the least common denominator, which is 7.

All Your Word Problems Solved

$$\frac{7 * 16 \text{ gallons}}{7 * 1 \text{ minute}} - \frac{80 \text{ gallons}}{7 \text{ minutes}} = \text{Rate of Leak}$$

$$\frac{112 \text{ gallons}}{7 \text{ minutes}} - \frac{80 \text{ gallons}}{7 \text{ minutes}} = \frac{32 \text{ gallons}}{7 \text{ minutes}} = \text{Rate of Leak}$$

	Rate	*	Time	=	Work
Faucet	$\dfrac{16 \text{ gallons}}{1 \text{ minute}}$				
Leak	$\dfrac{32 \text{ gallons}}{7 \text{ minutes}}$				
Faucet-Leak	$\dfrac{80 \text{ gallons}}{7 \text{ minutes}}$		7 minutes		80 gallons

Note, we did <u>not</u> need to fill in the other cells in the table to arrive at our answer for this question. Work smarter, not harder, and recognize when you need to **overcome the temptation to complete unnecessary tasks**, which are **time wasters** on standardized tests, especially on the GMAT.

HOW TO APPROACH DISTANCE-RATE PROBLEMS: 2 METHODS

You can use either or both of the following methods:

- Diagramming
- Tables & Labels

DIAGRAMMING: DRAW DIAGRAMS TO VISUALIZE INFORMATION

Some distance questions are harder than others to visualize, so you may want to draw simple diagrams to help you ensure you are correctly interpreting information from the word problem and incorporating this information into your equations.

Type of Distance Question	Wording Clues, Strategies, & Hints for Solving

When one car (or person) has a **head start**, and a second car or person must **catch up** and/or **overtake** the first. Both are moving in the same direction.	Think of this like a police chase, and instantly the question becomes a little more engaging and fun to solve.
	
	Create your diagram, which might be as simple as two arrows, both pointed to the right, with a gap between where one starts and the second one starts but both ending at the same point.
	
	Determine whether the first car's (or person's) head start is in <u>time</u> or in <u>distance</u>.
	
	• With <u>different physical starting points</u>: The head start is in distance.
	
	    o *Hint: The two will be traveling for the same amount of time.*
	
	    o *Hint: The rate at which the 2nd car catches up to the 1st car is the rate at which it "closes in on" the other, and is the difference between the two rates.*
	
	Closing speed = Rate of Faster Car − Rate of Slower Car
	
	• With the <u>same physical starting points</u>: The head start is in time.
	
	    o *Hint: The two cars (or people) will be traveling the same distance, if A catches up to B.*
	
	    o If you need to use variables to represent the time, make sure you represent the extra amount of time that the one with the head start has in the same units as the speeds. You'd need to convert 30 minutes to 0.5 hours (e.g., T hours and T+0.5 hours) so that the time will work with the rates presented in miles per hour.

Type of Distance Question	Wording Clues, Strategies, & Hints for Solving
When two cars or people traveling at different speeds are driving toward each other, or away from each other	Think of this like you're meeting a friend. If you each leave at the same time, but travel toward each other at different speeds, you will meet somewhere in between but not exactly at the halfway point. **Create your diagram**, which might be as simple as two arrows, pointed either toward or away from each other. Label each arrow with the information applicable to it. • *Hint: The two of you will be traveling for the same amount of time.* • *Hint: The sum of the distance driven by you and the distance driven by your friend will equal the total distance between your starting points.* • *Logic check: If the two of you are traveling for the same amount of time, the person who travels at a faster rate will end up traveling farther in that time. The meeting point will be closer to the person who travels at a slower rate.*
Moving in a direction, turning, and moving in another direction.	Many times, the question will include directions, such as North, East, South and/or West. • *Hint: When you see these directions, remember that North + West = form a **right angle**.* • *Hint: Draw a picture, connect the starting and stopping points, and you'll discover a **right triangle**.* **Create your diagram**, which might be as simple as two line segments, drawn according to the directions in the problem. Use this convention: North = Up, East = Right, South = Down, West = Left. Label your starting and ending points, then draw the line which would directly connect them. You can find the distance between the stopping point and the origin by drawing a diagonal line which connects them, then solving for this distance using the **Pythagorean theorem**.

Type of Distance Question	Wording Clues, Strategies, & Hints for Solving
When you must compare a multi-stop route to a more direct route.	If you see wording asking you to determine the time it would take to get from Point A to Point C "as the crow flies" then you'll need to draw a picture, and more than likely this distance will be the hypotenuse of a right triangle.
	Create your diagram, which might be as simple as two line segments, drawn according to the directions in the problem. Use this convention: North = Up, East = Right, South = Down, West = Left. Label your starting and ending points, then draw the line which would directly connect them.
	Be careful, though, if there are multiple changes in direction. For example, if along one of the sides of your triangle, the person traveled 6 miles west, then 3 miles north, then later traveled 2 miles east, then net this person is only (6-2) = 4 miles west of their point of origin. You'd then use 4 as the length of one of the legs of your triangle. Drawing a picture will make this more apparent.
	*Did you notice the **Pythagorean Triplet** incorporated into this example? The test makers love to sneak the Pythagorean Triplets into Distance questions involving travel in multiple directions!*
	In questions that ask you to solve for time, do not forget to add any time spent waiting at the stops into the total time it takes to get from one place to the other.

USE TABLES TO ORGANIZE INFORMATION

For all distance-rate problems, you should use tables for two purposes:

- To organize the information presented in the problem, and
- To help you figure out how to build any necessary formulas

How should you lay out your table?

- Row labels: Add meaningful labels to the rows, and skip a couple rows between each row label.

- Column labels: Use **rate * time = distance** across the top of the page, as your column headers. Be sure to leave a space at the left to add your row labels, and to make each space wide enough to allow you to fill in the values and units for each part of the table.

- Rates: Most rates are presented as **fractions**, which must be written on 2 lines (not crammed onto a single line) so you can more easily work with the fractions (e.g., finding a least common denominator and/or simplifying the fraction by cancelling out common terms).

USE LABELS TO ADD MEANING TO NUMBERS

Label your units in the table and in any equations related to this information. *Watch out for questions which provide given information in one unit, but present answers in terms of different units.*

Average speed: You <u>cannot</u> add, subtract, or simply take the average of the two speeds. You must find the average speed by taking the total time and dividing it by the total distance.

Here's an example of what the basic table layout might look like for this problem:

	Rate	*	Time	=	Distance
1st Leg of Trip					
2nd Leg of Trip					
Total Trip					

Next, **systematically transfer info** from the word problem into the table you laid out. You can start transferring the pieces of information in any order, but make sure you enter each piece into the correct place in the table.

All Your Word Problems Solved

Distance	Might be measured in any unit of distance, such as: • Kilometers or Meters • Miles, Yards or Feet
Time	May be given in seconds, minutes or hours. If time is given in mixed units, you <u>must</u> convert these mixed units to <u>one</u> of the two units, and You <u>must</u> also <u>use improper fractions</u> or <u>decimals</u> instead of mixed numerals. For example: <table><tr><td><u>Instead of this</u></td><td><u>Use one of these</u></td></tr><tr><td>1 hour 20 minutes</td><td>$\frac{4}{3}$ hours 80 minutes</td></tr><tr><td>5 minutes 30 seconds</td><td>5.5 minutes 330 seconds</td></tr></table>
Rate	A rate is any "something per something." In a Distance question, the speed may be provided in any of these units: • Miles per hour • Kilometers per hour • Meters per second You'll note that, in all your Distance problems, the rate is a <u>unit of distance</u> per a <u>unit of time</u>. **To find the rate, create a fraction which places the measure of distance over the amount of time.** For example, if it takes 3 hours to drive 135 miles, then: $$\text{Rate} = \frac{135 \text{ miles}}{3 \text{ hours}} = \frac{45 \text{ miles}}{1 \text{ hour}} = 45 \text{ mph}$$

Leave fractions in their factored and unsimplified form until you get to the very last step – solving for the specific piece of information that you need.

- Most of the time, you'll be able to cancel out some terms in the final equation to reduce the fractions and enable easy mental math.

Last, **fill in other blank spots in the table**, working up, down, left and/or right, based upon what information you have, and what information you need to find.

- **TIP**: Efficiently filling in the table should be more of a <u>Sudoku-like sequence of movements</u>

- If you try to always apply a linear, left-to-right, top-to-bottom approach, you're much more likely to get stumped on how to fill in portions of the table.

- *The approach for Distance-Rate problems is very similar to the approach for Work-Rate problems, <u>except</u> that there's a different box in the total / combined row of the table which must be solved for using the information in the row instead of the information in the column.*

  - *With Work-Rate, you can add (or subtract) the Rates in the column, and solve for the combined Time within the row.*

  - *With Distance-Rate, you can add (or subtract) the Times in the column, and solve for the average Rate within the row.*

- To solve for the Average Speed, you must <u>solve within the row, not the column</u>.

$$\text{Average Speed} = \frac{\text{Total Distance}}{\text{Total Time}}$$

Example #1: George's Commute To & From Work

George drives to work each morning at a constant speed of 60 miles per hour. If he returns home by the same route, it takes him an extra half hour and reduces his constant speed to 40 miles per hour. How far does George drive roundtrip each day?

Step 1: Start by setting up your table.

	Rate	*	Time	=	Distance
Going to work					
Coming home					
Roundtrip					

Step 2: Systematically transfer info from the word problem into the table, putting each piece into the right place. *Note: There may be <u>more than one way to represent the unknowns</u> in a word problem like this.*

For Distance:

- *If you decide to let D = the distance going to work, then the distance coming home by the same route will also equal D. The roundtrip distance will equal 2D.*

- *It is <u>equally valid</u> to assign D = the roundtrip distance, and then each of the one-way distances will be 0.5D (or ½ D).*

For Time:

- *You could represent the time in either hours or minutes. You could set the time going to work as H (for hours) and then the time coming home as H+0.5 or H+1/2. You could also choose to put the time in minutes, and set the time going to work as M (for minutes) and then the time coming home as M+30.*

- *These options are equally valid. The most important thing is that you are consistent and use meaningful variables to keep track of the units.*

	Rate	*	Time	=	Distance
Going to work	$\dfrac{60\ miles}{hour}$		H		D
Coming home	$\dfrac{40\ miles}{hour}$		H+0.5		D
Roundtrip					2D

Step 3: Fill in other cells in the table, based on what you have and what you need to find. Work backwards from the goal, so you see what you need to fill in.

- Your goal: Solve for <u>Total Distance</u>
- To find that, you need to find each Distance in terms of H hours.

	Rate	*	Time	=	Distance
Going to work	$60 \frac{miles}{hour}$		H hours		D = 60H
Coming home	$40 \frac{miles}{hour}$		H+0.5 hours		D = 40*(H+0.5)
Roundtrip					2D

Then, because George is returning home by the <u>same</u> route, we know that the distance of the trip going to work equals the distance of the trip coming home.

Set the two equations for Distance equal to each other.

$$60H = 40 * (H + 0.5)$$

Then, proceed through the order of operations and solve for H.

$$60H = 40H + 20$$

$$20H = 20$$

$$H = 1$$

Now, plug H = 1 back into either of the equations for distance to find D.

$$D = 60H$$

$$D = 60(1) = 60$$

The question asks us to find the distance George drives <u>roundtrip</u>. Based on how we chose to assign the variables, the roundtrip distance is **2D = 2*60 = 120 miles**.

*Using tables to organize our work and **keep track of exactly what the variables represent is mission-critical for Distance-Rate problems**, because we have up to 3 rates, 3 times, and 3 distances in each problem.*

All Your Word Problems Solved

RECOGNIZING A MIXTURE VS. A DILUTION PROBLEM

Many word problems involving **mixtures** and/or **dilutions** involve liquids with a percentage concentration, but you may also see questions which involve solid mixtures and a percentage or fraction by volume or weight which is one substance or another.

	Mixtures	Dilutions
Typical Problem: **Solutions with a Known Concentration**	Two liquids of different concentrations are combined into a single container	A liquid with a certain concentration must be diluted with water (or other solvent) to form an amount of liquid with a new, lower concentration.
Example	Six liters of a 10% acetic acid solution are combined with two liters of a 5% acetic acid solution. How concentrated is the combined solution?	Three liters of a 20% solution of bleach must be diluted with water to produce a final solution which is 8% concentrated. How many liters of water must be added?
Key Things to Remember	The amount of the new mix = the amount of mix A + the amount of mix B. In the example above, we'd have a combined 8 liters.	The amount of the diluted substance = the amount of the original liquid + the amount of water added. In the example above, if we assign the variable **W** for the unknown amount of water, we will end up with **3+W** liters of the new, weaker solution.
Logical Boundaries for your Answer *Sanity Check Your Work!*	The concentration of the new mix must be <u>between</u> the two concentrations of the original liquids. The concentration of the new mix is <u>usually not equal to the simple average</u> of the two original concentrations. It will only equal the simple average when we combine equal amounts of each solution. *Thus, the simple average is usually a trap answer!*	The amount of "interesting stuff" (i.e., bleach) does not change because we add pure water. The concentration of the new mix must be <u>less than</u> the concentration of the original mix, before water was added.

USE TABLES TO ORGANIZE INFORMATION

For both **mixture** and **dilution** problems, you can use tables for two purposes:
- To organize the information presented in the problem
- To help you figure out how to build any necessary formulas

How should you lay out your table?
- Row labels: Add meaningful labels to the rows, and skip a couple rows between each row label.

- Column labels: Use **Amount of Mix * % Interesting Stuff = Amount of Interesting Stuff** across the top of the page, as your column headers. Be sure to leave a space at the left to add your row labels, and to make each space wide enough to allow you to fill in the values and units for each part of the table.

- Percentages, Fractions, or Ratios: You can work with either fraction or decimal equivalents of what is presented in the word problem. Use whichever is easier to manipulate, given the specific numbers in the problem.

What's the "amount of interesting stuff"? It depends on the question, but it's whatever substance is mixed with or dissolved into another. "Interesting" refers to whatever the question wants you to focus upon.
- If you are mixing saline solutions, it's the amount of saline.
- If you are diluting an acetic acid solution with pure water, it's the amount of the acetic acid.
- If you are combining two mixes of an orange-flavored beverage, it's the amount of the orange powder (not the water).
- If you are blending two brands of mixed nuts, and one is 30% peanuts by weight and the other is 50% peanuts by weight, it's the peanuts.

USE LABELS TO ADD MEANING TO NUMBERS

Label your units in the table and in any equations related to this information. *Watch out for questions which provide given information in one unit, but present answers in terms of different units.*

The % of interesting stuff in the combined mix is a **weighted average** of the percentages in Mix A and in Mix B.

All Your Word Problems Solved

Here's an example of the basic table for a **mixture** problem:

	Amount of Mix	*	% Interesting Stuff	=	Amount of Interesting Stuff
Mix A					
Mix B					
Combined Mix					

Here's an example of the basic table for a **dilution** problem:

	Amount of Mix	*	% Interesting Stuff	=	Amount of Interesting Stuff
Mix A					
Add			n/a		n/a
Diluted Mix					

Next, **systematically transfer info** from the word problem into the table you laid out. You can start transferring the pieces of information in any order, but make sure you enter each piece into the correct place in the table.

Last, **fill in other blank spots in the table**, working up, down, left and/or right, based upon what information you have, and what information you need to find.

- **TIP**: Efficiently filling in the table should be more of a <u>Sudoku-like sequence of movements</u>

- If you try to always apply a linear, left-to-right, top-to-bottom approach, you're much more likely to get stumped on how to fill in portions of the table.

- *The approach for **Mixture** and **Dilution** problems is very similar to the approach for other 3-part formulas where there is a Part A and a Part B (such as Work-Rate, Distance-Rate, Principal & Simple Interest, etc.)*

- To solve for the % Interesting Stuff, you must <u>solve within the row, not the column</u>.

$$\% \text{ Interesting Stuff} = \frac{\text{Amount of Interesting Stuff}}{\text{Amount of Combined or Diluted Mix}}$$

Example #1: Dropping Acid...From 20% To 5%

Mike has 5 liters of a citric acid solution which is 20% concentrated. He needs to weaken the solution by adding distilled water, to make a final solution with a 5% concentration so he can use it in an experiment.

Step 1: Start by setting up your table. In this case, this is a **dilution** problem.

	Amount of Mix	*	% Interesting Stuff	=	Amount of Interesting Stuff
Mix A					
Add			n/a		n/a
Diluted Mix					

Step 2: Systematically transfer info from the word problem into the table, putting each piece into the right place.

	Amount of Mix	*	% Interesting Stuff	=	Amount of Interesting Stuff
Mix A	5 Liters		20%		
Add	W		n/a		n/a
Diluted Mix			5%		

Step 3: Fill in other cells in the table, based on what you have and what you need to find. Work backwards from the goal, so you see what you need to fill in.

- Your goal: Solve for W, the amount of water you must add to make the diluted mix only 5% concentrated.

- *Note: Converting percentages to fractions is helpful if you must do mental math.*

	Amount of Mix	*	% Interesting Stuff	=	Amount of Interesting Stuff
Mix A	5 Liters		20% or 1/5		1
Add	W		n/a		n/a
Diluted Mix	5+W		5% or 1/20		1

Step 4: Solve.

- In this problem, using the fraction equivalent is easier than using the percentage. We can quickly see that 5+W must equal 20 so that (5+W) * 1/20 = 1.

- If 5+W = 20, then W = 15.

- We must add **15 liters of water**.

	Amount of Mix	*	% Interesting Stuff	=	Amount of Interesting Stuff
Mix A	5 Liters		20% or 1/5		1
Add	W		n/a		n/a
Diluted Mix	5+W = 20 W = 15		5% or 1/20		1

Example #2: Mixing Saline Solutions

How many ounces of a 25% saline solution must be added to 6 ounces of a 10% saline solution to obtain a 15% saline solution?

Step 1: Start by setting up your table. In this case, this is a **mixture** problem.

	Amount of Mix	*	% Interesting Stuff	=	Amount of Interesting Stuff
Mix A					
Mix B					
Combined Mix					

Step 2: Systematically transfer info from the word problem into the table, putting each piece into the right place. Remember your **Words to Math** rules. Whenever you see a question phrase like "**how many**," there is an unknown value which you can represent with a variable.

	Amount of Mix	*	% Interesting Stuff	=	Amount of Interesting Stuff
Mix A	Q		25%		
Mix B	6 oz.		10%		
Combined Mix			15%		

All Your Word Problems Solved

Step 3: Fill in other cells in the table, based on what you have and what you need to find. Work backwards from the goal, so you see what you need to fill in. *Note: Converting percentages to fractions is helpful if you must do mental math. Cross-reference the section on Fractions, Decimals, and Percents.*

	Amount of Mix	*	% Interesting Stuff	=	Amount of Interesting Stuff
Mix A	Q		25% or $\frac{1}{4}$		$\frac{Q}{4}$ or $\frac{5Q}{20}$
Mix B	6 oz.		10% or $\frac{1}{10}$		$\frac{6}{10}$ or $\frac{12}{20}$
Combined Mix	$Q+6$		15% or $\frac{3}{20}$		

Step 4: Solve.

- Remember that the Amount of Interesting Stuff is the <u>same</u>, whether we calculate it using the row or the column.
    - Using the column:

$$\frac{5Q}{20} + \frac{12}{20} = \frac{5Q + 12}{20}$$

    - Using the row:

$$(Q + 6) * \left(\frac{3}{20}\right) = \frac{3Q + 18}{20}$$

- Remember your **Words to Math**. Because the amount is the <u>same</u> no matter which way we calculate it, these two expressions can be set equal to each other. Proceed through the order of operations to solve for Q.

$$\frac{5Q + 12}{20} = \frac{3Q + 18}{20}$$

- Now, because the denominators are the same, we can ignore them. *Note: this is equivalent to multiplying both sides of the equation by 20.* We know that the numerators must be the same as well.

$$5Q + 12 = 3Q + 18$$

$$2Q = 6$$

$$\mathbf{Q = 3}$$

Example #3: Store Brand Cereal

Sarah and Joe have two kids who prefer the name-brand cereal with raisins and bran flakes. There is also a less expensive store-brand cereal of the same type. The name-brand cereal is 20% raisins by weight, whereas the store-brand cereal is only 12% raisins by weight. The parents decide to mix the two cereals, because they know the kids will only notice the change if the raisins are less than 15% of the total weight. If the parents buy 12 ounces of the name-brand cereal, what is the greatest number of ounces of the store-brand cereal they can mix into it before the kids will notice and complain?

Step 1: Start by setting up your table. In this case, this is a **mixture** problem.

	Amount of Mix	*	% Interesting Stuff	=	Amount of Interesting Stuff
Name-Brand					
Store-Brand					
Combined Mix					

Step 2: Systematically transfer info from the word problem into the table, putting each piece into the right place. Remember your **Words to Math** rules. Whenever you see a question phrase like "**how many**," there is an unknown value which you can represent with a variable.

	Amount of Mix	*	% Interesting Stuff	=	Amount of Interesting Stuff
Name-Brand	12 ounces		$\dfrac{20}{100}$		
Store-Brand	Q		$\dfrac{12}{100}$		
Combined Mix	12+Q		$\dfrac{15}{100}$		

All Your Word Problems Solved

Step 3: Fill in other cells in the table, based on what you have and what you need to find. Work backwards from the goal, so you see what you need to fill in.

	Amount of Mix	*	% Interesting Stuff	=	Amount of Interesting Stuff
Name-Brand	12 ounces		$\dfrac{20}{100}$		$\dfrac{240}{100}$
Store-Brand	Q		$\dfrac{12}{100}$		$\dfrac{12Q}{100}$
Combined Mix	12+Q		$\dfrac{15}{100}$		

Step 4: Solve.

- Remember that the Amount of Interesting Stuff is the <u>same</u>, whether we calculate it using the row or the column.

  o Using the column:

  $$\frac{240}{100} + \frac{12Q}{100} = \frac{240 + 12Q}{100}$$

  o Using the row:

  $$(12 + Q) * \left(\frac{15}{100}\right) = \frac{180 + 15Q}{100}$$

- Remember your **Words to Math**. Because the amount is the <u>same</u> no matter which way we calculate it, these two expressions can be set equal to each other. Proceed through the order of operations to solve for Q.

  $$\frac{240 + 12Q}{100} = \frac{180 + 15Q}{100}$$

- Now, because the denominators are the same, we can ignore them. *Note: this is equivalent to multiplying both sides of the equation by 100.* We know that the numerators must be the same as well.

  $$240 + 12Q = 180 + 15Q$$

  $$60 = 3Q$$

  $$\mathbf{20 = Q}$$

If you think about it, both **mixtures** and **dilutions** are more complicated types of questions involving **weighted averages**. *Cross-reference the section on Statistics for Standardized Tests, which includes a discussion of weighted averages.*

Therefore, so long as you are accurate in how you interpret the question and assign variables for the unknown(s), you can solve questions about **mixtures** and **dilutions** using <u>any</u> of these approaches:

- Tables & Labels approach
- Weighted Averages formula
- Heuristics / reasoning approach for Weighted Averages

Some facts to remember about weighted averages, which are useful **heuristics** (or rules of thumb) to help you efficiently eliminate tempting-but-wrong answer choices:

- The weighted average cannot be less than the smallest of the group averages
- The weighted average cannot be more than the largest of the group averages
- The weighted average will only equal the average of the group averages if the groups are equally sized. Otherwise, the weighted average will not equal the average of the group averages. *Cross-reference the section on Mental Math Techniques, which discusses estimation using logical boundaries.*

ESSENTIAL FORMULAS & RELATIONSHIPS FOR RETAIL MATH

The term **Retail Math** refers to a set of terms and formulas which express the mathematical relationships between these concepts.

First, and most important, is to understand that the terms **Price** and **Cost** are <u>not interchangeable</u> in any standardized test.

- When you're speaking with friends about a recent purchase, you might ask "What was the price of your new sweater?" and your friend would respond "It cost me $40." It's OK to use the terms interchangeably with friends, but deadly on your standardized tests.

- **Cost vs. Price**. Make sure you understand the distinction:

    o **Cost** = What a business pays to purchase an item, which it will resell.

    o **Price** = What the business charges its customers to purchase the same item.

    o For example, if a retail store buys a sweater from a wholesaler for $20, and resells it for $60, then:

        ▪ The store's **cost** is $20, and

        ▪ The retail **price** is $60

Next, we need to understand the terms **Markup** and **Discount**.

Here, you'll need to understand the fundamental distinction: **markups** are applied/**added to cost**, but **discounts** are applied/**subtracted from price**. Knowing this distinction will help you retain and recall the formulas for markups and discounts accurately.

- **Markup** = The difference between the **price** a business charges for an item, and the **cost** the same business had to pay to buy that item. Said another way, a business buys a certain item at a **cost**, and adds a **markup**, to determine the **price** it will charge.

    o The **markup** can be expressed as either an <u>amount</u> or as a <u>percent</u>.

    o Thus, we have our first formulas:

        ▪ $Price = Cost + Markup\ Amount$

        ▪ $Markup\ Amount = Cost * Markup\ Percent$

    o Using substitution to put these together, we get:

        ▪ $Price = Cost + [Cost * Markup\ Percent]$

    o Notice here, that the Cost shows up in two places. That means this formula can also be re-expressed, by factoring out the Cost from each term, as:

        ▪ $Price = Cost * [1 + Markup\ Percent]$

- o This is important! Many students correctly figure out how to add a markup when the markup is less than 100%, but they get thrown off by markup percentages greater than 100%.
  - ▪ A "200% markup" means the price is actually "300% of" (3 times) the cost, <u>not</u> 2 times the cost.
- • **Discount** = The difference between the **original price** (also called **suggested retail price**, or **MSRP**) listed on an item's price tag or sticker, and the **sale price** a consumer actually pays for the item. Said another way, a business offers a certain item at an **original price**, and then offers a
  - o The **discount** can be expressed as either an <u>amount</u> or as a <u>percent</u>.
  - o Thus, we have our first formulas:
    - ▪ $Sale\ Price = Original\ Price - Discount\ Amount$
    - ▪ $Discount\ Amount = Original\ Price * Discount\ Percent$
  - o Using substitution to put these together, we get:
    - ▪ $Sale\ Price = Original\ Price - [Original\ Price * Discount\ Percent]$
  - o Notice here, that the Original Price shows up in two places. That means this formula can also be re-expressed, by factoring out the Original Price from each term, as:
    - ▪ $Sale\ Price = Original\ Price * [1 - Discount\ Percent]$

Next, we need to understand the terms **Percent Of** and **Percent Change**.

- • This is another fundamental difference you must understand: **The <u>percent of</u> a number is not the same thing as the <u>percent change</u>** (where a percent change could be either some <u>percent more</u> or some <u>percent less</u>). This leads us to another formula:
  - o $Percent\ Of = Original\ Amt + (Original\ Amt * Percent\ Change)$
  - o Notice here, that the Original Amount shows up in two places. That means this formula can also be re-expressed, by factoring out the Original Amount from each term, as:
  - o $Percent\ Of = Original\ Amt * (1 + Percent\ Change)$
  - o When we need to solve for the **percent change**, use whichever version of this formula is easier for you to grasp. *Most of the time when students get a question about percent change incorrect, it is because they have put the wrong number in the denominator.*
  - o $Percent\ Change = \frac{New - Original}{Original}\ or\ \frac{Focus - Basis\ of\ Comparison}{Basis\ of\ Comparison}$
- • Note, you enter a **percent increase as a positive number** for percent change, and a **percent decrease as a negative number**.
  - o A **markup** is one type of percent increase, so use a positive number
  - o A **discount** is one type of percent decrease, so use a negative number

All Your Word Problems Solved

Last, be aware that in a real-world business scenario, there are often multiple businesses involved supply chain from manufacturer to consumer.

Here's an example of a simple supply chain:

| Manufacturer | Distributor | Wholesaler | Retailer |

- Each of the businesses along the supply chain will add its own **markup** to its cost, before reselling a good to the next business along the supply chain.

- That means you may need to have a more than one **markup percent** factored into your equation!

- Let's say a certain item, such as a lamp, costs the manufacturer $30 to produce.

    - **Manufacturer markup**: The manufacturer will add a markup of 50% to the lamp to determine the price it will charge the distributor.

    - *Note: Because the distributor intends to resell the lamp to someone else, the **manufacturer's price = the distributor's cost**.*

    - **Distributor markup**: The distributor will, in turn, add a markup to cover its business expenses and make a profit. Let's say the distributor adds a markup of 20% to the price of the lamp, to determine the price it will charge the wholesaler.

    - *Note: Because the wholesaler intends to resell the lamp to someone else, the **distributor's price = the wholesaler's cost**.*

    - **Wholesaler markup**: The wholesaler will, in turn, add a markup to cover its business expenses and make a profit. Let's say the wholesaler adds a markup of 50% to the price of the lamp, to determine the price it will charge the retailer.

    - *Note: Because the retailer intends to resell the lamp to someone else, the **wholesaler's price = the retailer's cost**.*

    - **Retailer markup**: The retailer will, in turn, add a markup to cover its business expenses and make a profit. Let's say the retailer adds a markup of 200% to the price of the lamp, to determine the price it will charge the consumer.

    - *Note: Because the consumer intends to use the lamp, and does not intend to resell the lamp, we're at the end of the line. Let's find the **retail price paid by consumers**.*

    - You can create a single equation which strings together all the successive markups. And you wonder why things with high prices on the retail shelf are surprisingly cheap to manufacture! There are so many businesses in the supply chain that have their own expenses and profits to cover.

- With this much information given in the problem, it's easiest to **build your logic in words first, math second**:

$$Retail\ Price = Mfr.Cost * (1 + Mfr\ Markup\%) * (1 + Dist.Markup\%)$$
$$* (1 + Wholesaler\ Markup\%) * (1 + Retailer\ Markup\%)$$

$$Retail\ Price = \$30 * \left(1 + \frac{50}{100}\right) * \left(1 + \frac{20}{100}\right) * \left(1 + \frac{50}{100}\right) * \left(1 + \frac{200}{100}\right)$$

$$Retail\ Price = \$30 * \left(1 + \frac{1}{2}\right) * \left(1 + \frac{1}{5}\right) * \left(1 + \frac{1}{2}\right) * \left(1 + \frac{2}{1}\right)$$

$$Retail\ Price = \$30 * \left(\frac{3}{2}\right) * \left(\frac{6}{5}\right) * \left(\frac{3}{2}\right) * \left(\frac{3}{1}\right)$$

- And, don't forget, **always be cancelling**!

$$Retail\ Price = 3\ \cancel{\$30} * \left(\frac{3}{\cancel{2}}\right) * \left(\frac{\cancel{6}\ 3}{\cancel{5}}\right) * \left(\frac{3}{\cancel{2}}\right) * \left(\frac{3}{1}\right) = 3^5 = \$243$$

- Yes, that lamp which only cost $30 worth of materials and labor to produce, will be offered for sale in your local retailer for a whopping $243!!

HANDLING SUCCESSIVE PERCENT CHANGES

Let's say you're given the following problem:

> Greta's Gift Shop sells children's picture books. Greta buys picture books from a distributor for $5.00 per book. Her pricing strategy is to apply a 300% markup to determine her retail price, and then offer an everyday 20% discount off that retail price. What is the final selling price of one book at Greta's Gift Shop?

There is **more than one way to solve the problem**. You can use a **step-by-step approach**, or an **integrated approach**. Both approaches are equally valid (meaning, both get you to the same answer), but the integrated approach is usually more time-efficient.

Step-by-step approach

1. You're given Greta's cost per book and the markup percent she will add to determine the price. Use the relevant formula, starting with the **words first, math second** approach, so you can make sure to plug in the right information into the right places in the formula. *Tip: You can express those percentages as either a decimal, or a fraction with the percent placed over 100; use whichever method makes the computation easier for you. Putting the percentages into*

*fraction form is often helpful, because then you can employ the **always be cancelling** strategy to simplify the math.*

$$Retail\ Price = Cost * [1 + Markup\ Percent]$$

$$Retail\ Price = \$5 * \left[1 + \frac{300}{100}\right] = \$5 * [1 + 3] = \$5 * [4] = \mathbf{\$20}$$

2. Now that we know Greta's **retail price is $20**, we want to determine what her sale price will be. Use the given discount percent of 20% off, and plug that into the next formula.

$$Sale\ Price = Retail\ Price * [1 - Discount\ Percent]$$

$$Sale\ Price = \$20 * \left[1 - \frac{20}{100}\right] = \$20 * \left[1 - \frac{1}{5}\right] = \$20 * \left[\frac{4}{5}\right] = \mathbf{\$16}$$

Integrated approach

---

1. Here, you'll use the **substitution method** to adjust the algebraic formula to create a single, integrated formula, so you solve directly for the **sale price** <u>without</u> the intermediate step of solving for the original **retail price**.

$$Sale\ Price = Retail\ Price * [1 - Discount\ Percent]$$

2. We can use the formula for the Retail Price to substitute the components of Retail Price into this equation, so:

$$Sale\ Price = Cost * [1 + Markup\ Percent] \\ * [1 - Discount\ Percent]$$

3. Now, just plug in the right information into the right places in this combined equation.

$$Sale\ Price = \$5 * \left[1 + \frac{300}{100}\right] * \left[1 - \frac{20}{100}\right]$$

$$Sale\ Price = \$5 * [1 + 3] * \left[1 - \frac{1}{5}\right]$$

$$Sale\ Price = \$5 * [4] * \left[\frac{4}{5}\right] = \mathbf{\$16}$$

4. You can cancel out the 5's, so you're left with 4*4 = 16.

*The speed of computation is why you often want to **re-express percentages as fractions**, and employ the **always be cancelling** strategy to simplify the math.*

Example #1: Jewelry Boutique

Sarah, a boutique owner, purchases 20 necklaces from a wholesaler for $300 total.

Part A: If she adds a 250% markup to each necklace, what is the retail price of one necklace?

Part B: Now assume Sarah runs a holiday sale, with all jewelry discounted 20%. If Joe buys a necklace for his girlfriend, how much will he pay? *(You can ignore sales tax).*

You can solve the questions using either the **step-by-step approach** or the **integrated approach**.

Using the step-by-step approach

Step 1: Determine the wholesale cost per necklace.

$$Wholesale\ Cost\ per\ Necklace = \frac{Total\ Wholesale\ Cost}{\#\ of\ Necklaces} = \frac{\$300}{20} = \$15$$

Step 2: Add the markup to determine the retail price.

$$Retail\ Price = Cost * (1 + Markup\ Pct)$$

$$Retail\ Price = \$15 * \left(1 + \frac{250}{100}\right) = \$15 * \left(\frac{350}{100}\right) = \frac{\$525}{10} = \mathbf{\$52.50}$$

You have your answer for part A, the retail price is $52.50

Step 3: Subtract the discount from the retail price to determine the sale price. You'll need to plug in the retail price from above into this equation.

$$Sale\ Price = Retail\ Price * (1 - Discount\ Pct)$$

$$Sale\ Price = \$52.50 * \left(1 - \frac{20}{100}\right) = \$52.50 * \left(1 - \frac{1}{5}\right) = \$52.50 * \left(\frac{4}{5}\right) = \mathbf{\$42.00}$$

You have your answer for part B; the sale price is $42.00

All Your Word Problems Solved

Using the integrated approach

If, on the test, you're just asked the question in Part B, you would still need to solve for Part A along the way. Or, you can build an integrated equation to drive directly from the retail price to the sales price, adjusting for the markup and the discount as successive percent changes. *Due to the explanations, this will look like a lot of steps – but if you practice the skill of starting with the final equation, and progressively drilling down and replacing parts of the equation with equivalent expressions, this will become more intuitive and faster than solving a series of separate equations.*

Begin with the end in mind:

$$Sale\ Price = Retail\ Price * (1 - Discount\ Pct)$$

Because you know that the retail price equals cost times (1+markup), you can substitute that into the equation:

$$Sale\ Price = Cost * (1 + Markup\ Pct) * (1 - Discount\ Pct)$$

Because you know that the cost of one item is the total cost divided by the number of items, you can substitute that into the equation:

$$Sale\ Price = \frac{Total\ Cost}{\#\ of\ Items} * (1 + Markup\ Pct) * (1 - Discount\ Pct)$$

Now, plug in the information from the problem and solve directly for the sale price.

$$Sale\ Price = \frac{\$300}{20} * \left(1 + \frac{250}{100}\right) * \left(1 - \frac{20}{100}\right)$$

Proceed through the order of operations and cancelling to solve for the answer.

$$Sale\ Price = \frac{\$300}{20} * \left(\frac{350}{100}\right) * \left(\frac{80}{100}\right) = \$15 * \frac{35}{10} * \frac{4}{5} = 3 * \frac{7}{2} * 4 = 3 * 7 * 2 = \mathbf{\$42}$$

Example #2: Commercial Coffee Makers

A manufacturer producing commercial coffee makers does so at a cost of $150 per unit. These are sold through a network of distributors and wholesalers before final sale to independent local coffee shops. If the manufacturer requires a 100% markup, and the distributor and wholesaler each add a 50% markup, what is the final selling price to the local coffee shop?

You can solve the questions using either the **step-by-step approach** or the **integrated approach**.

Using the step-by-step approach

You'll notice that there's more than one markup added to the item, as each business in the supply chain needs to cover its costs and earn a profit. You should also realize that at each step in the supply chain, the seller's price equals the buyer's cost.

Step 1: Determine the <u>manufacturer's</u> price.

$$Mfr\ Price = Mfr\ Cost * (1 + Mfr\ Markup\ Pct)$$

$$Mfr\ Price = \$150 * \left(1 + \frac{100}{100}\right) = \$150 * 2 = \mathbf{\$300}$$

Step 2: Determine the <u>distributor's</u> price.

$$Dist\ Price = Dist\ Cost * (1 + Dist\ Markup\ Pct)$$

$$Dist\ Price = \$300 * \left(1 + \frac{50}{100}\right) = \$300 * \left(\frac{3}{2}\right) = \mathbf{\$450}$$

Step 3: Determine the <u>wholesaler's</u> price.

$$Whs\ Price = Whs\ Cost * (1 + Whs\ Markup\ Pct)$$

$$Whs\ Price = \$450 * \left(1 + \frac{50}{100}\right) = \$450 * \left(\frac{3}{2}\right) = \$225 * 3 = \mathbf{\$675}$$

The coffee shop will pay the wholesaler's price of **$675** to use this commercial coffee maker in the shop. *If the coffee shop were to resell this same coffee maker, it would add yet another markup before selling it to consumers or other coffee shops!*

All Your Word Problems Solved

Using the integrated approach

Due to the explanations, this will look like a lot of steps – but if you practice the skill of starting with the final equation, and progressively drilling down and replacing parts of the equation with equivalent expressions, this will become more intuitive and faster than solving a series of separate equations.

Begin with the end in mind: Finding the wholesaler's price.

$$Whs\ Price = Whs\ Cost * (1 + Whs\ Markup\ Pct)$$

Because you know that the wholesaler's cost equals the distributor's price, you can substitute that into the equation:

$$Whs\ Price = Dist\ Cost * (1 + Dist\ Mkup\ Pct) * (1 + Whs\ Mkup\ Pct)$$

Because you know that the distributor's cost equals the manufacturer's price, you can substitute that into the equation:

$$Whs\ Price = Mfr\ Cost * (1 + Mfr\ Mkup\%) * (1 + Dist\ Mkup\%) \\ * (1 + Whs\ Mkup\%)$$

Now, plug in the information from the problem and solve directly for the wholesaler's price.

$$Whs\ Price = \$150 * \left(1 + \frac{100}{100}\right) * \left(1 + \frac{50}{100}\right) * \left(1 + \frac{50}{100}\right)$$

Proceed through the order of operations and cancelling to solve for the answer.

$$Whs\ Price = \$150 * (2) * \left(\frac{3}{2}\right) * \left(\frac{3}{2}\right)$$

$$Whs\ Price = 75\ \cancel{150} * \cancel{(2)} * \left(\frac{3}{\cancel{2}}\right) * \left(\frac{3}{\cancel{2}}\right) = 75 * 9 = (75 * 10) - (75 * 1) = 750 - 75$$
$$= \$675$$

The coffee shop will pay the wholesaler's price of **$675** to use this commercial coffee maker in the shop.

Example #3: On Sale with Extra Coupon

A major department store sells men's merino wool sweaters for a regular price of $100. The sweaters are on sale for 40% off. There's also a coupon in the weekly advertisement for an extra 20% off all sale priced items. What is the total discount, as a percent of the regular price?

You can solve the questions using either the **step-by-step approach** or the **integrated approach**.

Using the step-by-step approach

If, like many consumers, you assume that you can simply add the two percentage discounts, 40% + 20% = 60%, then you have fallen for a classic retailer trick! The total discount after two or more successive discounts is never the sum of the individual percentages. *You can probably name two or three retailers who frequently use this to make shoppers think they're getting a better deal than they really are!!*

Step 1: Determine the sale price, before the coupon is applied.

$$Sale\ Price = Regular\ Price * (1 - Discount\ Pct)$$

$$Sale\ Price = \$100 * \left(1 - \frac{40}{100}\right) = \$100 * \left(\frac{60}{100}\right) = \$60$$

Step 2: Determine the after-coupon price.

$$After\ Coupon\ Price = Sale\ Price * (1 - Coupon\ Pct)$$

$$After\ Coupon\ Price = \$60 * \left(1 - \frac{20}{100}\right) = \$60 * \left(\frac{4}{5}\right) = \$12 * 4 = \$48$$

Step 3: Determine the cumulative (total) discount, after the sale and coupon.

$$Cume.\,Discount = \frac{After\ Coupon\ Price - Regular\ Price}{Regular\ Price} = \frac{\$48 - \$100}{\$100} = -52\%$$

Combining a 40% off sale with an extra 20% off coupon only gets you a 52% discount. That's good, but not quite the deal you originally thought it was!

Using the integrated approach

Due to the explanations, this will look like a lot of steps – but if you practice the skill of starting with the final equation, and progressively drilling down and replacing parts of the equation with equivalent expressions, this will become more intuitive and faster than solving a series of separate equations.

Begin with the end in mind: Finding the cumulative discount percentage.

$$Cumulative\ Discount = \frac{After\ Coupon\ Price - Regular\ Price}{Regular\ Price}$$

Because you know that the after-coupon price equals the sale price times 1 minus the coupon percentage, you can substitute that into the equation:

$$Cumulative\ Discount = \frac{[Sale\ Price * (1 - Coupon\ Pct)] - Regular\ Price}{Regular\ Price}$$

Because you know that the sale price equals the regular price times 1 minus the discount percentage, you can substitute that into the equation:

$$Cume.Disct\ Pct = \frac{[Reg.Price * (1 - Disct\ Pct) * (1 - Coupon\ Pct)] - Reg.Price}{Reg.Price}$$

Now, plug in the information from the problem and solve directly for the wholesaler's price.

$$Cume.Disct\ Pct = \frac{\left[100 * \left(1 - \frac{40}{100}\right) * \left(1 - \frac{20}{100}\right)\right] - 100}{100}$$

Proceed through the order of operations and cancelling to solve for the answer.

$$Cume.Disct\ Pct = \frac{\left[100 * \left(\frac{5}{5} - \frac{2}{5}\right) * \left(\frac{5}{5} - \frac{1}{5}\right)\right] - 100}{100}$$

$$Cume.Disct\ Pct = \frac{\left[100 * \left(\frac{3}{5}\right) * \left(\frac{4}{5}\right)\right] - 100}{100} = \frac{[4 * 12] - 100}{100} = \frac{48 - 100}{100} = \mathbf{-52}\%$$

Combining a 40% off sale with an extra 20% off coupon only gets you a 52% discount. That's good, but not quite the deal you originally thought it was!

ESSENTIAL FORMULAS & RELATIONSHIPS FOR INTEREST

You may be very familiar, or perhaps not-so-familiar, with the concept of **interest**. At its most basic, interest is the cost of using someone else's money. You can either pay or receive interest. Many of us do both, at different points in our lifetimes. You might earn interest on a bank account or pay interest on a student loan or car loan or do both.

- If you're a **borrower**, interest is the amount you pay to someone else, for the use of their money, for a defined period of time.

- If you're a **saver**, **investor**, **or lender**, interest is the payment you receive from someone else, for letting them use your money, for a defined period of time.

Like all economic transactions, there are two parties to the transaction. The interest paid by the borrower is equal to the interest received by the lender *(ignoring any fees paid to intermediaries, like banks or online payment companies. Those intermediaries earn their money by taking a small percent of each of the millions of transactions they process).*

There's some terminology on the next few pages which you'll want to study carefully, if you're not already familiar with them.

Term	Definition & Additional Info
Principal Amount	The original amount either borrowed or invested
Interest Rate	A percentage of the principal amount, which is the cost of borrowing the lender's money. Interest can be calculated either of two ways: • **Simple interest** – You pay (or earn) the interest on <u>only</u> the principal amount. • **Compound interest** – You pay (or earn) the interest on the principal amount <u>and</u> on any interest previously earned. Compound interest is commonly referred to as "**interest upon interest**." It's also, in finance courses, described as one of mankind's greatest inventions. You might agree or disagree! Compound interest is wonderful when it's working for you, such as in your 401k, but it's horrible when it's working against you on your student loans or credit cards. Either way, **compound interest** is a powerful force.

Term	Definition & Additional Info
Compounding Period & Compounding Frequency	The **compounding period** and **compounding frequency** are closely related concepts. • The **compounding period** expresses the amount of time that passes before the interest is accrued. • The **compounding frequency** expresses how many of those time periods occur per year. Common compounding periods & frequencies: • **Annual** compounding = **once per year** • **Semi-annual** compounding = **twice per year** • **Quarterly** compounding = **4 times per year** • **Monthly** compounding = **12 times per year** • **Daily** compounding = **365 times per year** *Note: for the standardized tests, you'll most likely need to handle semi-annual, quarterly, or monthly compounding, for a relatively short amount of time, such as 6 months or 2 years. (You'll use daily compounding more often in finance or accounting coursework).*
Interest Amount	The interest amount can be calculated using one of two formulas: **Simple interest** is a <u>linear</u> equation. The graph is a straight line. $$Interest\ Amt \ = \ Principal \ * \ Interest\ Rate$$ **Compound interest** is an <u>exponential</u> equation. The graph curves. $$Future\ Value = Principal * \left(1 + \frac{annual\ interest\ rate}{\#\ of\ periods\ per\ year}\right)^{(\#\ periods\ per\ year*\#\ Years)}$$ To find just the interest portion, use the formula above calculate the future value, which is the total of the principal and the interest, and subtract off the original principal amount.
Weighted average interest rate	Like other weighted averages, the overall interest rate is not equal to the simple average of the two interest rates. Instead, it's equal to the *total interest* divided by the *total principal.* To calculate the **weighted average interest rate**: $$Weighted\ Avg.\ Int.\ Rate = \frac{(Rate\ of\ A * Amt\ of\ A) + (Rate\ of\ B \ * \ Amt\ of\ B)}{Amt\ of\ A + Amt\ of\ B}$$

Term	Definition & Additional Info
APR vs. APY	There are two kinds of interest rates: • **APR**, or Annual Percentage Rate • **APY**, or Annual Percentage Yield What's the difference between APR and APY? It comes down to how often interest is accrued (calculated or accumulated). • **APR** is the rate, unadjusted for compounding • **APY** is the rate, after adjusting for compounding Whenever interest is compounded more often than once a year, **APR does <u>not</u> equal APY**. Instead, **APR < APY**. Banks earn extra profits from consumers who fail to understand the distinction between APR and APY, so banks will often present the rates on different financial products to the bank's advantage. Generally, here's how banks manipulate the way they present rates: • A bank will tell you the **APR** for any loans or credit cards, to make the amount of interest you'll have to pay seem <u>smaller</u>. • A bank will tell you the **APY** for any savings accounts or CDs, to make the amount of interest you'll receive seem <u>larger</u>. For example, if a credit card has an **APR of 19.99%**, with interest compounded monthly, the **APY is 21.93%**. The impact of frequent compounding is minimal on low-rate, short-term loans, but is more substantial on high-rate, long-term loans.

Cross-reference the sections on Exponential Equations and Weighted Averages.

Example #1: Investing in a Mix of Bonds

Brian has $40,000 to invest in a mix of corporate and municipal bonds. The corporate bond pays 10% simple annual interest, and the municipal bond pays 6% simple annual interest. If he expects to receive $3600 in interest payments this year, how much has Brian invested in the corporate bond?

First, note the type of interest indicated in the question: simple annual interest.

Second, realize that this question is asking us to determine Brian's allocation (mix) of his total investment to each of the two bonds. So, that $3600 is the combined interest amount.

Whenever you have a question asking you to find the allocation of two investments, based upon the interest rates and amounts, use the **Tables & Labels approach**.

All Your Word Problems Solved

Step 1: Start by setting up your table.

	Principal	*	Interest Rate	=	Interest Amount
Corp Bond					
Muni Bond					
Total Investment					

Step 2: Systematically transfer info from the word problem into the table, putting each piece into the right place.

	Principal	*	Interest Rate	=	Interest Amount
Corp Bond			10%		
Muni Bond			6%		
Total Investment	$40,000				$3600

Step 3: Fill in other cells in the table, based on what you have and what you need to find. Work backwards from the goal, so you see what you need to fill in.

You may need to choose variables for the unknown principal amounts.

	Principal	*	Interest Rate	=	Interest Amount
Corp Bond	C		10%		.10*C
Muni Bond	M		6%		.06*M
Total Investment	$40,000				$3600

You can use that last column of the table to create an equation. Here it is, using the **words first**, **math second** approach.

$$Int\ Amt\ from\ Corp\ Bond + Int\ Amt\ from\ Muni\ Bond = Total\ Interest\ Amt$$

$$(0.10 * C) + (0.06 * M) = \$3600$$

You've got one equation so far, and two variables.

Is there another equation? Yes. Again, using the **words first**, **math second** approach:

$$Principal\ in\ Corp\ Bond + Principal\ in\ Muni\ Bond = Total\ Principal$$

$$C + M = \$40000$$

Now we have two equation, and two variables, so we can solve this in one of three ways:

- Substitution method for solving systems of equations

- Combination method for solving systems of equations

- A modified form of the substitution method – re-expressing the principal invested in muni bonds, M, in terms of the principal invested in corp bonds, C. Update the table.

$$M = \$40000 - C$$

	Principal	*	Interest Rate	=	Interest Amount
Corp Bond	C		10%		.10*C
Muni Bond	~~M~~ **(40000-C)**		6%		.08*~~M~~ **(40000-C)**
Total Investment	$40,000				$3600

Now you'll have an equation with one variable, which you can solve for the amount invested in the corporate bond.

$$Int\ Amt\ from\ Corp\ Bond + Int\ Amt\ from\ Muni\ Bond = Total\ Interest\ Amt$$

$$(0.10 * C) + (0.06 * (40000 - C)) = \$3600$$

$$(0.10C) + (2400 - 0.06C) = \$3600$$

$$0.04C = \$1200$$

$$C = \$1200 * \frac{100}{4} = \mathbf{\$30,000}$$

Example #2: Certificate of Deposit

Shawna invests $10,000 in a certificate of deposit (CD) that offers a 4% interest rate, compounded quarterly. How much interest will she have earned, in total, after 6 months?

First, note the type of interest indicated in the question: quarterly compound interest.

Second, realize that a stated interest rate of 4% means that Shawna earns 1% every quarter *(a quarter = 3 months)*. This means that she'll earn:

	Interest on Principal	Interest upon Interest	Total Interest
1st Qtr	$10000 * \frac{1}{100} = \$100$	none	$100
2nd Qtr	$10000 * \frac{1}{100} = \$100$	$100 * \frac{1}{100} = \$1$	$101
Total in 6 months			**$201**

Shortcut to solving <u>compound interest</u> problems: Estimate & Eliminate

- Determine the amount of simple interest earned during the stated amount of time – that's your **estimate**.

- Use the simple interest (in this case, $200) to **eliminate** wrong answer choices.

  o Is the amount of simple interest among the answer choices? Eliminate it.

  o Any amounts that are smaller than the simple interest? Eliminate it / them.

  o Are any amounts that are much larger than the simple interest? Eliminate it / them. *"Much larger" is relative to the amount you're dealing with. $45 is "much larger" than $200, but not so compared to $50K.*

- After you've used this approach, you might only have one answer choice remaining.

- If there's more than one, the correct answer is usually the smaller of the two answers that are close to, but slightly more than, the simple interest amount.

- If you had these options, each of which assumes certain missteps in either interpreting the words or using the formula, you'd have quickly gotten the right answer <u>without</u> calculating!

(A) $100, (B) $101, (C) $200, (D) $201, (E) $406

ESSENTIAL TERMS & FORMULAS FOR PROFIT, REVENUE & COST

You may be very familiar, or perhaps not-so-familiar, with the concept of **profit**. At its most basic, profit is the difference between the **revenue** earned and **costs** incurred by a business. Profit can be positive, negative, or zero. When profit is negative, that's called a **loss**. When profit is zero, that's called the **break-even** point.

Profits, revenues, and costs can all be calculated on an **aggregate basis**, on a **per-unit basis**, on a **percentage basis**. There are several adjectives which you need to know are synonyms.

- "Aggregate" is a term that's synonymous with "total" or "overall"
  - Aggregate Profit = Total Profit = Overall Profit
- "Per unit" is synonymous with "each" or "for one unit"
  - Profit per Unit = Profit Each = Profit from selling one unit
- "Percentage" can be calculated using either the aggregate or the per-unit figures, because of the constant ratio.

On standardized tests, the test maker might try to make Profit questions harder by providing some of the information on an aggregate basis and other information on a per-unit basis. Pay careful attention to any adjectives that should prompt you to adapt your approach and your equation! You should be prepared to slice-and-dice profit, revenue, and cost in a variety of ways, and to move nimbly among the concepts. The test makers expect that you can progressively and quickly drill down from the basic formula to a more detailed formula, by knowing how the different concepts fit together.

For example, you might see a question which gives you total revenue, but then lists four different types of costs. You'll need to add up all the costs to figure out the total costs, and then use that in the profit equation.

There's more terminology on the next few pages which you'll want to study carefully, if you're not already familiar with them.

Term	Definition & Additional Info
Profit	The difference between a company's Revenues and Costs. Profit can be calculated on an aggregate basis, or a per-unit basis. • *Total Profit = Total Revenue – Total Cost* • *Profit Per Unit = Revenue per Unit – Cost per Unit*
Break-Even	The break-even point occurs when a company's profit equals zero. This happens when Total Revenue equals Total Cost.

Term	Definition & Additional Info
Revenue	The income generated by a business from the sale of goods and services. Revenue can be calculated on an aggregate (total) or per-unit basis. • $Total\ Revenue\ =\ Price\ *\ Quantity\ Sold$ • $Revenue\ Per\ Unit\ =\ Price$ Here, price means the actual selling price, not the regular or original price.
Cost	The expenses which a business must pay for, to hire staff, make products, sell products, etc. There are two kinds of costs: • **Fixed Costs**, which do not change with the level of output or number of units produced. Common fixed costs include rent and management salaries. Together, fixed costs may also be called overhead. • **Variable Costs**, which change directly with the level of output or number of units produced. Common variable costs include labor (wages) and materials (ingredients). A firm's total costs can be calculated as follows: $$Total\ Cost = Fixed\ Cost + Variable\ Cost$$ Often, the firm's fixed cost is provided as an aggregate amount and the variable cost is provided as a per-unit amount. In that case, we must modify our formula a bit: $$Total\ Cost = Fixed\ Cost + (VC\ per\ Unit\ *\ \#\ of\ Units)$$
Gross vs. Net	Gross and Net are two related adjectives which can be inserted in front of several other profit-related terms. For any particular profit-related term, **gross is greater than net**. • **Gross income** = Income <u>before</u> taxes, deductions, product returns, and other adjustments • **Net income** = Income <u>after</u> taxes, deductions, product returns, and other adjustments

Term	Definition & Additional Info
Marginal vs. Average	Marginal and Average are two related adjectives which can be inserted in front of several other profit-related terms.
	Marginal means "incremental" and rarely equal to the average. This is true because in the real world, the cost per unit changes as quantity changes – firms may get volume discounts on materials, or may start to incur higher costs as supplies of key resources become less available.
	• **Marginal cost** = the cost of producing the *next* unit of a good. In other words, to produce just one more, what will it cost? If you were producing 300 units, what is the marginal cost of producing the 301st unit?
	• **Average cost** = the total cost of producing a certain number of units, divided by the number of units.

Example #1: Making Boots

A company that makes hiking boots has fixed costs of $30,000. Each pair of boots requires $20 of materials and $40 of labor to produce. If the company plans to make 6,000 pairs of boots this year, and wants to earn a profit of $60,000, what price must the company charge per pair of boots?

Notice, here, that some of the information is provided on an aggregate basis, whereas other pieces of information are provided on a per-unit basis. As long as you get each piece of the Profit Equation in common terms (either all aggregate or all per-unit), both methods will get you to the correct answer.

Using the integrated approach – with aggregate values

Begin with the end in mind:

$$Total\ Profit = Total\ Revenue - Total\ Cost$$

Because you know that the Total Revenue equals Price times Quantity, you can substitute that into the equation. You also know that Total Cost equals Fixed Cost + Total Variable Cost, which you can also substitute into the equation.

$$Total\ Profit = (Price * Qty) - (Fixed\ Cost + Total\ Variable\ Cost)$$

Because you know that Total Variable Cost equals Variable Cost per Unit times Quantity, you can substitute that into the equation.

$$Total\ Profit = (Price * Qty) - [Fixed\ Cost + (Variable\ Cost\ per\ Unit * Qty)]$$

Now, plug in the information from the problem and solve directly for the sale price.

$$\$60000 = (Price * 6000) - [30000 + ((40 + 20) * 6000)]$$

Proceed through the order of operations and cancelling to solve for the answer.

$$\$60000 = 6000P - [30000 + (60 * 6000)]$$

$$\$60000 = 6000P - [30000 + 360000]$$

$$\$60000 = 6000P - [390000]$$

$$\$450000 = 6000P$$

$$Price = \frac{450000}{6000} = \$75\ per\ pair$$

Using the integrated approach – with per-unit values

Begin with the end in mind:

$$Profit\ per\ Unit = Price - Total\ Cost\ per\ Unit$$

Because you know that the Profit per Unit equals the Total Profit divided by the Quantity, you can substitute that into the equation. You also know that the Total Cost per Unit equals the Total Cost divided by the Quantity, which you can also substitute into the equation.

$$\frac{Total\ Profit}{Quantity} = Price - \frac{Total\ Cost}{Quantity}$$

Because you know that Total Cost equals Fixed Cost + Total Variable Cost, you can substitute that into the equation.

$$\frac{Total\ Profit}{Quantity} = Price - \frac{Fixed\ Cost + Total\ Variable\ Cost}{Quantity}$$

You can split that second fraction into two parts, to separate Fixed Cost per Unit and Variable Cost per Unit.

$$\frac{Total\ Profit}{Quantity} = Price - \left(\frac{Fixed\ Cost}{Quantity} + \frac{Total\ Variable\ Cost}{Quantity}\right)$$

If you take Total Variable Cost and divide it by Quantity, that's the same thing as Variable Cost per Unit.

$$\frac{Total\ Profit}{Quantity} = Price - \left(\frac{Fixed\ Cost}{Quantity} + Variable\ Cost\ per\ Unit\right)$$

Now, plug in the information from the problem and solve directly for the sale price.

$$\frac{\$60000}{6000} = Price - \left(\frac{\$30000}{6000} + (\$40 + \$20)\right)$$

Proceed through the order of operations and cancelling to solve for the answer.

$$\$10 = Price - (\$5 + \$60)$$

$$\$10 = Price - \$65$$

$$\mathbf{\$75} = Price$$

Example #2: Erin's Bakery

Erin's bakery sells two products, bread and cupcakes. Each loaf of bread sells for $6, and a single cupcake sells for $3. The ingredients cost $3 per loaf of bread and $18 per dozen cupcakes. If Erin's rent, labor, and other expenses total $80,000 per year, what is her expected profit, assuming she will sell 20,000 loaves of bread and 30,000 cupcakes this year?

Using the integrated approach – with aggregate values

Begin with the end in mind:

$$Total\ Profit = Total\ Revenue - Total\ Cost$$

Because Erin has two products which have different prices and costs, you'll need to modify the profit equation to look at these two products separately in the revenue and variable cost components of the overall equation. Because her rent, labor, and other expenses cannot be attributed to either product, you'll want to leave that as an aggregate value.

$$Total\ Profit = [Bread\ Rev + Cupcake\ Rev] - [FC + Bread\ TVC + Cupcake\ TVC]$$

Because you know that Revenue equals Price times Quantity, you can substitute that into the equation for both Bread and Cupcakes. Also, you know that the Total Variable Cost equals the Variable Cost per Unit times Quantity, you can substitute that into the equation for both Bread and Cupcakes.

$$Total\ Profit = [(Bread\ P * Q) + (Cupcake\ P * Q)] - [FC + [(Bread\ VC * Q) + (Cupcake\ VC * Q)]$$

Now, plug in the information from the problem and solve directly for the total profits.

$$Total\ Profit = [(\$6 * 20000) + (\$3 * 30000)] - \left[\$80000 + \left[(\$3 * 20000) + \left(\frac{\$18}{12} * 30000\right)\right]\right]$$

Proceed through the order of operations and cancelling to solve for the answer.

$$Total\ Profit = [\$120000 + \$90000] - \left[\$80000 + \left[\$60000 + \left(\frac{\$3}{2} * 30000\right)\right]\right]$$

$$Total\ Profit = [\$210000] - [\$80000 + [\$60000 + \$45000]]$$

$$Total\ Profit = \$210000 - \$185000 = \mathbf{\$25000}$$

WHAT IS COORDINATE GEOMETRY?

Coordinate Geometry refers to all the concepts and questions about points, lines, parabolas, circles, and other 2-dimensional shapes which can be drawn in the **XY-coordinate plane**. You'll need a combination of Algebra and Geometry concepts and skills.

COORDINATE GEOMETRY BASICS: PLOTTING POINTS IN THE XY-PLANE

The term **XY-plane** refers to the 2-dimensional graph with an **X-axis** and a **Y-axis**, shown in the diagram below. Refer to this image as you read the text descriptions and match each description back to the diagram, to make sure you understand both in words and visually what is being described.

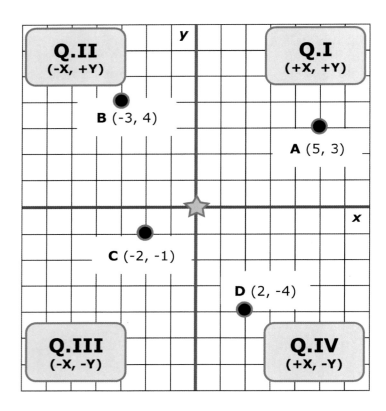

- The **X-axis**, shown in purple, is the horizontal axis. The <u>Y-axis is our dividing line</u>, which separates the X-axis into its positive and negative portions.

    - A point with an **X-coordinate** which has a <u>positive value</u> is plotted (drawn) <u>to the right side of the Y-axis</u>.

- A point with an **X-coordinate** which has a <u>negative value</u> is plotted (drawn) <u>to the left side of the Y-axis</u>.
- A point with an **X-coordinate** which has a <u>value of zero</u> is plotted (drawn) <u>on the Y-axis</u>.

- The **Y-axis**, shown in green, is the vertical axis. The <u>X-axis is our dividing line</u>, which separates the Y-axis into its positive and negative portions.
  - A point with a **Y-coordinate** which has a <u>positive value</u> is plotted (drawn) <u>above the X-axis</u>.
  - A point with a **Y-coordinate** which has a <u>negative value</u> is plotted (drawn) <u>below the X-axis</u>.
  - A point with a **Y-coordinate** which has a <u>value of zero</u> is plotted (drawn) <u>on the X-axis</u>.

- The **origin**, indicated with a yellow star, is the <u>intersection</u> of the X-axis and the Y-axis.
  - When plotting points, drawing lines, drawing parabolas, or anything else in the XY-coordinate plane, <u>always start at the origin</u>, because that is our reference point, and then move directionally right, left, up, or down from the origin.
  - The **coordinate points of the origin** are **(0, 0)**.

- The **XY-coordinate plane** is divided into four **quadrants**, and each quadrant is defined in relation to the origin. The standard naming convention is as follows:
  - **Quadrant I**: <u>Top-right</u> quadrant. The rest of the quadrants are numbered sequentially, working counter-clockwise from Quadrant I.
    - Positive X-values
    - Positive Y-values
  - **Quadrant 2**: <u>Top-left</u> quadrant.
    - Negative X-values
    - Positive Y-values
  - **Quadrant 3**: <u>Bottom-left</u> quadrant.
    - Negative X-values
    - Negative Y-values
  - **Quadrant 4**: <u>Bottom-right</u> quadrant.
    - Positive X-values
    - Negative Y-values

- **Interpreting X, Y coordinates**: Every point in the XY-coordinate plane has both an X-coordinate and a Y-coordinate, which are presented in parentheses:
  - (X-coordinate, Y-coordinate)
    - If **point A** is located at (5, 3), then:
      - The X-coordinate of point A is +5, and
      - The Y-coordinate of point A is +3.
      - Start at the origin. Because the <u>X-coordinate is positive, move right</u> 5 units. Then, because the <u>Y-coordinate is positive, move up</u> 3 units. Mark point A.
    - If **point B** is located at (-3, 4), then:
      - The X-coordinate of point B is -3, and
      - The Y-coordinate of point B is +4.
      - Start at the origin. Because the <u>X-coordinate is negative, move left</u> 3 units. Then, because the <u>Y-coordinate is positive, move up</u> 4 units. Mark point B.
    - If **point C** is located at (-2, -1), then:
      - The X-coordinate of point C is -2, and
      - The Y-coordinate of point C is -1.
      - Start at the origin. Because the <u>X-coordinate is negative, move left</u> 2 units. Then, because the <u>Y-coordinate is negative, move down</u> 1 unit. Mark point C.
    - If **point D** is located at (2, -4), then:
      - The X-coordinate of point D is +2, and
      - The Y-coordinate of point D is -4.
      - Start at the origin. Because the <u>X-coordinate is positive, move right</u> 2 units. Then, because the <u>Y-coordinate is negative, move down</u> 4 units. Mark point D.

FINDING THE DISTANCE BETWEEN TWO POINTS IN THE XY-PLANE

There are <u>two ways</u> you can find the distance between two points located in the XY-coordinate plane.

1. **Using the Distance Formula – a valid but** high-risk approach

    *   The Distance Formula looks like this:

$$Distance\ between\ two\ points = \sqrt{(x_2 - x_1)^2 + (y_2 - y_1)^2}$$

    *   It is difficult to remember all the parts of the Distance Formula correctly.

    *   Worse, it is difficult to apply the Distance Formula when one or more of the coordinates is negative, because you have to be very conscientious to <u>avoid making mistakes with handling the signs and any sign changes</u> (e.g., 5 minus -2 is 7, because minus a negative is the same thing as adding the positive).

    *   **Memorizing and using the Distance Formula is not recommended.**

2. **Using logic + the Pythagorean Theorem – also valid and lower-risk approach**

    *   Whenever you are working with points in the XY-coordinate plane, you should realize that every intersection of a horizontal grid line and a positive grid line <u>occurs at a 90° angle</u>, because the grid lines are perpendicular.

    *   Think about it! Graph paper is made up of tiny squares...and squares always have <u>90° angles.</u>

    *   So, instead of using the valid-but-awful Distance Formula, you can draw a horizontal line from one of the points and a vertical line from the other point. Where these lines intersect, you'll have a <u>90° angle.</u>

    *   Then, draw the diagonal distance between the two points you want to find, and BAM! These lines you just drew **form a right triangle**, where the <u>diagonal distance connecting the two points is the</u> **hypotenuse** of the right triangle.

    *   Now you can use the **Pythagorean Theorem** to solve for the distance between the two points.

$$a^2 + b^2 = hypotenuse^2$$

    *   *You might realize now that the* **Distance Formula** *is simply a transformation of the* **Pythagorean Theorem**, *where the hypotenuse is expressed in terms of the other variables. The <u>two approaches are mathematically identical</u>.*

    *   *The* **Pythagorean Theorem, however, is much easier to remember** *and apply on test day!*

    *   **This technique is also applicable to word problems in which you see compass directions* **North/East/South/West** *used. For example, "Joe left home, walked north for 3 miles, then turned east and walked 4 miles. How far is he from home, in straight-line distance?" <u>Look for the right triangle</u> and solve!*

Let's go back to our XY-coordinate plane, but now focus on using the logic + Pythagorean Theorem to solve for the **distance between points A and C**.

1. You can draw your horizontal and vertical lines starting from either point.

    a. Let's draw the horizontal line from point C toward point A. Shown in **blue**.

    b. Let's draw the vertical line from point A toward point C. Shown in **orange**.

    c. Now, draw the diagonal line connecting points A and C. Shown in **black**.

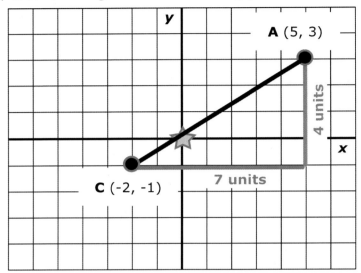

2. Find the distance of each of the sides of the triangle.

    a. The **horizontal distance** from **X= -2** to **X= +5** is **7 units**. *We travel right 2 units from -2 to zero, then another 5 units from zero to 5, for a total of 7 units.*

    b. The **vertical distance** from **Y= -1** to **Y = +3** is **4 units**. *We travel up 1 unit from -1 to zero, then another 3 units from zero to 3, for a total of 4 units.*

    c. The **diagonal distance between points A and C** is the hypotenuse of the triangle.

3. Use the Pythagorean Theorem to solve for the diagonal distance between A and C.

$$a^2 + b^2 = hypotenuse^2$$
$$7^2 + 4^2 = hypotenuse^2$$
$$49 + 16 = hypotenuse^2$$
$$65 = hypotenuse^2$$
$$\sqrt{65} = hypotenuse = distance\ AC$$

4. *Note: For some problems, you may need to perform an <u>extra step, to simplify the radical</u>. In this question, however, the square root of 65 cannot be simplified.*

All Your Word Problems Solved

LINEAR EQUATIONS IN THE XY-PLANE

Any 2-variable **linear equation** can be graphed in the XY-plane, using the **y-intercept** value and the **slope** of the line.

- Sometimes, the linear equation will be provided in the **slope-intercept form**. This form of the linear equation makes it easy and obvious to identify the **slope** and the **y-intercept** of the line. The slope-intercept form is the formal name of the familiar equation shown below. *Refer to the section on* ***Linear Equations.***

$$y = mx + b$$

  - For example, if we see the following equation, we can quickly identify the **slope (m)** and the **y-intercept (b)**.

$$y = mx + b$$
$$y = -\frac{2}{3}x + 4$$

    - **Slope**: m = -2/3
    - **Y-intercept**: b = +4
    - **Coordinate points of the Y-intercept** = (0, 4)

  - To graph this line, use the following process:

    - Plot the y-intercept first. Find the origin, and move up the Y-axis 4 units, to plot the y-intercept at the point (0,4).

    - Using the slope, add the next one or two points, then connect them by drawing a straight line.

      - Remember that the **slope** equals "**rise over run**," so our slope of -2/3 means a "rise of negative 2" and a "run of 3"

      - From the y-intercept, **move down 2 units** (because a negative "rise" means you must go down, not up). Then, from this point, **move right 3 units** (because a positive "run" means you must go right).

      - We mark our 2nd point at the coordinates **(3, 2)** and connect this point with the y-intercept **(0, 4)** with a straight line, extended through both points and beyond.

- Other times, the linear equation will be provided in a different form, which must be transformed through **variable manipulation** into the slope-intercept form.

  - For example, if you are given the following equation, you'll need to **isolate y to** transform this into the slope-intercept form:

$$5x - 2y = 6$$

    - Using the order of operations (PEMDAS), rearrange the equation to isolate Y.

$$-2y = -5x + 6$$

$$\frac{-2y}{-2} = \frac{-5x}{-2} + \frac{6}{-2}$$

$$y = \frac{5x}{2} - 3$$

    - Now our equation is in the slope-intercept form.

    - **Slope**: m = +5/2

    - **Y-intercept**: b = -3

    - **Coordinate points of the Y-intercept** = (0, -3)

  - To graph this line, use the following process:

    - Plot the y-intercept first. Find the origin, and move down the Y-axis 3 units, to plot the y-intercept at the point (0, -3).

    - Using the slope, add the next one or two points, then connect them by drawing a straight line.

      - Remember that the **slope** equals "**rise over run,**" so our slope of +5/2 means a "rise of 5" and a "run of 2"

      - From the y-intercept, **move up 5 units**. Then, from this point, **move right 2 units**.

      - We mark our 2nd point at the coordinates **(2, 2)** and connect this point with the y-intercept **(0, -3)** with a straight line, extended through both points and beyond.

- In still other problems, you may be **given a graph and asked to identify the equation** which represents the line shown.
  - To identify the equation from the graph, start by finding the two key pieces of information about all linear equations:
    - **Y-intercept**: At what value of Y does the line cross the X-axis? The coordinate points for the intercept are (0, Y).
    - **Slope**: Identify another point on the line. Compare this point to the y-intercept.
      - What is the "rise" (vertical change) between these two points?
      - What is the "run" (horizontal change) between these two points?
      - Then, plug these two numbers into the slope:

$$\text{Slope} = \frac{\text{Rise}}{\text{Run}}$$

  - Then, plug the values you found for the **y-intercept** and the **slope** into the **slope-intercept form** of the equation.
  - Depending upon the format of the available answer choices, you <u>may need to transform</u> the slope-intercept form of the equation into an equivalent but different form using variable manipulation and the order of operations.

LINES & ANGLES

Use these facts to help keep straight the definitions of and the difference between the various terms and relationships related to lines and angles. *To visualize the terms, grab some graph paper and create sketches as you follow along.*

Term	Definition	Additional Notes & Tips
Parallel Lines	• Two lines with the <u>same slope</u>, but different Y-intercepts • Because parallel lines have the same slope, they will <u>never intersect</u> • When a pair of parallel lines are crossed by a 3rd line, that 3rd line is called a <u>transversal</u>	Questions may ask about parallel lines either in the XY-coordinate plane -or- in some sort of diagram.
Perpendicular Lines	• Two lines which intersect at a 90° angle (right angle) • The slope of the 2nd line will be the <u>negative reciprocal of the slope</u> of the 1st line • A triangle formed by a pair of perpendicular lines and a 3rd line will always be a <u>right triangle</u>. *Often, it will be one of the <u>special right triangles</u> (discussed on subsequent pages)*	Questions may ask about perpendicular lines either in the XY-coordinate plane -or- in some sort of diagram. If you get questions about the height of a ladder leaned against a building, you can assume that the building exterior is perpendicular to the ground. *The complete diagram would form a right triangle.*
Supplementary Angles	• If two angles share one side, and the other sides are formed by a straight line, then these two angles are supplementary • Supplementary angles sum to 180°	In any polygon, an interior angle and an exterior angle touching the same corner of the polygon will be supplementary.
Complementary Angles	• If two angles share one side, and the other sides are formed by a 90° angle (such as the corner of a square), then these two angles are complementary • Complementary angles sum to 90°	In any rectangle or any square, a line drawn into one of its corners will form two angles which are complementary.

All Your Word Problems Solved

Term	Definition	Additional Notes & Tips
Vertical Angles	<ul><li>If a pair of straight lines intersect, forming an "X", then each pair of vertical angles will be equal measure. That means:</li><ul><li>The top-and-bottom pair of angles are vertical to one another.</li><li>**Top ∠ = Bottom ∠**</li><li>The left-and-right pair of angles are vertical to one another.</li><li>**Left ∠ = Right ∠**</li></ul><li>We also know that these pairs of angles will be supplementary:</li><ul><li>**Top ∠ + Left ∠ = 180°**</li><li>**Top ∠ + Right ∠ = 180°**</li><li>**Bottom ∠ + Left ∠ = 180°**</li><li>**Bottom ∠ + Right ∠ = 180°**</li></ul></ul>	Vertical angles are most likely to show up in complex diagrams, but are tested less frequently than the other types of angles.

POLYGONS

Use these facts to help keep straight the definitions of and the difference between many of the different geometric shapes which may show up on your test.

Term	Definition	Additional Notes & Tips
Polygon	<ul><li>Any closed shape with 3 or more sides</li><li>Formed by only straight lines</li><li>The roots of the word polygon translate to "many sides"</li></ul>	Polygon is the most generic term for a multi-sided, 2-dimensional closed shape. All of the following are considered polygons: triangles, squares, rectangles, trapezoids, pentagons, octagons, etc. Circles are <u>not</u> considered polygons.

Triangles		
Term	**Definition**	**Additional Notes & Tips**

Triangle	<u>The following apply to all triangles</u>:
	
	• Formed by only straight lines
	
	• Angles can be any measure, as long as the sum equals 180
	
	• **Perimeter = SideA + SideB + SideC**
	
	• **Area = ½ * Base * Height**
	
	• Any of the 3 sides can be a base, but the height must be drawn perpendicular (at 90º) to that base
	
	• The longest side is opposite the largest angle
	
	• The shortest side is opposite the smallest angle
	
	• *Triangle Inequality Rule*: The sum of the lengths of any two sides must be greater than the length of the 3rd side. For a triangle with sides of lengths A, B, and C:
	
	   ○ A + B > C
	
	   ○ A + C > B
	
	   ○ B + C > A
		<u>Do not assume</u> that a given triangle is one of the <u>special types</u> listed below. Make sure!
		
		Use the <u>logic of proofs</u> to discern whether the triangle shown happens to be one of the special types of triangles.
		
		Look for <u>hidden triangles</u> in other types of shapes. Sometimes, drawing a new line creates triangle(s), which unlocks the path to an answer about another shape. For example, drawing a diagonal inside a quadrilateral will form two triangles.

All Your Word Problems Solved

Special Triangles Based on Sides-<u>and</u>-Angles

Term	Definition	Additional Notes & Tips

Isosceles Triangles	• 2 of the 3 sides are the same length
	• 2 of the 3 angles are the same measure
	• The pair of equal sides are opposite the pair of equal angles
	• A line drawn from the angle with a unique measure to the side with a unique length will:
	    ○ Bisect (cut in half) the unique angle measure
	    ○ Bisect (cut in half) the unique side length
	    ○ Form a height (also called altitude), which is a line that is perpendicular to the base
	    ○ Form two smaller triangles which have equal areas, each of which is a right triangle
		If you know that the triangle is <u>isosceles</u> *and* is a <u>right triangle</u>, then it is a special right triangle, the 45-45-90 triangle.

Equilateral Triangles	• All 3 sides are the same length
	• All 3 angles are the same measure, 60°
	• A line drawn from any angle the side opposite that angle will:
	    ○ Bisect (cut in half) the angle
	    ○ Bisect (cut in half) the side
	    ○ Form a height (also called altitude), which is a line that is perpendicular to the base
	    ○ Form two smaller triangles which have equal areas, each of which is a special right triangle, the 30-60-90 triangle.
		You need to know and use the properties of the <u>30-60-90 Triangle</u> in order to solve for the height of the Equilateral Triangle.

Scalene Triangles	• Each of the 3 sides has a different length • Each of the 3 angles has a different measure	*Scalene triangles appear less frequently on the various standardized tests.*

Term	Definition	Additional Notes & Tips
Similar Triangles	• Two triangles are <u>similar</u> if the 3 angles of the 2nd triangle have the same measurements as the 1st triangle. • Each pair of <u>corresponding sides</u> will be in the same proportion as each other pair of corresponding sides. • Thus, the lengths of the <u>corresponding sides</u> of <u>similar triangles</u> are <u>proportional</u> to one another.	If a diagram appears such that one triangle seems "stuffed inside of" another triangle, in that they share one angle (corner) and share a pair of sides, <u>and</u> the third side of the bigger triangle opposite the shared angle is <u>parallel</u> to the third side of the smaller triangle, then the bigger and smaller triangles are <u>similar</u> and thus <u>proportional</u>. This type of diagram may not explicitly state that the third side of each triangle is <u>parallel</u> to the other. Instead, you might see that each third side is <u>perpendicular</u> to one of the shared sides. From this information, however, you can conclude that those lines are parallel, and that the two triangles are similar & proportional.

All Your Word Problems Solved

Right Triangles

Term	Definition	Additional Notes & Tips
Right Triangle	<ul><li>1 of the angles is 90°</li><li>The other 2 angles add up to 90°</li><li>The longest side, which is opposite the right angle, is called the <u>hypotenuse</u></li><li>The pair of sides adjacent (touching/forming) the right angle will be the base and the height, which you may use to find the area</li><li>If you know the length of any 2 sides, you can use the <u>Pythagorean Theorem</u> to solve for the length of the unknown 3rd side. **$A^2 + B^2 = C^2$**, where C is always the <u>hypotenuse</u></li></ul>	There are several specific kinds of right triangles, listed separately, which have special properties you must know. <u>Do not assume</u> that you have one of the <u>special right triangles</u>. Make sure!
Pythagorean Triplet	<ul><li>1 of the angles is 90°</li><li>All 3 sides have lengths which are <u>integers</u>, and the triplets are named by the ratios of the sides</li><li>If you memorize the Pythagorean Triplets, you can avoid extra computation needed to use the Pythagorean Theorem to find the length of the 3rd side (when given 2 of the lengths.</li><li>There are lots of Pythagorean Triplets, but a handful are tested frequently. The <u>ratio of the 3 sides</u>, from smallest to largest / the hypotenuse listed <u>last</u>, is as follows:<ul><li>3:4:5</li><li>5:12:13</li><li>8:15:17</li><li>7:24:25</li></ul></li><li>We would need trigonometry (SOHCAHTOA) to solve for the angle measures…that's not the issue in play</li></ul>	You should also be able to <u>recognize multiples</u> of the frequently tested Pythagorean Triplets, such as: 9:12:15 (triple the 3:4:5) or 10:24:26 (double the 5:12:13)

Right Triangles

Term	Definition	Additional Notes & Tips
45-45-90 Triangle	• This is a special right triangle, because of its angle measures. 1 of the angles is 90º. The other 2 angles are each 45º. • The pair of sides opposite the two 45º angles have equal length • This may also be called the <u>isosceles right triangle</u> • The <u>ratio of the 3 sides</u>, from smallest to largest / the hypotenuse listed <u>last</u>, is: $X : X : X\sqrt{2}$	All the rules for and special properties of triangles, right triangles, and isosceles triangles also apply to the 45-45-90 Triangle. Watch out for questions where the test gives you an integer value for the side that has the radical (square root) in the ratio of the 3 sides. *You're expecting $X\sqrt{2}$ but instead the test tells you it's an integer, in an attempt to throw you off.* When that happens, set that integer equal to $X\sqrt{2}$. You'll need to divide both sides by $\sqrt{2}$ to isolate X. *Don't forget how to get the radical out of the denominator.*
30-60-90 Triangle	• This is a special right triangle, because of its angle measures. 1 of the angles is 90º. The smallest angle is 30º. The medium angle is 60º • The <u>ratio of the 3 sides</u>, from smallest to largest / the hypotenuse listed <u>last</u>, is: $X : X\sqrt{3} : 2X$ All the rules for and special properties of triangles and right triangles also apply to the 30-60-90 Triangle. You need to know and use the properties of the 30-60-90 Triangle in order to solve for the height of the <u>Equilateral Triangle</u>.	Watch out for questions where the test gives you an integer value for the side that has the radical (square root) in the ratio of the 3 sides. *You're expecting $X\sqrt{3}$ but instead the test tells you it's an integer, in an attempt to throw you off your game.* When that happens, set that integer equal to $X\sqrt{3}$. You'll need to divide both sides by $\sqrt{3}$ to isolate X. *Make sure you remember how to get the radical out of the denominator.*

All Your Word Problems Solved

4-Sided Shapes		
Term	**Definition**	**Additional Notes & Tips**
Quadrilateral	• Formed by only straight lines • Sides can be any length • Angles can be any measure, as long as the sum equals 360 degrees	Quadrilateral is the most generic term for a 4-sided, 2-dimensional closed shape. All of the other 4-sided shapes listed on this page & next are specific kinds of quadrilaterals.
Rectangle	• Formed by 2 pairs of parallel lines • Opposite pairs of parallel sides have the same length, but Pair A does not necessarily equal Pair B • All four angles are 90 degrees • Symmetric along horizontal or vertical axes, but not diagonal • **Perimeter = 2*Length + 2*Width** • **Area = Length * Width**	A rectangle is a specific kind of parallelogram (w/ all angles = 90)
Square	• Formed by 2 pairs of parallel lines • All four sides are the same length • All four angles are 90 degrees • Symmetric along horizontal, vertical, and diagonal • **Perimeter = 4*Side** • **Area = Side^2**	A square is a specific kind of rhombus (w/ all angles = 90) A square is a specific kind of rectangle (w/ all sides = same) A square is a specific kind of parallelogram (w/ all angles = 90 and all sides = same) A <u>square</u> will <u>maximize the area</u> inside of a 2-dimensional object, given a finite amount of materials, and <u>including a constraint</u> that the object must be formed using straight lines / rigid materials.

4-Sided Shapes

Term	Definition	Additional Notes & Tips
Trapezoid	• Formed by 1 pair of parallel lines, and 1 pair of non-parallel lines • Sides can be any length • Angles can be any measure, as long as the sum equals 360 degrees • **Perimeter = Base1 + Base2 + Side1 + Side2** • **Area = (Average of Bases) * Height = (Base1+Base2)/2 * Height** • *Not necessarily symmetric*	Note, in a trapezoid, you may need to draw a new line to find the height. The <u>height</u> of a trapezoid is a line drawn perpendicular to the pair of parallel bases of the trapezoid <u>Do not assume</u> that the pair of non-parallel sides are the same length.
Parallelogram	• Formed by 2 pairs of parallel lines • Opposite pairs of parallel sides have the same length, but Pair A does not necessarily equal Pair B • Opposing pairs of angles are the same measure, but Pair C does not necessarily equal Pair D • **Perimeter = 2*Base + 2*Side** • **Area = Base * Height** • *Think of it as "rectangle in the wind"*	Note, in a parallelogram, you may need to draw a new line to find the height. The <u>height</u> of a parallelogram is a line drawn perpendicular to the base of the parallelogram.
Rhombus	• Formed by 2 pairs of parallel lines • All four sides are the same length • Opposing pairs of angles are the same measure, but Pair C does not necessarily equal Pair D • Symmetric along diagonal only • **Perimeter = 4*Side** • **Area = Side * Height** • *Think of it as "square in the wind"*	A rhombus is a specific kind of parallelogram. A square is a specific kind of rhombus. Note, in a rhombus, you may need to draw a new line to find the height. The <u>height</u> of a rhombus is a line drawn perpendicular to the base of the rhombus

All Your Word Problems Solved

Other Polygons		
Term	**Definition**	**Additional Notes & Tips**

Pentagon	• Has 5 sides
	
	• Sides are not necessarily the same length
	
	• Angles are not necessarily the same measure
	
	• **Sum of interior angles = (5-2) *180 = 540 degrees**
	
	• **Sum of exterior angles = 360**
	
	• A *regular pentagon:*
	
	    o Each side is the same length
	
	    o Each interior angle is 540/5 = 108 degrees
	
	    o Each exterior angle is 360/5 = 72 degrees	

Hexagon	• Has 6 sides
	
	• Sides are not necessarily the same length
	
	• Angles are not necessarily the same measure
	
	• **Sum of interior angles = (6-2) *180 = 720 degrees**
	
	• **Sum of exterior angles = 360**
	
	• A *regular hexagon:*
	
	    o Each side is the same length
	
	    o Each interior angle is 720/6 = 120 degrees
	
	    o Each exterior angle is 360/6 = 60 degrees
		To find the area of a regular hexagon, you can first break it up into 6 equilateral triangles (each will be the same size).
		
		Then, you can cut one of the equilateral triangles in half, into a pair of 30-60-90 triangles, to find the height.
		
		The area of the hexagon will be 6 times the area of this single equilateral triangle.

Other Polygons		
Term	**Definition**	**Additional Notes & Tips**

Octagon	• Has 8 sides
	
	• Sides are not necessarily the same length
	
	• Angles are not necessarily the same measure
	
	• **Sum of interior angles** = (8-2) *180 = 1080 degrees
	
	• **Sum of exterior angles** = 360
	
	• A *regular octagon:*
	
	    ○ Each side is the same length
	
	    ○ Each interior angle is 1080/8 = 135 degrees
	
	    ○ Each exterior angle is 360/8 = 45 degrees
		Visualize a stop sign.
		
		To find the area of a regular octagon, you can draw two horizontal and two parallel lines to break it up into 5 squares and 4 45-45-90 triangles.

CIRCLES

Understand the different parts of a circle, and the inter-relationships of these concepts.

Term	**Definition**	**Additional Notes & Tips**
Radius	• The distance from the center of a circle to any point on the circle itself • A straight line • All possible radii of the circle have the same length • **Radius = ½*Diameter**	A triangle formed by two radii of the circle and a third line which does not pass through the center will <u>always form an isosceles triangle</u> because the two sides formed by the two radii are equal length. The two angles not at the center of the circle will be equal. This triangle <u>can be an equilateral</u>, if either the chord is the same length as the radius <u>or</u> the angle at the center is 60 degrees.

Term	Definition	Additional Notes & Tips
Diameter	• The distance from one point on the circle to another point on the circle, which <u>passes through the center</u> of the circle • A straight line • All possible diameters of the circle have the same length • The diameter has the greatest possible straight-line distance between two points on the circle. • **Diameter = 2*Radius**	A diameter is a specific kind of chord. A triangle formed by the diameter of the circle and two additional lines which do not pass through the center but do meet at any point on the circle will always be a <u>right triangle</u>. The angle opposite the diameter will be 90 degrees. The sum of the other two angles will be 90 degrees.
Circumference	• The <u>complete</u> distance around the outside of the circle • A curved line that forms a closed loop • **Circumference = 2*Pi*Radius** • **Circumference = Pi*Diameter** • *Think of it as the <u>crust</u> on an <u>entire</u> pizza.*	Do not mix up the formulas for circumference & area.
Area of Circle	• The measure of total space inside of the circle. • **Area of Circle = Pi*Radius²** • *Think of it as the <u>cheese</u> on an <u>entire</u> pizza.*	Do not mix up the formulas for circumference & area.

Term	Definition	Additional Notes & Tips
Arc Length	• The <u>partial</u> distance around the outside of the circle. It is a fraction of the circumference. • A curved line • <u>Major Arc</u> vs. <u>Minor Arc</u> – if a circle is presented with two points A and B which lie on the circle, then: o <u>Major Arc</u> AB = goes more than 180° around the circle. In other words, the major arc AB goes the "long way" between points A and B o <u>Minor Arc</u> AB = goes less than 180° around the circle. In other words, the minor arc AB goes the "short way" between points A and B • **Arc Length = (Degrees/360)*Circumference** • *Think of it as the <u>crust</u> on a <u>slice</u> of pizza. If you eat ¼ of a pizza, you'll eat ¼ of the total crust on the pizza.* • *If you remember the classic video game Pac Man™, think of:* o *Major Arc AB as Pac Man's back, and* o *Minor Arc AB as Pac Man's mouth.*	Do not mix up arc & chord.
Area of Sector	• The measure of a fraction of the total space inside of the circle. • **Area of Sector = (Degrees/360)*Area of Circle** • *Think of it as the <u>cheese</u> on a <u>slice</u> of pizza. If you eat ¼ of a pizza, you'll eat ¼ of the total cheese on the pizza.*	

All Your Word Problems Solved

Term	Definition	Additional Notes & Tips
Chord	• The distance from one point on the circle to another point on the circle, which <u>does not necessarily pass through the center</u> of the circle • A straight line • If a chord <u>does not</u> pass through the center of the circle, then: **chord < diameter.** • If a chord <u>does</u> pass through the center of the circle, then: **chord = diameter.**	Do not mix up chord & arc.
Line Tangent to a Circle	• A line drawn tangent to a circle will touch the circle at <u>exactly one</u> point. • A line drawn tangent to a circle will be <u>perpendicular</u> to the radius of the circle at the point of tangency.	

SOLIDS

Proportional volume is the most important and commonly tested concept about solids. To compute proportional volume, plug in the multiplier for each of the dimensions into the equation for the volume of the shape. *Remember, the exponent applies to the coefficient as well as the dimension. For example, in the formula for the volume of a sphere, $(2R)^3 = 8R^3$. The 4/3 * Pi part of the formula would not change.*

Term	Definition	Additional Notes & Tips
Cube	<ul><li>A solid shape where all six faces are squares.</li><li>**Surface Area of Cube = 6 * Area of Square**</li><li>**Volume of Cube = Side³**</li></ul>	A <u>cube</u> will <u>maximize the volume</u> inside of a 3-dimensional object, given a finite amount of materials, and <u>including a constraint</u> that the object must be formed using straight lines / rigid materials. If you <u>double just one of the dimensions</u> and keep the other two the same, you will <u>double the volume</u>. If you <u>double all dimensions</u> (length, width, and height), you will get <u>8 times the volume</u>.
Sphere	<ul><li>A solid round shape</li><li>Visualize a basketball, volleyball, etc.</li><li>**Volume of Sphere = 4/3 * Pi * Radius³**</li></ul>	A <u>sphere</u> will <u>maximize the volume</u> inside of a 3-dimensional object, given a finite amount of materials, if you <u>remove the constraint</u> that the object must be formed using straight lines. If you <u>double the radius</u>, you will get <u>8 times the volume</u>.

All Your Word Problems Solved

Term	Definition	Additional Notes & Tips
Rectangular prism	• A solid shape where all six faces are either rectangles or squares. • Each corresponding pair of faces has the same area; i.e., top=bottom, left=right, front=back. • **Surface Area of Rectangular Prism = 2*Area of Top + 2*Area of Left + 2*Area of Front** • **Volume of Rectangular Prism = Length * Width * Height**	When asked about <u>proportional volume</u> between two objects of the same type, make sure you plug the relative dimensions into the formulas appropriately. If you <u>double just one of the dimensions</u> and keep the other two the same, you will <u>double the volume</u>. If you <u>double all dimensions</u> (length, width, and height), you will get <u>8 times the volume</u>.
Cylinder	• A solid shape where two bases are formed by circles. • **Surface Area of Cylinder = 2*Area of Circle + Circumference*Height** • **Volume of Cylinder = Area of Circle * Height** • *Visualizing this as a can of soup is particularly helpful if you need to find the surface area. You have a lid, a bottom, and a wrapper.* • *If you removed the wrapper, you'd have a rectangle. The length of this rectangle = the circumference of the circle.*	If you <u>double the height</u> of a cylinder, you will <u>double the volume</u>. If you <u>double the radius</u> of a cylinder, you will get <u>4 times the volume</u> (because the radius term is squared).
Pyramid	• **Volume of Right Rectangular Pyramid = 1/3 * Volume of Rectangular Prism**	*Rarely tested on the major standardized tests.*
Cone	• **Volume of Right Circular Cone = 1/3 * Volume of Cylinder** • *Visualize this as a party hat. The height is perpendicular to the circular base.*	*Rarely tested on the major standardized tests.*

Sometimes you will encounter geometry questions on standardized tests which ask you to solve for the area of a shaded region within a diagram.

In this type of problem, the shape of the shaded region is usually one for which you cannot solve for its area <u>directly</u>, using a single formula.

You can, however, solve these <u>indirectly</u>. You can use an approach which is similar to the displacement method you may recall from your high school science courses.

DISPLACEMENT METHOD FROM SCIENCE CLASS

Think back to your high school chemistry course. Early in the course, you probably spent some time learning about measurement tools and different approaches to taking measurements.

Let's say you want to determine the <u>volume</u> of an object, which is a <u>cylinder</u>. There's a single, known formula you can use to solve for its volume. With relative ease, you can measure the radius and the height. You can therefore find the volume of the cylinder <u>directly</u>.

$$Volume \ of \ Cylinder = \pi * (radius^2) * height$$

Let's say you want to determine the <u>volume</u> of another object, which is a <u>small plastic horse figurine</u>. There's no single, known formula you can use to solve for its volume. There's not even an obvious way to cut the shape into a set of simpler, more easily solvable shapes. What can you do? You must find a way to find the volume of the small plastic horse figurine <u>indirectly</u>. Your teacher probably even had a lab experiment in which you and your lab partner practiced using the displacement method, which worked like this:

- Get a beaker
- Fill the beaker with a known volume of water, perhaps 200 mL
- Drop the plastic horse figurine into the water
- Measure the volume of the water and the plastic horse figurine combined.
- Let's say this reading is 237 mL
- You determine the volume of the plastic horse figurine as follows:

$$Vol. of \ Figurine = (New \ Vol. of \ Water \ \& \ Figurine) - (Original \ Vol. of \ Water)$$

$$Vol. of \ Figurine = 237 \ mL - 200 \ mL$$

$$Vol. of \ Figurine = 37 \ mL$$

Essentially, the **displacement method** is an **indirect approach** to finding the volume (or area, or other measurement) of the shape which cannot be measured directly using a standard formula.

DISPLACEMENT METHOD APPLIED TO GEOMETRY QUESTIONS

Now, whenever you see a geometry question which asks you to solve for the length, area, or volume of a line, shape, or solid <u>which you cannot measure directly</u>, you must **solve for it indirectly** using a variation of the **displacement method.**

Standardized test questions may or may not provide a diagram.

- If a diagram is provided, you probably need to **interpret** some written information and **combine** it with the information already marked on the diagram.

- If a diagram is not provided, you should draw one. Then, **interpret** the written information and **combine** it with the information already marked on the diagram.

Wording	Translation	Details & Examples
Inscribed	Drawn within/inside	A circle **inscribed** in a square = the circle is drawn inside the square Visualize: A pizza inside its box.
Circumscribed	Drawn around/outside	A circle **circumscribed** around an equilateral triangle = the circle is drawn around the equilateral triangle Visualize: The triangular prism mirror inside a kaleidoscope tube (in cross-section). The round tube goes around the triangular prism.
Tangent to...	A curve or circle touches a straight line at exactly one point	Often, when you see questions that describe one shape either inscribed in or circumscribed around another, you'll also see the phrase **tangent at exactly (some number of) points**. This means that the two shapes just barely touch where the edges of the straight-sided shape meet the curves of the rounded shape.
Concentric	Centered at the same point	Visualize these everyday examples of **concentric circles**: • A dart board and its multiple rings • A wheel of a car and its tire
Uniform Constant Consistent	Same measurement	Often, you will see questions which refer to a **border of uniform width.** This means that the border has the same dimensions on all sides of / all the way around the object.

The easiest way to remember to use the displacement method in geometry questions is:

$$Area\ of\ Shaded\ Region = Area\ of\ Big\ Shape - Area\ of\ Small\ Shape$$

And

$$Volume\ of\ Shaded\ Region = Volume\ of\ Big\ Shape - Volume\ of\ Small\ Shape$$

Next, you will want to be intentional about which shape is the "big" shape and which shape is the "small" shape. From there, you can drill-down the formula. Let's look at a few examples.

Example #1: Picture in a Frame

A rectangular photo which is 5 inches wide by 7 inches tall is inside a wooden frame. The outside of the wooden frame is 8 inches wide by 10 inches tall. What is the area of the wooden frame?

$$Area\ of\ Shaded\ Region = Area\ of\ Big\ Shape - Area\ of\ Small\ Shape$$
$$Area\ of\ Wooden\ Frame = Area\ of\ Whole\ Object - Area\ of\ Photo$$
$$Area\ of\ Wooden\ Frame = (Width * Height) - (Width * Height)$$
$$Area\ of\ Wooden\ Frame = (8\ in * 10\ in) - (5\ in * 7in)$$
$$Area\ of\ Wooden\ Frame = 80\ in^2 - 35\ in^2$$
$$Area\ of\ Wooden\ Frame = 45\ in^2$$

Example #2: Concentric Circles

Two concentric circles have radii of 4 and 6, respectively. If the smaller circle, which is white, is placed on top of the larger circle, which is blue, what fraction of the blue circle is visible?

Note: If you think you should draw a picture, you should draw a picture. It can be as simple as the one below. These help you think logically and concretely about the information in geometry word problems.

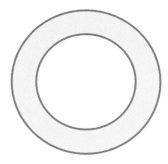

Note: This is a multi-step question.

- First, realize you're solving for what portion of the blue circle is visible. Set up that equation so you remind yourself to do this extra step.

$$Fraction\ of\ Blue\ Visible = \frac{Area\ of\ Blue\ Visible}{Total\ Area\ of\ Blue} = \frac{???}{\pi r^2} = \frac{???}{\pi 6^2} = \frac{???}{36\pi}$$

- Next, go use the shaded region formula to solve for the part you need to find.

$$Area\ of\ Shaded\ Region = Area\ of\ Big\ Shape - Area\ of\ Small\ Shape$$

$$Area\ of\ Blue\ Visible = Area\ of\ Blue\ Circle - Area\ of\ White\ Circle$$

$$Area\ of\ Blue\ Visible = (\pi r^2) - (\pi r^2)$$

$$Area\ of\ Blue\ Visible = 36\pi - 16\pi$$

$$Area\ of\ Blue\ Visible = 20\pi$$

- Now, plug this information back into the placeholder you left in the 1st equation above, then simplify.

$$Fraction\ of\ Blue\ Visible = \frac{Area\ of\ Blue\ Visible}{Total\ Area\ of\ Blue} = \frac{20\pi}{36\pi} = \frac{5}{9}$$

- **5/9**, or **55.55%** of the blue circle is visible.

Example #3: Garden Path

An elementary school has a community garden which is surrounded by a 2-meter wide paved path. If the rectangular community garden measures 16 meters by 10 meters, what is the total surface area of the paved path?

Note: If you think you should draw a picture, you should draw a picture. It can be as simple as the one below. These help you think logically and concretely about the information in geometry word problems.

The diagram helps you avoid one very common mistake:

What's the total width of the garden & path? The garden is 16 meters and the path is 2 meters wide. But the path is on <u>both</u> sides (top/bottom pair, left/right pair) of the garden, so the outer length is 16+(2*2) and the outer width is 10+(2*2).

- **Correct outer dimensions: 20 by 14** (adding 2 <u>twice</u> to each dimension)
- **Common mistake dimensions**: **18 by 12** (only adding 2 <u>once</u> to each dimension)

$$Area\ of\ Shaded\ Region = Area\ of\ Big\ Shape - Area\ of\ Small\ Shape$$

$$Area\ of\ Paved\ Path = Area\ of\ Whole\ Object - Area\ of\ Garden$$

$$Area\ of\ Paved\ Path = (Length * Width) - (Length * Width)$$

$$Area\ of\ Paved\ Path = (20\ m * 14\ m) - (16\ m * 10\ m)$$

$$Area\ of\ Paved\ Path = (280\ m^2) - (160\ m^2)$$

$$Area\ of\ Paved\ Path = 120\ m^2$$

All Your Word Problems Solved

Example #4: A Square Inscribed in a Circle

A square is inscribed in a circle, and each corner of the square is tangent to the circle. If each side of the square is 6 centimeters long, by approximately what percent is the area of the circle larger than the area of the square?

Note: If you think you should draw a picture, you should draw a picture. It can be as simple as the one below. These help you think logically and concretely about the information in geometry word problems.

Note: This is a multi-step problem. It also combines geometry concepts with percents.

- First, set up the equation for what you ultimately are solving for, so you remind yourself to do this extra step.
  - By approximately <u>what percent</u> is the area of the circle <u>larger</u> than the area of the square?
  - The keywords "what percent larger..." means we are dealing with **percent change** (<u>not</u> **percent of** – a common logical error). With this approach, you actually do not need to <u>use</u> the **shaded region formula**.

$$Area\ of\ Circle = Area\ of\ Square * (1 + Percent\ Change)$$

  - Alternatively, you could approach this problem using the shaded region formula. Both methods are valid and mathematically identical.

$$Percent\ Change = \frac{New - Original}{Original}$$

$$Percent\ Change = \frac{Area\ of\ Circle - Area\ of\ Square}{Area\ of\ Square} = \frac{Area\ of\ Shaded\ Region}{Area\ of\ Square}$$

- Next, go solve for the parts you need to find, based on the approach you chose.
  - In either case, you need to find the area of the circle. You know you need the radius to find the area of a circle. How can you find the radius?
  - Hint: **Always look for hidden triangles** in geometry problems.

- o Adding the **diagonal of the square** to the diagram reveals the **hidden triangle**.
  - The diagonal of a square cuts it into two 45-45-90 triangles.
  - The ratio of the sides of any 45-45-90 triangle is **X:X:X√2**
  - Because each side of the square is 6 centimeters, the diagonal of the square will be 6√2
- o Now, how does knowing the diagonal of the square help you?
  - Realize that in complex diagrams, the same line can serve multiple functions.
  - Here, the diagonal of the square is also the diameter of the circle. So, the diameter of the circle is 6√2.
  - By its definition, the radius is half the diameter. So, the radius of the circle is 3√2.
- o You have all the information you need to plug into the equation for whichever approach you chose.
- o Then, follow the order of operations and solve.

$$Area\ of\ Circle = Area\ of\ Square * (1 + Percent\ Change)$$

$$\pi r^2 = side^2 * (1 + Percent\ Change)$$

$$\pi(3\sqrt{2})^2 = 6^2 * (1 + Percent\ Change)$$

$$18\pi = 36 * (1 + Percent\ Change)$$

$$\frac{18\pi}{36} = (1 + Percent\ Change)$$

$$\frac{18\pi}{36} - 1 = Percent\ Change$$

$$\frac{\pi}{2} - 1 = Percent\ Change$$

$$\frac{3.14}{2} - 1 = Percent\ Change$$

$$1.57 - 1 = Percent\ Change$$

$$\mathbf{0.57\ or\ 57\%} = Percent\ Change$$

$$Percent\ Change = \frac{Area\ of\ Circle - Area\ of\ Square}{Area\ of\ Square}$$

$$Percent\ Change = \frac{\pi r^2 - side^2}{side^2}$$

$$Percent\ Change = \frac{\pi(3\sqrt{2})^2 - 6^2}{6^2}$$

$$Percent\ Change = \frac{18\pi - 36}{36}$$

$$Percent\ Change = \frac{18(\pi - 2)}{36} = \frac{\pi - 2}{2} = \frac{3.14 - 2}{2} = \frac{1.14}{2} = \boldsymbol{0.57\ or\ 57\%}$$

PARABOLAS: MULTIPLE FORMS OF THE SAME EQUATION

A **parabola** is one of several **conic sections** (slices of a cone) learned in Algebra 2.

The parabolic equation can be expressed in one of several <u>equivalent forms</u>. A parabolic equation may be presented in any of these forms, and you may be asked to determine:

- The <u>coordinates of the vertex</u>.

- The <u>x-intercepts</u> of the parabola.

- The correct <u>graph of the equation</u>, given the equation.

- The correct <u>equation</u>, given the graph of the equation.

- The <u>minimum</u> or <u>maximum</u> value of the equation (especially in word problems).

- <u>When</u> the minimum or maximum value occurs (especially in word problems).

Form	Equation	Each Letter Stands For	Use This Form to...
Standard Form	$y = ax^2 + bx + c$ A standard quadratic equation	**a** = coefficient of x² term **b** = coefficient of x term **c** = constant	Easily determine the **y-intercept** of the parabola The **y-intercept** of the parabola will be located at the point (0, c). Why? We would let x = 0 and solve for y. In this equation, y = c when x = 0.
Intercept Form	$y = a(x - p)(x - q)$ A factored form of the quadratic equation	**a** = coefficient **p** = one of the x-intercepts of the parabola **q** = the other x-intercept of the parabola The **x-intercept** is where the graph of the parabola crosses the x-axis, and y = 0.	Easily determine the **x-intercepts** of the parabola The **x-intercepts** of the parabola will be located at the points (p, 0) & (q, 0). Why? We would let y = 0 and solve for x. In this equation, x = either h or k when y = 0.

All Your Word Problems Solved

Form	Equation	Each Letter Stands For	Use This Form to...
Vertex Form	$y = a(x - h)^2 + k$	**a** = coefficient **h** = horizontal shift of the vertex away from the origin. It is also the x-coordinate of the vertex. **k** = vertical shift of the vertex away from the origin. It is also the y-coordinate of the vertex.	Easily determine the <u>coordinates of the **vertex**</u> of the parabola The **vertex** will be located at the point (h, k).

PARABOLAS: INTERCEPT FORM

The **Intercept Form of the Parabolic Equation** is this:

$$y = a(x - p)(x - q)$$

We use this form to determine where the graph crosses the x-axis.

- The graph will cross the x-axis at either 2, 1, or zero points.
    - If there are <u>2 points</u> where the parabola crosses the x-axis, then either:
        - The vertex is <u>below</u> the x-axis, <u>and</u> the parabola opens <u>upward</u>, OR
        - The vertex is <u>above</u> the x-axis, <u>and</u> the parabola opens <u>downward</u>.
    - If there is <u>only 1 point</u> where the parabola crosses the x-axis (meaning, p and q are the same value), then the **vertex** is located <u>on</u> the x-axis.
    - If there are <u>zero points</u> where the parabola crosses the x-axis, then either:
        - The vertex is <u>above</u> the x-axis, <u>and</u> the parabola opens <u>upward</u>, OR
        - The vertex is <u>below</u> the x-axis, <u>and</u> the parabola opens <u>downward</u>.
- We set y = 0, then solve for the two values of x which could make either of the factors in parentheses equal zero.

PARABOLAS: VERTEX FORM

The **Vertex Form of the Parabolic Equation** is this:

$$y = a(x - h)^2 + k$$

We use this form to determine how to graph the parabola and/or to choose the correct graph that matches the equation.

- First, determine coordinates of the **vertex** of the parabola. The coordinates of the vertex are **(h, k)**. Plot the vertex at (h, k).
    - The y-coordinate of the vertex is equal to...
        - The **minimum** of a parabola which opens <u>upward</u>.
        - The **maximum** of a parabola which opens <u>downward</u>.
        - In other words, the value of **k** is our <u>minimum</u> or <u>maximum</u> point.
    - The h-coordinate of the vertex is equal to...
        - The value of our **x** at which point the equation *reaches* its minimum or maximum.
    - In word problems related to parabolas:
        - The value of **x (and h)** is the independent variable which most commonly represents <u>elapsed time</u>. *Elapsed time = 5 seconds after a ball is thrown, or 10 hours after an experiment is begun.*
        - The value of **y (and k)** is the dependent variable, which might represent <u>the depth of water in a tank, the height of a ball thrown upward, or some other observed measurement</u>.
        - Thus, **k** commonly represents the <u>maximum height</u> of a ball thrown upward (or <u>minimum</u> of some other observation).
        - Thus, **h** commonly represents the <u>time at which</u> the minimum or maximum observation <u>occurs</u>.
    - The x-coordinate of the vertex allows us to find the **axis of symmetry**.
- Next, determine whether the parabola will open upward or downward.
    - If the **coefficient a** is <u>positive</u>, then the parabola opens <u>upward</u>.
    - If the **coefficient a** is <u>negative</u>, then the parabola opens <u>downward</u>.
    - If the <u>absolute value</u> of the **coefficient a** is <u>greater than 1</u>, then the parabola will be <u>narrow</u> (like a champagne flute), because y will increase much faster than x increases.
    - If the <u>absolute value</u> of the **coefficient a** is <u>less than 1</u>, then the parabola will be <u>wide</u> (like a fruit bowl), because y will increase slower than x increases.
- These steps are usually sufficient to select the correct graph from several available in the answer choices on your standardized tests.

Example: Multi-part Question About Parabolas

The height of a ball thrown in the air measured in feet, t seconds after it is thrown, is given by the function $f(t)$:

$$f(t) = -12(t-5)^2 + 300$$

    a. What is the maximum height of the ball?

    b. At what time does the ball reach this height?

    c. What is the height of the ball 2 seconds before it reaches its maximum height?

    d. What is the height of the ball 3 seconds after it reaches its maximum height?

    e. After how many seconds will the ball hit the ground?

The five related questions above are designed to help you think, step-wise, through a question like this one to understand how the parabolic equation is applicable to real-life situations. A visualization of the parabola is shown on a subsequent page, for reference.

Question Part	How to Approach and Solve
What is the maximum height of the ball?	If you look at the formula for f(t), notice: 1) The coefficient on the squared term is negative; this means the parabola opens downward. 2) This makes sense intuitively, if you have ever thrown a ball. The ball will go up in the air, but after a few seconds, it will continue going up but not as quickly as at first (thanks to gravity!). Then, the ball will reach a maximum height before coming back down to the ground. 3) Because the parabola opens downward, our maximum height will be the y-coordinate of the vertex. Comparing the formula in this question to the vertex form of the equation, our **k=300**. Our **maximum height is 300 feet**. If the first term of the equation is anything other than zero, then the height will be something less than 300 feet.
At what time does the ball reach this height?	The maximum height of 300 feet is reached when the first term of the equation equals zero. When does that happen? At **t=5**. This is the same thing as finding the x-coordinate of the vertex. Comparing the formula in this question to the vertex form of the equation, our **h=5**.

Question Part	How to Approach and Solve
What is the height of the ball 2 seconds before it reaches its maximum height?	What is the time, of "2 seconds before the ball reaches its maximum height"? If the maximum height occurs at t=5, then two seconds <u>before that</u> means **t=3**. Plug in **t=3** into the function and solve for the $f(3)$. $$f(3) = -12\,(3-5)^2 + 300$$ $$f(3) = -12\,(-2)^2 + 300$$ $$f(3) = -12*4 + 300$$ $$f(3) = -48 + 300$$ $$\mathbf{f(3) = 252}$$
What is the height of the ball 3 seconds after it reaches its maximum height?	What is the time of "3 seconds after the ball reaches its maximum height"? If the maximum height occurs at t=5, then three seconds <u>after that</u> means **t=8**. Plug in **t=8** into the function and solve for the $f(8)$. $$f(8) = -12\,(8-5)^2 + 300$$ $$f(8) = -12\,(3)^2 + 300$$ $$f(8) = -12*9 + 300$$ $$f(8) = -108 + 300$$ $$\mathbf{f(8) = 192}$$
After how many seconds will the ball hit the ground?	To "hit the ground" the ball must reach a height of zero. Let $f(t) = 0$, then solve for the values of t which make the function equal zero. $$f(t) = -12\,(t-5)^2 + 300$$ $$0 = -12\,(t-5)^2 + 300$$ $$12\,(t-5)^2 = 300$$ $$(t-5)^2 = 25$$ $$(t-5) = 5$$ $$t = 10$$

All Your Word Problems Solved

Visualizing the parabola, in the graphic below, we can see:

- The parabola opens downward, so the **vertex** is the <u>maximum</u> of the function for the height of the ball (rather than a minimum).

- The vertex of the parabola is at the coordinates (5, 300).

- These values for (h, k) are visible in the equation as well.

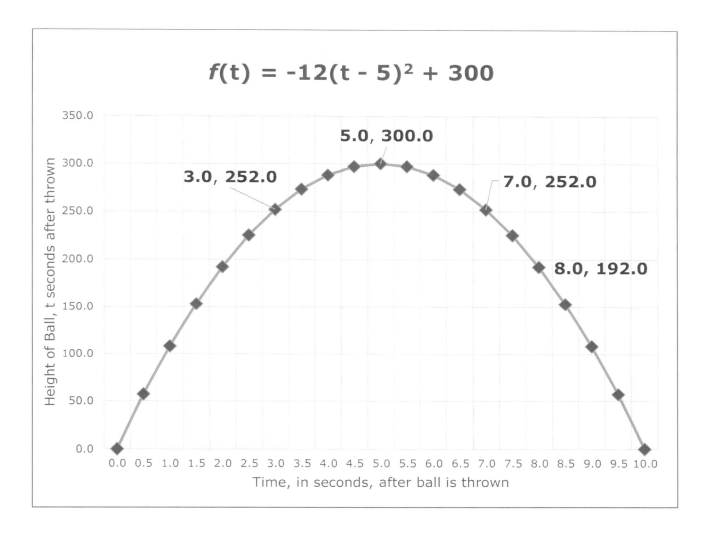

$$f(t) = -12(t - 5)^2 + 300$$

Term	Definition & Additional Info
Probability	At its simplest, **probability** refers to the likelihood that something occurs. The **probability** of any event happening ranges from: • 0%, or impossible/never --- to --- • 100%, or guaranteed/always The probability of an event happening is the simplified fraction or percentage of the number of **desired outcomes** out of the total number of **possible outcomes**. $$P(Event\ happens) = \frac{\#\ of\ desired\ outcomes}{\#\ of\ possible\ outcomes}$$ The probability of an event happening always equals 100% minus the probability of that event not happening. $$P(Event\ happens) = 1 - P\ (Event\ doesn't\ happen)$$
Event	What's an **event**? It's some activity of interest. *We're using the term of interest loosely here, folks!* Some examples of common **events** used in probability questions include: • Rolling a 5 on a single fair die (or "number cube") • Selecting a Heart from a standard deck of 52 playing cards • Raining on Tuesday The probability of an event happening can be expressed as either a fraction or a percent. In most cases on the standardized tests, you will want to use the fraction form so that you can take advantage of cancelling.
When to add vs. multiply probabilities of multiple events	When approaching all **Probability** questions, as well as any **Combinatorics** questions, the words: ▪ **AND means "multiply"** ▪ **OR means "add"** Think about it logically: If two uncertain events need to both "go your way," the likelihood that both do so is lower than if you only needed one of the two events to "go your way." We represent probabilities as either fractions or decimals between 0 and 1, or percentages between 0% and 100%. Anything multiplied by a positive fraction or decimal less than 1 will become smaller.

All Your Word Problems Solved

Term	Definition & Additional Info

Independent vs. Dependent Events	Probability questions can involve more than one event. You must determine from the question whether the events are **independent** of one another, or **dependent** on one another.
	
	• **Independent events**: Two events are independent of one another if one event happening does not influence or impact the likelihood that the other. They're unrelated. For example:
	
	  ○ The probability that you draw a card that's 7 or lower from a standard deck of 52 cards, and the probability that you roll a total of 8 on a pair of dice (number cubes).
	
	• **Dependent events**: Two events are dependent on one another if one event happening makes another event more or less likely to happen. They're related. For example:
	
	  ○ The probability that it is raining outside, and the probability that you bring an umbrella to work.

Mutually Exclusive vs. Not Mutually Exclusive Events	Probability questions can involve more than one event. You must determine from the question whether the events are **mutually exclusive** of one another, or **not mutually exclusive**.
	
	• **Mutually exclusive events**: Two events are mutually exclusive of one another if one event happens, then the other event definitely does not happen. The two events cannot occur at the same time. For example:
	
	  ○ Raining vs. not raining
	
	  ○ Happy vs. not happy
	
	• **Not mutually exclusive events**: Two events are not mutually exclusive of one another if it is possible that both events can happen at the same time. For example:
	
	  ○ Wearing shorts and wearing sandals. You can wear shorts with sneakers but you can also wear them with sandals. So, these events are not mutually exclusive.
	
	  ○ Going to grad school and working full-time. You can obviously do one, both, or neither at the same time. So, these events are also not mutually exclusive.

Odds of *something happening*	Clue words or (trigger phrase) that a word problem deals with **Probability**.
Equal chance of *something happening*	Clue words (trigger phrase) that a word problem deals with Probability, and that two or more events have the <u>same probability</u> of occurring.

Term	Definition & Additional Info
Probability of Multiple Events	For any situation with two events, A and B, we have multiple scenarios to evaluate: • Neither Event A nor Event B happens (Neither) • Event A happens, but Event B does not happen (A only) • Event B happens, but Event A does not happen (B only) • Both Event A and Event B happen (A and B) When we have more than one event, we can determine the **probability that at least 1 of the 2 events happens**, which means either-or-both, using the following formula. We subtract off the probability of both A and B happening because it will otherwise be double-counted. *This potential double-counting is similar to what we see in Venn Diagram problems; in both situations, simply adding the instances of both events separately would cause you to double-count the overlap.* $$P(at\ least\ 1\ of\ the\ events) = P(A) + P(B) - P(A\ and\ B)$$ You could restate this in plain language as: $$P(at\ least\ 1\ of\ the\ events) = P(A) + P(B) - P(both)$$ We can also determine the **probability that either A or B happens, but not both**, using the following formula. In other words, this is the **probability of exactly one of the events happening**. We subtract off two times the probability of both A and B happening because it is double-counted, and we want to fully exclude it. $$P(either\ A\ or\ B) = P(A) + P(B) - 2 * P(A\ and\ B)$$ You could restate this in plain language as: $$P(either) = P(A) + P(B) - 2 * P(both)$$ If events A and B are **mutually exclusive**, then: • The last term, P(both) will equal zero If events A and B are **not mutually exclusive**, then: • The last term, P(both) will not equal zero • You'll need to find P(both) by multiplying the individual probabilities of events A and B. $$P(both) = P(A) * P(B)$$

All Your Word Problems Solved

THINKING THROUGH THE LOGIC: WORDS FIRST, MATH SECOND

The basic question, "**What is the probability of**...*a certain situation(s) with various parameters or constraints*?" are the clue words which should trigger you to think in terms of Probability.

- The activity or context of the question <u>will change</u> – flipping one or more coins; rolling one or more "number cubes" (aka, dice); drawing one or more cards from a standard 52-card deck; rain or no rain; drawing a marble of a certain color from a bag of several marbles; drawing names from a raffle; selecting the Powerball jackpot numbers; the odds of winning certain casino games; and others.

- The parameters or constraints <u>will change</u> – and you must pay strict attention to these details.

  - Are you making **one or more than one selection**?

  - If there are **multiple events**, does outcome of one event <u>have an impact</u> or <u>no impact</u> on the probability of the second event? In other words, are the two events **independent** or **dependent**?

  - Is **replacement** allowed or not?

    - The best example to understand **replacement** vs. **no replacement**: A raffle with sequential drawings for several prizes.

    - If your name is drawn for the first prize, will your name "go back in the hat" to be eligible for any of the other, often bigger/better, prizes, or will you become ineligible for the subsequent drawings?

  - If the events are **sequential**, whether the ability to be chosen on the 3rd selection is predicated upon not being chosen for the 1st or 2nd selection.

    - For example, if there are 3 student council positions of President, Vice President, and Secretary, and the 3 positions are elected in sequential order, the probability that a certain person is selected for the role of Secretary means that to become Secretary, this person:

      - Must <u>not</u> be selected for the role of President, and

      - Must also <u>not</u> be selected for the role of VP, and

      - <u>Is</u> selected for the role of Secretary

      - Thus, the logic in **Words First, Math Second** becomes:

        $$P(\text{elected Sec}) = P(\text{Not Pres}) * P(\text{Not VP}) * P(\text{Yes Sec})$$

    - The example above is really another way of saying "there is no replacement."

- When you encounter more complex scenarios, try to articulate the scenario(s) which fit the question in your own words. You will want to pay attention to where you include the words which trigger math operations:

  - **EITHER / OR** = Add, often the probability of two cases which fit the described scenario

- o **AND** = Multiply, often that <u>this-AND-that</u> need to happen in scenario.

You should use the **Words First, Math Second approach** for structuring your approach.

Some of the most common scenarios described in word problems testing your understanding of Probability include:

- Flipping one or more coins

- Rolling one or more number cubes (i.e., a single die or ≥ 2 dice)

- Drawing colored marbles from a jar

- Drawing names from a hat

- Selecting a certain color of shirt or pants from a closet or drawer

FYI: There is quite a bit of cross-over in the logic needed to solve Probability questions and the logic needed to solve Permutations & Combinations questions.

The hardest problems you may encounter will <u>combine the concepts of Probability and Permutations & Combinations.</u>

- For example, what are your odds of winning the Powerball Jackpot with a single ticket?

- As of October 2017: **1 in 292,201,338**

- The number of Desired outcomes = how many tickets you bought 😊

- The number of Possible outcomes = your challenge problem!

  - o Read the rules of the Powerball jackpot game

  - o Translate the logic using Words First, Math Second

  - o Use a calculator or Excel to solve this one!

  - o The answer is provided on the last page, but try it yourself before you read the explanation.

Some examples of the more common Probability questions and the logic required to solve them are explained on the following pages.

EXAMPLES: COIN FLIPS

In nearly all Probability word problems about coin flips, you will find a reference to the fact that the coin is "fair" which is another way of saying "the odds of heads and tails are equal, and thus the probability of each is 1/2."

Example #1: Flipping a Coin, All Heads

A fair coin is <u>flipped three times</u> in a row. What is the probability that <u>all three flips</u> result in <u>heads</u>?

Try to articulate the scenario in your own words. In this case, we could achieve the desired outcome in only one way. Each coin flip must result in a heads.

- The 1st flip is a heads AND the 2nd flip is a heads AND the 3rd flip is a heads.

Flipping a Coin Three Times: Getting All Heads				
1st Flip = Heads	and	2nd Flip = Heads	and	3rd Flip = Heads
$\dfrac{1}{2}$	x	$\dfrac{1}{2}$	x	$\dfrac{1}{2}$

Note: The probability that all three flips result in tails is the same as the probability that all three flips result in heads. You would use the same approach as above.

Also, the probability of getting 2 heads and 1 tail is the same as getting 1 heads and 2 tails. You would need to modify the approach from above because you must deal with the possibility of getting the 2 heads and 1 tail in different orders, such as HHT, HTH, and THH. When there are more than 2 or 3 coin flips, it becomes too difficult to just write out all the possible variations; in those cases, we must combine Probability with Combinatorics.

Cross-reference sections on Permutations & Combinations.

Example #2: Flipping a Coin, 1 Head and 1 Tail

A fair coin is flipped two times in a row. What is the probability of receiving exactly one heads and one tails?

Try to articulate the scenario in your own words. In this case, we could achieve the desired outcome in one of two ways. Either:

- The 1st flip results in a heads AND the 2nd flip results in a tails, OR
- The 1st flip results in a tails AND the 2nd flip results in a heads

Pay attention to how you articulate the scenario in your own words.

- The OR is the primary split between the two ways of achieving the desired outcome.
- The AND in each of the two scenarios is the secondary split.
- This helps us determine where to place the parentheses.

Flipping a Coin Two Times: Getting One Heads & One Tails						
(1st = Heads	and	2nd = Tails)	or	(1st = Tails	and	2nd = Heads)
$\dfrac{1}{2}$	x	$\dfrac{1}{2}$	+	$\dfrac{1}{2}$	x	$\dfrac{1}{2}$

All Your Word Problems Solved

EXAMPLES: NUMBER CUBES (DICE)

In nearly all Probability word problems about number cubes (dice), you will find a reference to the fact that the six sides of each number cube are numbered one through six. This appears to be a way of making a question about dice culture-neutral, as not everyone has experience playing games with dice. The question may also include wording to specify that the probability of each is equally likely.

In other words, the probability of rolling a certain number on a single number cube is 1/6.

Some questions about 2 (or more) number cubes may ask about:

- Each cube's value individually, e.g., what is the probability of rolling two 5's?

- The sum of the values of the two cubes equaling a number, e.g., what is the probability that the sum of the numbers showing on the two number cubes equals 8?

  - This type of question requires a different approach than the coin flips.

  - It is advisable to **de-couple the numerator and the denominator** of the probability, and think through each separately.

    - **Numerator = Desired Outcomes**, which match the scenario described

    - **Denominator = Possible Outcomes**, which are all possible, inclusive of the desired ones.

  - Finding the total number of Possible outcomes is usually easier to solve, so **start with the denominator first**.

  - **Next, think through all the ways which the Desired outcomes can be achieved**.

  - Then, use substitution to replace these values you found for **Desired** and **Possible** into each part of the Probability fraction.

  - Last, simplify the fraction into its lowest common terms.

- The sum of the values of the two cubes being within a range of certain values, or being above or below a certain threshold.

  - E.g., what is the probability that the sum of the numbers showing on the two number cubes is less than 11?

  - E.g., what is the probability that the sum of the numbers showing on the two number cubes is at least 4, but at most 11?

  - When you encounter wording similar to either of the examples above, you need to think through the **multiple scenarios** which could satisfy the criteria for the number of **Desired** outcomes.

    - Try to articulate the scenario in your own words.

    - Pay attention to how you articulate the scenario in your own words.

    - Structure your logic in **Words First, Math Second**.

Example #1: Number Cubes, Sum Equals 10

Two number cubes, each of which is numbered 1 through 6 on its sides, are rolled. What is the probability that the <u>sum of the numbers</u> showing on the two number cubes <u>equals 10</u>?

- Finding the total number of Possible outcomes is usually easier to solve, so **start with the denominator first**.
    - 6 ways to roll the 1st AND 6 ways to roll the 2nd =
    - **36 Possible** outcomes
- **Then, think through all the ways which the Desired outcomes can be achieved**. The sum of 10 could occur in several ways:
    - 1st = 4, 2nd = 6
    - 1st = 6, 2nd = 4
    - 1st = 5, 2nd = 5
    - **3 Desired** outcomes.
- Now, use substitution to replace these values into each part of the Probability fraction, then simplify the fraction to its lowest common terms:
    - $P(Sum\ of\ 2\ cubes = 10) = \dfrac{Desired}{Possible} = \dfrac{3\ Desired}{36\ Possible}$
    - $P(Sum\ of\ 2\ cubes = 10) = \dfrac{1}{12}$

All Your Word Problems Solved

Example #2: Number Cubes, Sum is Less Than 11

Two number cubes, each of which is numbered 1 through 6 on its sides, are rolled. What is the probability that the <u>sum of the numbers</u> showing on the two number cubes is <u>less than 11?</u>

- Finding the total number of Possible outcomes is usually easier to solve, so **start with the denominator first**.
    - 6 ways to roll the 1st AND 6 ways to roll the 2nd =
    - **36 Possible** outcomes
- **Then, think through all the ways which the Desired outcomes can be achieved**. A sum of <u>less than 11</u> could occur in several ways:
    - The sum could be either 2 or 3 or 4 or 5 or 6 or 7 or 8 or 9 or 10 *(but not 11, because the question says, "less than 11," not "less than or equal to 11")*.
    - Trying to identify and count all the scenarios that this event <u>happens</u> is effortful and high-risk that you make a mistake. There is a better way!
    - It is easier to identify and count the scenarios in which the event <u>does not happen</u>. Then, plug that information into the formula:

    $$P(Event\ happens) = 1 - P\ (Event\ doesn't\ happen)$$

    $$P(Sum\ of\ 2\ cubes < 11) = 1 - P(Sum\ of\ 2\ cubes \geq 11)$$

    - What are all the ways that "a sum of <u>less than 11</u>" does <u>not happen</u>?
        - The sum is <u>at least</u> 11. Thus, the sum could be either 11 or 12.
        - The sum of 11 could occur in two ways:
            - 1st = 5, 2nd = 6
            - 1st = 6, 2nd = 5
        - The sum of 12 could occur in only one way, if both are a 6:
            - 1st = 6, 2nd = 6
        - Thus, there are **3 Desired** outcomes for the probability that the event <u>does not happen</u>.
- Now, use substitution to replace these values into each part of the Probability fraction, then simplify the fraction to its lowest common terms, and combine like terms:
    - $P(Sum\ of\ 2\ cubes < 11) = 1 - P(Sum\ of\ 2\ cubes \geq 11)$
    - $P(Sum\ of\ 2\ cubes < 11) = 1 - P(Sum\ of\ 2\ cubes = 11\ or\ 12)$
    - $P(Sum\ of\ 2\ cubes < 11) = 1 - \frac{3\ Desired}{36\ Possible}$
    - $P(Sum\ of\ 2\ cubes < 11) = 1 - \frac{1}{12}$
    - $P(Sum\ of\ 2\ cubes < 11) = \frac{11}{12}$

Example #1: Mutually Exclusive Events, There's No Rain

If the probability of rain on any single day in November is 0.25, what is the probability that it does not rain until the 5th day of November?

Try to articulate the scenario in your own words. In this case, for it to not rain until the 5th day means:

- On the 1st, it does not rain, AND

- On the 2nd, it does not rain, AND

- On the 3rd, it does not rain, AND

- On the 4th, it does not rain, AND

- On the 5th day, it rains.

Pay attention to how you articulate the scenario in your own words.

- Remember, AND means multiply.

- Fractions are more compatible with mental math than are decimals, so we can convert the probability of rain from 0.25 to its fraction equivalent, 1/4.

- Because "it rains" and "it does not rain" are mutually exclusive events, we know:

$$P(does\ not\ rain) = 1 - P(does\ rain)$$

$$P(does\ not\ rain) = 1 - \frac{1}{4}$$

$$P(does\ not\ rain) = \frac{3}{4}$$

- Now, plug these values into the structure you created using the Words First, Math Second approach. *Both approaches – either fractions or decimals – are equally valid.*

Does not rain until the 5th day of November								
1st = No Rain	and	2nd = No Rain	and	3rd = No Rain	and	4th = No Rain	and	5th = Yes Rain
$\frac{3}{4}$	X	$\frac{3}{4}$	X	$\frac{3}{4}$	X	$\frac{3}{4}$	X	$\frac{1}{4}$
0.75	X	0.75	X	0.75	X	0.75	X	0.25

Example #2: Mutually Exclusive Events, No Rain on Vacation

If the probability of rain on any single day in July is 0.10, what is the probability that it does not rain at all during your three-day weekend vacation?

Try to articulate the scenario in your own words. In this case, for it to not rain until the 5th day means:

- On the 1st, it does <u>not rain</u>, AND
- On the 2nd, it does <u>not rain</u>, AND
- On the 3rd, it does <u>not rain</u>, AND

Pay attention to how you articulate the scenario in your own words.

- Remember, AND means multiply.
- Fractions are more compatible with mental math than are decimals, so we can convert the probability of rain from 0.10 to its fraction equivalent, 1/10.
- Because "it rains" and "it does not rain" are mutually exclusive events, we know:

$$P(does\ not\ rain) = 1 - P(does\ rain)$$

$$P(does\ not\ rain) = 1 - \frac{1}{10}$$

$$P(does\ not\ rain) = \frac{9}{10}$$

- Now, plug these values into the structure you created using the **Words First, Math Second** approach. *Whether you choose to use fractions or decimals, remember that both are equally valid, but using fractions makes the mental math easier.*

Does not rain on any of 3 days of vacation				
1[st] = No Rain	and	2[nd] = No Rain	and	3[rd] = No Rain
$\frac{9}{10}$	X	$\frac{9}{10}$	X	$\frac{9}{10}$
0.9	X	0.9	X	0.9

It is common that students who find math and probability interesting also take a keen interest in understanding the application of <u>both</u> **probability** and **combinatorics** concepts to understanding the odds of various casino games.

Note: These examples assume you know the rules of common casino games, and therefore are **not indicative of questions you might see on any standardized tests**.

Instead, these are presented to spark your curiosity to dig into these topics to understand them better. Consider these "challenge problems" and try to translate the rules of various casino games and lotteries from **Words to Math**.

Example #1: Let's Play Poker

What is the probability of getting <u>4 of a Kind</u> in the game 5-card stud poker, assuming a single, standard deck of 52 playing cards is used?

Note: 4 of a Kind means the same number or face card, i.e., four 2's or four Queens.

- Finding the total number of Possible outcomes is usually easier to solve, so **start with the denominator first**.
  - You will receive 5 cards from the 52 cards in the deck.
  - Order does not matter with 5-card stud poker, so you will need to use the Combinations formula to count all the Possible outcomes.

$$Possible\ outcomes = \ _{52}C_5$$

$$Possible\ outcomes = \frac{52!}{5!\,(52-5)!}$$

$$Possible\ outcomes = \frac{52!}{5!\,47!}$$

$$Possible\ outcomes = \frac{52*51*10\ \cancel{50}*49*2\ \cancel{48}*\cancel{47!}}{\cancel{5}*4*\cancel{3}*\cancel{2}*1*\cancel{47!}}$$

$$Possible\ outcomes = \frac{52*51*10*49*2}{1}$$

$$Possible\ outcomes = 2,598,960$$

- **Then, think through all the ways which the Desired outcomes can be achieved.** To get 4 of a Kind, this means you would receive 4 cards all the same, and 1 card different from the other 4:

$$Desired\ Outcomes = 4\ cards\ same\ AND\ 1\ different\ card$$

- Because there are 13 different numbered/face cards in the deck, from Ace through King, there are <u>13 different ways you could receive a set of four of a kind</u>.

- Assuming you have been dealt 4 cards already, there are 48 cards remaining in the deck. (52 – 4 =48). Thus, there are <u>48 ways to receive the one card which is different</u> from the other 4 cards.

- Plug these into the formula we laid out above for Desired outcomes:

$$Desired\ Outcomes = 4\ cards\ same\ AND\ 1\ different\ card$$

$$Desired\ Outcomes = 13 * 48$$

$$Desired\ Outcomes = 624$$

- Now, use substitution to replace these values into each part of the Probability fraction, then use a calculator to arrive at the final answer:

$$P(4\ of\ a\ Kind) = \frac{Desired}{Possible} = \frac{624\ Desired}{2,598,960\ Possible}$$

$$P(4\ of\ a\ Kind) = 0.0002401, or\ 0.024\%$$

- You can see that it is extremely rare to get 4 of a Kind in the casino game 5-card stud poker. That's why this hand beats almost all other hands!

- *4 of a Kind beats everything except the even-lower probability hands of the Straight Flush and Royal Flush.*

Example #2: Let's Play Powerball®

What is the probability of <u>winning the Powerball® Jackpot</u> if you buy a single ticket?

Powerball® Rules
as of October 2017
Five white balls are drawn out of a drum with 69 balls
One red ball is drawn out of a drum with 26 balls
The Powerball® Jackpot is won by matching all five white balls in any order and the red Powerball

- This is an example of the rare probability question for which it is easier to solve for the number of Desired outcomes than for the number of Possible outcomes!

- The number of Desired outcomes = the number of tickets you purchased.

$$Desired\ outcomes = 1$$

- Now, identify the number of Possible outcomes.

  - Structure the logic in **Words First**, **Math Second**.

  $$Possible\ outcomes = Match\ 5\ White\ Balls\ AND\ Match\ 1\ Red\ Ball$$

  - Order does not matter to win the Powerball® Jackpot. You will need to use the Combinations formula to count the ways the 5 white balls can be drawn, then multiply this by the ways the red ball can be drawn. Because only 1 red ball is drawn, there are just 26 ways the red ball can be drawn.

  $$Possible\ outcomes = Match\ 5\ White\ Balls\ AND\ Match\ 1\ Red\ Ball$$

  $$Possible\ outcomes = {}_{69}C_5 * 26$$

  $$Possible\ outcomes = \frac{69!}{5!\,(69-5)!} * 26$$

  $$Possible\ outcomes = \frac{69!}{5!\,64!} * 26$$

  $$Possible\ outcomes = \frac{69 * 17\ \cancel{68} * 67 * 11\ \cancel{66} * 13\ \cancel{65} * \cancel{64!}}{\cancel{5} * 4 * \cancel{3} * \cancel{2} * 1 * \cancel{64!}} * 26$$

  $$Possible\ outcomes = \frac{69 * 17 * 67 * 11 * 13}{1} * 26$$

  $$Possible\ outcomes = 292,201,338$$

- Now, use substitution to replace these values into each part of the Probability fraction, then use a calculator to arrive at the final answer:

$$P(\text{Jackpot}) = \frac{Desired}{Possible} = \frac{1\ Desired}{292,201,338\ Possible}$$

- Thus, your odds of winning the Powerball® Jackpot = just 1 in 292 million!

All Your Word Problems Solved

WHICH APPROACH DO I USE, WHEN?

When you encounter a question with wording similar to this:

How many ways can you choose ... from ....?

How many different ways can you order...?

There are two things you should immediately ask yourself:

- Are the items different components of something, which are non-substitutes?
    - If <u>yes</u>, then **just multiply**.
    - For example, you have 5 flavors of ice cream and 3 toppings, and you can pick one of each, you cannot substitute an additional scoop of ice cream for a topping.
    - If <u>no</u>, ask yourself the next question.
- Are the items substitutes or replacements for one another?
    - If yes, then it's either a **permutation** or a **combination** problem.
- Now, ask yourself: Does order matter? *The question probably will not tell you directly. You must infer from the context whether order does or does not matter.*
    - If **order matters**, then this is a **permutation** problem. Examples:
        - <u>Horse race</u>: How many ways can six different horses receive 3 ribbons for win, place, and show?
        - <u>Olympic medals</u>: How many ways can fifteen athletes win the individual medals for the high dive?
        - <u>Elected officers</u>: If there are 12 members on the City Council, and the President, Vice President, Secretary, and Treasurer are elected from the existing council members, how many different ways can these positions be elected?
    - If **order does not matter**, then this is a **combination** problem. Examples:
        - <u>Roommates</u>: Joe needs to choose two of his six closest friends to share an apartment for the summer. How many different ways can he choose his roommates?
        - <u>Team members for a school project</u>: How many ways can the teacher assign four of her 15 students to form a single team?
        - <u>Choosing what to pack for vacation</u>: Miranda has eight shirts in her closet. She wants to pick five of them to pack for a long weekend trip. How many ways can she choose five of her eight shirts to take on the trip?

The formula for a **permutation** is <u>almost the same</u> as the formula for a **combination**. The combination formula has an extra term in the denominator, to remove the duplicates from permutations.

For example, if we had 3 letters A, B, and C, and want to choose just 2 of them:

- There are six different <u>permutations</u>: AB, AC, BA, BC, CA, CB

- But there are only 3 different <u>combinations</u>: AB, AC, BC

  - Why? If order doesn't matter, then these pairs are identical:

    - AB = BA

    - AC = CA

    - BC = CB

  - So, the extra term in the denominator of the combination formula serves to remove these duplicates.

- In the formula, you'll see these variables:

  - **N** = the **number of options** you have

  - **K** = the **number of items chosen**, from the total set of options

- You'll also see an exclamation point after a number, like this: **5!** or **n!**

  - When you see a number followed by an exclamation point, it is called a **factorial**. Thus, 5! is said aloud as "five factorial" and n! is said aloud as "n factorial" and k! is said aloud as "k factorial"

  - A **factorial** of a number is that number times each of the positive integers smaller than it. You can use either factorial notation or expanded notation:

Factorial Notation	Expanded Notation
2!	2 x 1
3!	3 x 2 x 1
4!	4 x 3 x 2 x 1
5!	5 x 4 x 3 x 2 x 1
6!	6 x 5 x 4 x 3 x 2 x 1
7!	7 x 6 x 5 x 4 x 3 x 2 x 1
8!	8 x 7 x 6 x 5 x 4 x 3 x 2 x 1

COMPARING PERMUTATIONS & COMBINATIONS

	Permutation	Combination
Does order matter?	Order matters	Order does <u>not</u> matter
Examples	• Olympic medals • Elected positions (e.g., President, VP, Treasurer)	• Choosing roommates • Deciding which of several items to buy
Formula	$$_nP_k = \frac{n!}{(n-k)!}$$	$$_nC_k = \frac{n!}{k!\,(n-k)!}$$
Detailed example	How many different ways can 5 athletes win 3 medals in the Olympics? *Here, order does matter. Winning a silver medal is not the same as winning bronze or gold.* We have 5 choices of athletes. The judges will award 3 medals. *In our formula, then:* • n = 5 • k = 3 $$_5P_3 = \frac{5!}{(5-3)!}$$ *Now, expand out the factorial only as far as needed to cancel:* $$= \frac{5*4*3*\cancel{2!}}{\cancel{2!}} = 5*4*3 = 60$$ 3 medals can be awarded to 5 athletes in **60 different ways**.	Nick likes a certain shirt, which comes in 5 colors. He would like to buy 3 shirts, all in different colors. In how many different ways can Nick choose which shirts to buy, assuming he will not buy two of the same color? *Here, order does not matter. A choice of red, blue, brown is the same as blue, red, brown.* Nick has 5 choices of colors: red, blue, green, brown, grey And Nick will choose 3 of them. *In our formula, then:* • n = 5 • k = 3 $$_5C_3 = \frac{5!}{3!\,(5-3)!}$$ *Now, expand out the factorial only as far as needed to cancel:* $$= \frac{5*4*\cancel{3}*\cancel{2!}}{\cancel{3}*2*\cancel{2!}} = (20/2) = 10$$ 3 different colors of shirts can be chosen from 5 available colors in **10 different ways**.

Here are some of the common ways the test maker can make a permutations or combinations problem harder on your standardized test:

1. Writing questions that **combine another topic**, such as probability, with a permutation or combination.

2. Inserting wording which indicates the **choices are selected from separate pools**, not from a single pool, which increase the complexity of the question. To solve these correctly, you'll need to write your logical structure in **words first, math second**.

   - For example: A debate class is made up of both juniors and seniors. There are 8 juniors and 12 seniors in the class. If the teacher must select a team of 3 juniors and 3 seniors to represent their school at a local debate competition, how many different ways can she select this team?

   - Here, you must discern from the content of the question that the juniors and seniors are different pools of students from which the teacher can select debate team members.

   - You'll need to **multiply** the number of ways the teacher can choose juniors by the number of ways the teacher can choose seniors.

     # ways to choose Juniors X # ways to choose Seniors

   - Also, the question wording does <u>not</u> mention any positions, such as team captain, or include any other wording which suggests that order would matter, so you should assume that order does not matter.

     Choose 3 of 8 Juniors AND 3 of 12 Seniors = $_8C_3$ * $_{12}C_3$

3. Inserting wording such as **at least**, **at most**, or **up to**, which increases the complexity of the question.

   - For example: A local pizza place has 6 different toppings on the menu. If Sarah chooses <u>at least</u> 2, but <u>at most</u> 4, different toppings for her pizza, how many different ways can she select the toppings?

   - **Add up** the ways to choose exactly 2, OR exactly 3, OR exactly 4 toppings.

     # ways to choose 2 + # ways to choose 3 + # ways to choose 4

     Order doesn't matter for pizza toppings, so these are combinations.

     At least 2, but at most 4 toppings = $_6C_2$ + $_6C_3$ + $_6C_4$

EXPLORING VARIATIONS OF COMBINATIONS QUESTIONS

Now that you have read and understood the introductory Permutations & Combinations section, let's explore how you need **adjust the structure of your approach** based on subtle changes in the wording.

We will use one <u>extended example</u> – ordering pizza – to explore several different variations the GMAT or GRE may show you. *Students taking the PSAT/NMSQT, SAT, or ACT most likely will not encounter questions that this level of difficulty, but can still attempt these questions for extra practice to improve logical thinking skills.*

THINKING THROUGH THE LOGIC: WORDS FIRST, MATH SECOND

Let's say you and a friend are planning to order a pizza.

The basic question, "**<u>How many different ways can you</u>** order a pizza with...*various parameters or constraints*?" are the clue words which should trigger you to think in terms of Combinatorics (a term which collectively refers to the counting principle, permutations, and combinations).

- The activity or context of the question <u>will change</u> – ordering pizza, a burrito, an ice cream sundae; buying an outfit; redesigning your kitchen, etc.

- The parameters or constraints <u>will change</u> – and you must pay strict attention to these details.

  - Are you choosing exactly one of each option? The question may or may not state this explicitly.

    - For example: it is <u>logical</u> that you can choose *only one pizza crust*, so the test may <u>expect you to make this conclusion on your own</u>. It *probably will not* say "if a pizza consists of one crust..."

      - For any part of a pizza, where you logically <u>pick just one of that</u> type of thing, you **just multiply** the options. (kinds of crust, sauce, etc.)

      - For any part of an ice cream sundae, where you logically <u>pick just one of that</u> type of thing, you **just multiply** the options. (types of cones)

    - On the other hand: it is also <u>logical</u> that you could choose *none, one, or more than one toppings*. For this type of item, the test will explicitly tell you how many options you are allowed to choose from the list.

      - For any part of a pizza, where you pick more than one of that type of thing, such as the toppings, you need to **use the combination formula**.

      - With pizza toppings, or most food items, **<u>order does not matter</u>**. *Bacon + Sausage is the same as Sausage + Bacon.*

      - If you have the option <u>OMIT</u> something that is an extra option! If you have 3 kinds of cheese but can choose <u>no</u>

<u>cheese</u>, then you have 4 ways to choose what kind of cheese you want.

- Putting it all together: you will use the **counting principle** for the part of the problem where you choose one of this and one of that, and you will use the **combinations formula** for the part(s) where you choose more than one of something.

You should use the **Words First, Math Second approach** for structuring your approach. A few examples are shown below.

You may have noticed that more and more fast-casual restaurants have menus designed like "pick one of these, pick one of these, pick up to 4 of these..."

Why is this menu design so popular? Because consumers like choice, and this menu design means restaurants can offer <u>thousands of variations</u> with a "simple" menu.

Ordering a Pizza							
Ways to Choose Crust	x	Ways to Choose Sauce	x	Ways to Choose Cheese	x	Ways to Choose Toppings *Usually the complex part*

DIY Stir-Fry							
Ways to Choose Carb	x	Ways to Choose Protein	x	Ways to Choose Sauce	x	Ways to Choose Vegetables *Usually the complex part*

Ice Cream Bar							
Ways to Choose a Cone or Dish	x	Ways to Choose Flavors of Ice Cream *May be one or more than one*	x	Ways to Choose Syrup	x	Ways to Choose Toppings *Usually the complex part*

Pizza menu

- <u>Crusts</u>: Crispy Thin Crust, Hand Tossed, Pan, Garlic Butter Crust*
- <u>Sauces</u>: Marinara, Alfredo*, Spicy Marinara, BBQ
- <u>Cheese</u>: Mozzarella*, Four Cheese Blend*, Vegan Cheese
- <u>Toppings</u>:
    - <u>Meats</u>: Pepperoni, Sausage, Bacon, Grilled Chicken, Ground Beef, Canadian Bacon
    - <u>Veggies & Fruits</u>: Tomatoes, Black Olives, Pineapple, Mushrooms, Spinach, Roasted Red Peppers, Banana Peppers

Allergy warning: Contains dairy

Example #1: Using the Counting Principle & Combinations Formula

If a pizza consists of one crust, one sauce, one cheese, and toppings, how many different ways can you order a pizza with <u>3 different toppings</u>?

- <u>Counting principle</u>: Because we can only choose one each from our options for crusts, sauces, and cheeses, we **just multiply** these options.
- <u>Combinations</u>: If you count all of the meats, veggies, and fruits, we have 13 total options for toppings. We are asked to choose 3 different toppings from those 13 options.
    - The combinations formula is $_nC_k$
    - N represents the number of options available, so N = 13
    - K represents the number of choices we make, so K = 3

Ordering a Pizza						
Crust	x	**Sauce**	x	**Cheese**	x	**Toppings**
4	x	4	x	3	x	$_{13}C_3$

Example #2: Choosing from Separate "Pools"

If a pizza consists of one crust, one sauce, one cheese, and toppings, how many different ways can you order a 4-topping pizza with <u>2 different meat and 2 different non-meat toppings</u>?

- <u>Counting principle</u>: Because we can only choose one each from our options for crusts, sauces, and cheeses, we **just multiply** these options.
- <u>Combinations</u>: If you count all of the meats, veggies, and fruits, we have 13 total options for toppings. 6 of these are meats, and 7 of these are non-meats.
   - For our toppings, we are asked to choose 2 different meats from the 6 options available, and choose 2 different non-meats from the 7 options available.
      - So, we can replace sausage with pepperoni, but we cannot replace sausage with pineapple.
      - This means we are choosing our toppings from separate "pools."
   - The combinations formula is $_nC_k$
   - The question asks us to select meat <u>and</u> non-meat toppings, so we "break the logic" into two parts – ways to pick meat <u>and</u> ways to pick non-meat.
      - *The word AND, when it shows up in Combinations questions, means "multiply."*
      - *Whenever we "break the logic" into parts, use parentheses around the total of the ways to pick that part of the pizza (e.g., around Toppings).*
   - For the meat toppings:
      - N represents the number of options available, so N = 6
      - K represents the number of choices we make, so K = 2
   - For the non-meat toppings:
      - N represents the number of options available, so N = 7
      - K represents the number of choices we make, so K = 2

Ordering a Pizza								
Crust	**x**	**Sauce**	**x**	**Cheese**	**x**	**Toppings**		
						Meats	and	Non-Meats
4	x	4	x	3	x	($_6C_2$	x	$_7C_2$)

Example #3: Changing the # of Choices We Make (Several Values of K)

If a pizza consists of one crust, one sauce, one cheese, and toppings, how many different ways can you order a pizza with <u>at least 2, but at most 4, different toppings</u>?

- <u>Counting principle</u>: Because we can only choose one each from our options for crusts, sauces, and cheeses, we **just multiply** these options.

- <u>Combinations</u>: If you count all of the meats, veggies, and fruits, we have 13 total options for toppings.
  - For our toppings, the phrasing "at least 2, but at most 4" means we can choose either 2 toppings, or 3 toppings, or 4 toppings.
  - The combinations formula is $_nC_k$
  - Because we can pick different numbers of toppings we "break the logic" into two parts – ways to pick 2 toppings <u>or</u> ways to pick 3 toppings <u>or</u> ways to pick 4 toppings.
    - *The word OR, when it shows up in Combinations questions, means "add."*
    - *Whenever we "break the logic" into parts, use parentheses around the total of the ways to pick that part of the pizza (e.g., around Toppings).*
  - For the toppings:
    - N represents the number of options available, so N = 13
    - K represents the number of choices we make, so K = 2 or 3 or 4

Ordering a Pizza										
Crust	**x**	**Sauce**	**x**	**Cheese**	**x**	**Toppings**				
						2 topp's	OR	3 topp's	OR	4 topp's
4	x	4	x	3	x	($_{13}C_2$	+	$_{13}C_3$	+	$_{13}C_4$)

Example #4: Choices Do Not Always Have To Be "Different"

If a pizza consists of one crust, one sauce, one cheese, and toppings, how many different ways can you order a pizza with 3 toppings?

- Counting principle: Because we can only choose one each from our options for crusts, sauces, and cheeses, we **just multiply** these options.
- Combinations: If you count all of the meats, veggies, and fruits, we have 13 total options for toppings.
    - Notice here, the question does not say the toppings are different.
        - So, we could get triple pepperoni!
        - Or double chicken with black olives
        - Or three different toppings
    - Because we can pick 3 toppings that are not necessarily different, we "break the logic" into three parts – ways to pick 3 of the same toppings or ways to pick 2 the same and 1 different or ways to pick 3 different toppings.
        - *The word OR, when it shows up in Combinations questions, means "add."*
        - *Whenever we "break the logic" into parts, use parentheses around the total of the ways to pick that part of the pizza (e.g., around Toppings).*
    - For the toppings:
        - If we pick 3 of the same thing, then we have as many ways to do this as we have options on the menu. 13 toppings available = 13 ways to pick 3 of the same thing.
        - If we pick 2 of the same and 1 different, we have 13 ways to pick the first "doubled" topping, which eliminates one option for the different topping. Thus, we have 12 ways to pick the 3rd topping.

Ordering a Pizza										
Crust	**x**	**Sauce**	**x**	**Cheese**	**x**	**Toppings**				
						3 same	OR	2 same AND 1 different	OR	3 different
4	x	4	x	3	x	[13	+	(13 * 12)	+	$_{13}C_3$]

All Your Word Problems Solved

Example #5: Omitting Something Still Counts as a Choice!

If a pizza consists of one crust, one sauce, one cheese, and toppings, how many different ways can you order a pizza with <u>up to 2 different toppings</u>?

- <u>Counting principle</u>: Because we can only choose one each from our options for crusts, sauces, and cheeses, we **just multiply** these options.
- <u>Combinations</u>: If you count all of the meats, veggies, and fruits, we have 13 total options for toppings.
    - ○ For our toppings, the phrasing "up to 2 different toppings" means we can choose either 2 toppings, or 1 topping, or <u>zero</u> toppings.
    - ○ Because we can pick different numbers of toppings we "break the logic" into two parts – ways to pick 2 toppings <u>or</u> ways to pick 1 topping <u>or</u> ways to pick <u>zero</u> toppings.
        - ▪ *The word OR, when it shows up in Combinations questions, means "add."*
        - ▪ *Whenever we "break the logic" into parts, use parentheses around the total of the ways to pick that part of the pizza (e.g., around toppings).*
        - ▪ *There is only <u>one way to pick zero toppings</u> – omit all of them!*
    - ○ For the toppings:
        - ▪ N represents the number of options available, so N = 13
        - ▪ K represents the number of choices we make, so K = 2 or 1 or 0

Ordering a Pizza										
Crust	**x**	**Sauce**	**x**	**Cheese**	**x**	**Toppings**				
						2 toppings	OR	1 topping	OR	No toppings
4	x	4	x	3	x	($_{13}C_2$	+	13	+	1)

Example #6: Constraining Options & Forced Choices

If a pizza consists of one crust, one sauce, one cheese, and toppings, how many different ways can you order a pizza with 2 different toppings, if your friend has a dairy allergy?

- <u>Counting principle</u>: Because we can only choose one each from our options for crusts, sauces, and cheeses, we **just multiply** these options.
  - The number of options for your crust, sauce, and cheeses is constrained by your friend's dairy allergy. Look at the asterisks on the menu!
  - <u>Crusts</u>: Because the Garlic Butter Crust contains dairy, you only have 3 viable options for the crust.
  - <u>Sauces</u>: Because the Alfredo sauce contains dairy, you only have 3 viable options for the sauce.
  - <u>Cheeses</u>: Because both Mozzarella and Four Cheese Blend contain dairy, you only have one option – the Vegan Cheese. In other words, this is a "forced choice."
    - If you feel more comfortable including it in your Words First, Math Second logical structure, then do so, but it's just multiplying by 1
    - You can therefore also <u>omit</u> Cheese from the list of choices you can make.
- <u>Combinations</u>: If you count all of the meats, veggies, and fruits, we have 13 total options for toppings.
  - For the toppings:
    - N represents the number of options available, so N = 13
    - K represents the number of choices we make, so K = 2

Ordering a Pizza – No Dairy, option A						
Crust	**x**	**Sauce**	**x**	**Cheese**	**x**	**Toppings**
3	x	*3*	x	*1*	x	$_{13}C_2$

Ordering a Pizza – No Dairy, option B				
Crust	**x**	**Sauce**	**x**	**Toppings**
3	x	*3*	x	$_{13}C_2$

All Your Word Problems Solved

Example #7: Unlimited Toppings

If a pizza consists of one crust, one sauce, one cheese, and toppings, how many different ways can you order a pizza with <u>unlimited different toppings</u>?

- <u>Counting principle</u>: Because we can only choose one each from our options for crusts, sauces, and cheeses, we **just multiply** these options.

- <u>Combinations</u>: If you count all of the meats, veggies, and fruits, we have 13 total options for toppings.
  - For our toppings, the phrasing "unlimited different toppings" means we can choose either all 13 toppings, or 12 toppings, or 11 toppings, or 10 toppings...or 2 toppings, or 1 topping, or <u>zero</u> toppings.
    - $_{13}C_{13} +\ _{13}C_{12} +\ _{13}C_{11} +\ _{13}C_{10} \cdots\ _{13}C_2\ _{13}C_1 + 1$
    - Attempting to calculate "unlimited toppings" this way, however, quickly gets tedious and there's a high risk that you'll make errors somewhere in the calculation.
  - Fortunately, we can **simplify** how we think about "unlimited toppings" as making a **Yes-or-No decision** about each of the 13 toppings.
    - For the <u>first</u> topping on the list, we have two ways to choose – either yes or no
    - For the <u>second</u> topping on the list, we have two ways to choose – either yes or no
    - For the <u>third</u> topping on the list, we have two ways to choose – either yes or no
    - So that is 2 * 2 * 2...and so on.
    - This allows us to think about toppings as making a binary (2 option, Yes-or-No) decision, repeated 13 times (once about each topping), which **simplifies our calculation to 2^{13}**

Ordering a Pizza						
Crust	**x**	**Sauce**	**x**	**Cheese**	**x**	**Toppings**
4	x	4	x	3	x	2^{13}

If you're preparing for one of the standardized tests, **statistics** is probably one of the topics which seems more daunting than it really is. That's because these topics are often glossed over in our high school math classes, and not all college majors require a course in statistics.

Fortunately, there's a fairly limited scope of statistics concepts tested on the major college and graduate admissions standardized tests. You'll need to be familiar with how to find, utilize, and compare:

- The **measures of centrality**: finding and using the mean, median, and mode
- The **measures of dispersion**: finding and using the range

$$Range\ of\ a\ set = Maximum\ Value - Minimum\ Value$$

- The **normal distribution** (bell curve) and its components: mean, standard deviation, variance, and percentile.
- Other measures of **relative standing / ranking**: decile, quintile, and quartile

For the GRE, you will also need to be able to interpret certain graphs and visualizations of statistical information, such as:

- The **box-and-whisker plot**: a way of presenting the range, quartiles, and median of a data set. You can also infer the interquartile ranges from this plot.

Note: As of 2017, the box-and-whisker plot does <u>not</u> appear on the GMAT (subject to change by the GMAC).

WHAT ARE THE MEASURES OF CENTRALITY?

Here's what you need to know about the three measures of centrality used to describe a data set (or a population):

	Mean	Median	Mode
Definition	The **arithmetic average** of a data set	The **middle value**, when the data set is listed in order from smallest to largest	The term which **appears most frequently** in the data set
How to find this measure	= (Sum of terms) / (# of terms)	• First, list them in order by size • If the set has an <u>odd</u> number of terms, it's the <u>term in the middle</u>. • If the set has an <u>even</u> number of terms, take the <u>average of the two terms in the middle</u>.	If the <u>set is provided in a list</u> like this: {a, b, c, c, d, c, e} Then it's the term which appears most frequently. If the data is presented in a <u>histogram</u>, look for the tallest column.
Practical usage	The **mean** is the most commonly used of the three measures of centrality. It is most useful and relevant <u>when the data set is *reasonably symmetric*</u>, and/or there is both a minimum and a maximum possible value for the data. You're probably quite familiar with means (arithmetic averages): • Your GPA • Average test scores (range of 0 to 100) for your classes • Average height	The **median** is most useful and relevant <u>when the data set is skewed</u>, and there are a few outliers (extremes) which cause the "average" to be overstated. **Household income (HHI)** is the most common stat that uses median, instead of an average. Why? If you include the income of billionaire CEOs, the "average" HHI of your state is very high. The median is more relevant for planning things like public transportation.	The **mode** is used much less often than the mean or median. It's more relevant for things like consumer surveys, where you're looking for frequency of an answer more than an exact value (or where the answers are split into two camps).

WHAT IS THE NORMAL DISTRIBUTION? WHAT DO I NEED TO KNOW?

The **normal distribution** is the academic term for what many of us call the "**bell curve**." You should know these key facts about the normal distribution:

- The normal distribution has a **mean**, a number of observations (or population size) a **standard deviation**, and a **variance**.
  - You need to know what these terms mean and how to use them, but you will not be expected to calculate the individual variances to find the standard deviation.
    - **Individual Variance** = the square of the distance between one of the data points and the mean of the set of data points.

      $$Individual\ Variance = (Value - Mean)^2$$

    - **Standard Deviation** = the square root of the mean (arithmetic average) squared variances (individual variances).

$$Std.\ Deviation = \sqrt{\frac{(a_1 - Mean)^2 + (a_2 - Mean)^2 + (a_3 - Mean)^2 \dots + (a_n - Mean)^2}{n}}$$

  - Instead, you might be given a couple of the parts and asked to calculate the other one. (This is much less work than finding the variance from the individual data points!)
  - Special relationships:
    - $Total\ Variance = Mean\ Squared\ Variance = (Std.\ Deviation)^2$
    - If all values or terms in a set are identical, then:
      - Each term equals the mean
      - Each of the individual variances is zero
      - The standard deviation is also zero
- The normal distribution is **symmetrical** around the mean (arithmetic average)
  - 50% of the observations / population lie <u>below</u> the mean. That can be further broken down as follows: *Note: the GRE uses less-precise percentages than a Statistics course will use, so the 14% and 2% are rounded. Other tests may use 13.5% and 2.5% for these values, respectively.*
    - 34% of the population is between the mean & 1 standard deviation below the mean
    - 14% of the population is between 1 standard deviation & 2 standard deviations below the mean
    - 2% of the population is more than 2 standard deviations below the mean

All Your Word Problems Solved

- 50% of the observations / population lie <u>above</u> the mean. That can be further broken down as follows:
    - 34% of the population is between the mean & 1 standard deviation above the mean
    - 14% of the population is between 1 standard deviation & 2 standard deviations above the mean
    - 2% of the population is more than 2 standard deviations above the mean
- Note: If a test question asks you what percent of the population falls <u>within 1 standard deviation of the mean</u>, the **words to math** translation of that means you need to <u>add</u> the percent of the population between the mean & 1 standard deviation <u>below</u> the mean AND the percent of the population between the mean & 1 standard deviation <u>above</u> the mean.
    - Population between mean & 1 standard deviation below it = 34%
    - Population between mean & 1 standard deviation above it = 34%
    - Total population within 1 standard deviation of the mean = 68%
- A normal distribution can be "tight" around the mean (indicating a small standard deviation) or "spread out" from the mean (indicating a large standard deviation).
    - If two data sets, both described by the normal distribution, have the same mean (arithmetic average) and the same population size, but one is more "tall and narrow" and the other is more "short and wide", then:
        - Short & wide (see fig. 1 below) = larger standard deviation
        - Tall & narrow (see fig. 2 below) = smaller standard deviation

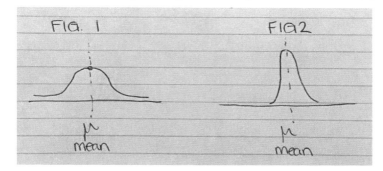

WEIGHTED AVERAGES

A **weighted average** is an overall average across two or more groups. For example, if a large middle school has three 7th grade math teachers:

- Each teacher will have his or her own class average on the final exam.

- The average of all 7th grade math students is **probably not** equal to the simple average of the three class averages. Why? Because the classes may not be equally sized. One class may have a few more students than the other two classes. Let's call these classes Groups A, B, and C.

- There are **two variations of the weighted average formula**. You can use <u>either</u> the **number of observations** or the **percent of observations** in each group.

$$Wtd.Avg = \frac{(Group\ A\ avg\ *\ \#\ in\ A) + (Group\ B\ avg\ *\ \#\ in\ B) + (Group\ C\ avg\ *\ \#\ in\ C)}{\#\ in\ A + \#\ in\ B + \#\ in\ C}$$

OR

$$Wtd.Avg = (Group\ A\ avg\ *\ \%\ in\ A) + (Group\ B\ avg\ *\ \%\ in\ B) + (Group\ C\ avg\ *\ \%\ in\ C)$$

- From the first formula, we can see that to find the weighted average – or the average of all 7th graders – we need to know each of the three class averages and the number of students in each class.

- Using the data below, we'll find the average score for all 7th grade math students.

Teacher	# of Students	Class Average
Ms. Anderson	30	75
Mr. Baker	20	88
Ms. Cook	25	84

$$Weighted\ Avg = \frac{(75*30) + (88*20) + (84*25)}{30+20+25}$$

$$Weighted\ Avg = \frac{2250 + 1760 + 2100}{75} = \frac{6110}{75} = \mathbf{81.46}$$

- Some facts to remember about weighted averages, which are useful **heuristics** (or rules of thumb) to help you efficiently eliminate tempting-but-wrong answer choices:

  o The weighted average <u>cannot be less than the smallest</u> group average

  o The weighted average <u>cannot be more than the largest</u> group average

  o The weighted average will <u>only equal the average of the group averages if the groups are equally sized</u>. Otherwise, the weighted average will not equal the average of the group averages.

PERCENTILES, DECILES, QUINTILES, AND QUARTILES

In a data set with any kind of distribution (normal or otherwise), we use one of three terms to express a person or observation's **relative standing** compared to all others in the same set.

You might already be familiar with **percentiles** from your past experience with standardized tests – you'll get a numeric score and a percentile ranking.

- **Percentile**: The percentile associated with a particular score or data point expresses what percent of the sample population scored the same or less than that person or observation. This could be restated as the person scored the same or better than what percent of the sample population. You can multiply your percentile rank times the size of the sample population to get an exact value for the number of students whom you beat.

  - For example, on a recent administration of the ACT, a composite score of 26 would give you an 83rd percentile rank. That means, this student who scored a 26 performed the same or better than 83% of all students taking that test on the same date.

  - If 50,000 students took the ACT on the same date, then this student scored the same or better than 83% * (50,000) = 41,500 other students.

  - *Note: absolute scores on standardized tests can fluctuate up or down over time, or across different exam dates, so the percentile ranking is what gives meaning to your absolute score.*

Sometimes, we would prefer to cluster or group the sample population into equally sized units. For that purpose, we use Decile, Quintile, and/or Quartile.

In the real world, you may see **deciles** used to describe various types of population or market segments.

- **Decile**: Using the Latin roots, we know that calculating deciles means splitting the population into 10 groups, when ordered from least to greatest. So, each decile contains (100%/10) = **10%** of the population.

  - The 1st decile would represent the lowest score up to the 10th percentile;

  - The 2nd decile would represent the 11th percentile up to the 20th percentile;

  - The 3rd decile would represent the 21st percentile up to the 30th percentile;

  - And so on…

In the real world, you may see **quintiles** used to describe household income data and its association to socioeconomic classes, with such terms as "Working Class", "Lower Middle Class", "Middle Class", "Upper Middle Class" and "Affluent" (or other similar terms).

- **Quintile**: Using the Latin roots, we know that calculating quintiles means splitting the population into 5 groups, when ordered from least to greatest. So, each quintile contains (100%/5) = **20%** of the population.

  - The 1st quintile would represent the lowest score up to the 20th percentile;

- The 2nd quintile would represent the 21st percentile up to the 40th percentile;
- The 3rd quintile would represent the 41st percentile up to the 60th percentile;
- And so on…

In the real world, you may see **quartiles** used to provide information about the range of the middle of the data set, after eliminating the upper and lower ends of the set. For example, many colleges present their **25th and 75th percentile** test scores and GPAs for admitted students (also called the "**middle 50 percent**", which is found by finding the scores at the bottom of the 2nd quartile and the top of the 3rd quartile) to help students understand whether their application is competitive for their desired school. For example, if a school had an average ACT score of 31.3, some students with a 29 or 30 might be too intimidated to apply, so if the same school shares a middle 50 percent range of scores from 27 to 33, those students with a 29 or 30 would better understand that they're right in the sweet spot of that school's applicant pool.

- **Quartile**: Using the Latin roots, we know that calculating quartiles means splitting the population into 4 groups, when ordered from least to greatest. So, each quartile contains 25% of the population.
  - The 1st quartile would represent the lowest score up to the 25th percentile
  - The 2nd quartile would represent the 26th percentile up to the 50th percentile
  - The 3rd quartile would represent the 51st percentile up to the 75th percentile
  - The 4th quartile would represent the 76th percentile up to the 100th percentile

All Your Word Problems Solved

BOX-AND-WHISKER PLOTS

The **box-and-whisker plot** is one way of visually conveying lots of information about a population's scores on some dimension (such as height, test scores, etc.). From a **box-and-whisker plot**, you can determine these important statistics of a sample:

- Overall minimum, maximum, and total range
- Middle 50% range
- Median
- Cutoff scores between quartiles

A **box-and-whisker** plot will not, however, give you an exact percentile associated with a specific score. In other words, you might know if your score falls within the 2nd quartile or 3rd quartile, but you will not know if it is the 33rd or 47th percentile.

Let's look at an example, with hypothetical data. Suppose a health and fitness researcher identified a sample of 200 women, and measured the maximum weight (in excess of their own body weight) which each of them could lift in a specific exercise, such as squats.

If we wanted to visualize the full distribution of the researcher's observations, we could plot them on a graph.

You'll see there's a wide variation, with some women squatting as few as 10 pounds and others squatting 200 or more pounds.

Here's the same data, presented in a table. The second column lists the exact number of observations for a specific squat weight. The third column lists the number of **cumulative observations**, which is determined by summing the number of observations for that squat weight *plus* all the squat weights equal to or less than that one.

For any given sample size or population size, we can determine the **quartile cutoffs** by finding:

$$\text{Quartile Cutoff} = \text{Sample Size} * \frac{1}{4} = \text{Cumulative \# of Observations}$$

Here, because our sample contains a total of 200 observations, then our quartile cutoffs occur at 50, 100, and 150 cumulative observations.

Squat Weight	# of Observations	Cumulative # of Observations	Quartile Cutoffs
10	23	23	Start of 1st Quartile
20	20	43	
30	7	50	End of 1st Quartile
40	16	66	Start of 2nd Quartile
50	11	77	
60	13	90	
70	10	100	End of 2nd Quartile
80	3	103	Start of 3rd Quartile
90	12	115	
100	13	128	
110	18	146	
120	4	150	End of 3rd Quartile
130	5	155	Start of 4th Quartile
140	2	157	
150	14	171	
160	6	177	
170	3	180	
180	3	183	
190	0	183	
200	0	183	
210	2	185	
220	3	188	
230	1	189	

240	5	194	
250	0	194	
260	0	194	
270	2	196	
280	1	197	
290	0	197	
300	0	197	
310	0	197	
320	2	199	
330	0	199	
340	0	199	
350	1	200	End of 4th Quartile

Let's recap the important statistics we now know about our sample observations.

- Overall minimum = 10 pounds
- Overall maximum = 350 pounds
- Total range = max-min = (350 - 10) = 340 pounds
- Middle 50% range = bottom of 2nd Quartile to top of 3rd Quartile, or 40 to 120 pounds
- Median = 75 pounds

Now, let's draw that as a **box-and-whisker plot**. We mark the lowest and the highest observations at either end of the diagram. The box, then, indicates the lowest value that falls within the 2nd quartile and the highest value that falls within the 3rd quartile.

75 lb

10 lb   40 lb   120 lb   350 lb

Let's say the <u>only</u> information you have is the box-and-whisker plot, and you do not have the underlying data. How do you interpret a box-and-whisker plot?

From our **box-and-whisker plot**, above, you can infer:

- The range of observations goes from a **minimum** of 10 pounds to a **maximum** of 350 pounds.
- The underlying data set is **skewed toward the lower end** of the range.
- The **middle 50 percent** of the sample goes from 40 pounds to 120 pounds.

- The **median** is 75 pounds.

In addition to identifying the total range of the sample observations, you can determine what are called the **interquartile ranges**, or the cutoff values associated with being in either the first, second, third, or fourth quartile.

- Interquartile range of 1st quartile: 10 to 40 pounds, or (40-10) = 30 pounds
- Interquartile range of 2nd quartile: 40 to 75 pounds, or (75-40) = 35 pounds
- Interquartile range of 3rd quartile: 75 to 120 pounds, or (120-75) = 45 pounds
- Interquartile range of 4th quartile: 120 to 350 pounds, or (350-120) = 230 pounds

Because the interquartile ranges are smaller (narrower) in the first couple of quartiles, we can infer that the underlying data is relatively concentrated here. The much larger interquartile range of the last quartile shows that there is much **more variability within the high end** of the sample population (presumably, women who strength train and/or compete in bodybuilding activities).

FUNCTIONS & SYMBOL PROBLEMS ARE JUST EQUATIONS

Functions and **Symbol Problems** seem intimidating at first, because they are unfamiliar, but these two types of math problems are just equations in disguise.

All the rules of <u>substitution</u> and <u>order of operations</u> (PEMDAS) that apply to manipulating variables and numbers in equations also apply to Functions and to Symbol Problems.

FUNCTIONS

What's a function? An equation with a name. See the examples below.

How Equations & Functions are Related	Equation	Function
Given this:	y = 4x + 3	$f(x) = 4x + 3$
Remember:	**y** and **f(x)** mean the same thing!	
Example question: What you do: Given a value of X, solve for the value of Y	If x = 5, what is y?	What is the $f(5)$? Evaluate the function $f(x)$ when x = 5.
Plug in X = 5 & solve for Y	Y = 4(5) + 3 Y = 23	$f(5) = 4(5) + 3$ $f(5) = 23$

How Equations & Functions are Related	Equation	Function
Given this:	$y = x^2 + 8x + 12$	$g(x) = x^2 + 8x + 12$
Remember:	**y** and **g(x)** mean the same thing!	
Example question: What you do: Given a value of Y or *g(x)*, solve for X	If y = 45, what is x?	If $g(x) = 45$, what is the value of x?
Plug in Y = 45, then solve for X Plug in *g(x)* = 45, then solve for X	$y = x^2 + 8x + 12$ $45 = x^2 + 8x + 12$ $0 = x^2 + 8x - 33$ $0 = (x + 11)(x - 3)$ X = -11 or +3	$g(x) = x^2 + 8x + 12$ $45 = x^2 + 8x + 12$ $0 = x^2 + 8x - 33$ $0 = (x + 11)(x - 3)$ X = -11 or +3

UNDERSTANDING THE DOMAIN & RANGE OF A FUNCTION

Every function has both a **domain** and a **range**.

- **Domain** = all the valid (possible) values of X.
- **Range** = all the valid (possible) values of Y or *f(x)*.

IDENTIFYING THE DOMAIN OF A FUNCTION

- For many "pure math" functions, the domain of that function will consist of **all real numbers**. *See the section on Number Properties for an explanation of real numbers.*
  - Sometimes, the domain will consist of all real numbers <u>except</u> one or two values.
  - Usually, these <u>exceptions</u> are the values of X that would make the denominator of a fraction equal zero, and therefore be undefined.
  - Example: in the function $f(x) = \frac{4x+3}{x-2}$
    - We find the exceptions by setting the denominator equal to zero, and solving for X.
      - X-2 = 0
      - If X = +2, then the denominator would equal zero.
      - Thus, X cannot equal +2, but it can get very close to it (such as 1.99 or 2.03)

All Your Word Problems Solved

- The domain of *f(x)* consists of all real numbers X, such that X ≠ 2.
  - Note: the phrase "such that" indicates a constraint
- Example: in this function $g(x) = \frac{4x+3}{x^2-2x-15}$
  - We find the exceptions by setting the denominator equal to zero, and solving for X.
    - $x^2 - 2x - 15 = 0$
    - It's a quadratic, so we need to factor it.
    - $(x - 3)(x + 5) = 0$
    - Either factor could make the equation equal zero, so we set each factor equal to zero and solve for X.
    - If X = +3 or -5, then the denominator would equal zero.
    - Thus, X cannot equal +3 or -5, but it can get very close to either of them.
  - The domain of *g(x)* consists of all real numbers X, such that X ≠ +3 or -5.

- For many "real-world" functions, the domain of that function will consist of **only positive numbers**. Depending upon what real-world scenario the function describes, the domain might consist of <u>either</u> **only positive integers** or **all positive numbers**. Why positive?
  - Because you cannot produce negative units of a good.
  - Because you cannot sell negative units of a good.
  - Because you cannot run a negative distance.
  - Because you cannot earn negative income. (*Net income, on the other hand, is a different story, because it is the result of taking Income-Expenses. You can spend more than you earn.*)

If the Domain consists of...	...Only Positive Integers	...All Positive Numbers
Examples of "real world" scenarios of each type	• Production of inventory • Number of items purchased	• Household income • Tax revenue • Distance run, in miles per week • Miles traveled for work
If the domain is THIS, it is also called THAT type of function	**Discrete function**	**Continuous function**
What does that mean?	**Discrete functions** mean you can make and sell either 8 or 9 or 10 units of a good, but you cannot make and sell partial units... ...so 8.2 or 9 ½ or 10.333 units are not possible values for the number of units made and sold. This logic is why the functions listed above are considered **discrete functions**, and the **domain** of each function consists of **all positive integers X**.	**Continuous functions** mean both integer and non-integer values are valid... ...so you can have a household income of exactly \$65,000, but \$64,897.23 and \$65,204.11 are also possible values. This logic is why the real-world functions listed above are considered **continuous functions**, and the **domain** of each function consists of **all positive numbers X**.

All Your Word Problems Solved

IDENTIFYING THE RANGE OF A FUNCTION

- For many "pure math" functions, the range of that function may:
    - Consist of **all real numbers**, if the function is **linear**. *Cross-reference the section on Number Properties for an explanation of real numbers.*
    - Have a **minimum** or **maximum**, if the function is **quadratic** or the graph is a **parabola**.
- You will need to identify the type of function, then use any of these strategies to determine the range:
    - Using <u>math rules</u>, such as the vertex form of the equation for a parabola to find its minimum or maximum
    - Using a <u>patterns, logic, and reasoning approach</u>, such as testing various values of X to determine if a pattern emerges in the possible values of Y.

MULTIPLE FUNCTIONS, NESTED FUNCTIONS & PEMDAS

What's a nested function? It's a function-of-a-function. All of the usual rules of the Order of Operations (PEMDAS) apply. Start solving the functions "from the inside out" or "from the innermost parentheses" and work your way outward. See the examples below.

How to Solve Nested Functions	Nested Functions
Given this... *Don't get intimidated! Nested Functions are easier than they look.*	$f(x) = 3x - 2$ $g(x) = 4x^2 - 1$ $h(x) = 2x$
Remember:	• Start from the inside out. • The result of the innermost function becomes the x-value you plug into the next function.
Example question:	If $f(x) = 3x - 2$, $g(x) = 4x^2 - 1$, and $h(x) = 2x$, what is $h\big(f(g(2))\big)$?
Work through each step in the order of operations	$h\big(f(g(2))\big)$ Start with the function g(x), when x = 2 $h\big(f(4 * 2^2 - 1)\big)$ $h\big(f(4 * 4 - 1)\big)$ $h\big(f(16 - 1)\big)$ The result of g(2) = 15. Now, use the function f(x), and solve for when x = 15. $h\big(f(15)\big)$ $h(3 * 15 - 2)$ $h(45 - 2)$ The result of f(15) = 43. Now, use the function h(x), and solve for when x = 43. $h(43)$ 2*43 **=86**

How to Solve Nested Functions	Nested Functions
Given this... *Don't get intimidated! Nested Functions are easier than they look.*	$$a(x) = 2x^2 + 5x$$ $$b(x) = 12 - x$$ $$c(x) = 4x - 10$$
Remember:	• Start from the inside out. • The result of the innermost function becomes the x-value you plug into the next function.
Example question:	If $a(x) = 2x^2 + 5x$, $b(x) = 12 - x$, and $c(x) = 4x - 10$, what is $a(3) - c(b(4))$?
Work through each step in the order of operations *Note: you can actually perform the operations for a(3) and c(8) in the same row, as long as your work is organized. That's not shown here because it would be more complex to explain the simultaneous steps than the table permits.*	$$a(3) - c\big(b(4)\big)$$ Start with the function b(x), when x = 4 $$a(3) - c\big(b(4)\big)$$ $$a(3) - c(12 - 4)$$ $$a(3) - c(8)$$ The result of b(4) = 8. Now, use the function c(x), and solve for when x = 8. $$a(3) - c(8)$$ $$a(3) - (4*8 - 10)$$ $$a(3) - (32 - 10)$$ $$a(3) - (22)$$ The result of c(8) = 22. Now, solve the function a(x), and solve for when x = 3. $$a(3) - (22)$$ $$(2*3^2 + 5*3) - (22)$$ $$(2*9 + 5*3) - (22)$$ $$(18 + 15) - (22)$$ $$(33) - (22)$$ The result of a(3) = 28. Now, combine like terms and solve for your final answer. $$33 - 22 = \mathbf{11}$$

SYMBOL PROBLEMS

What's a symbol problem? A function with a goofy symbol as its name. Think of a symbol problem as "the function formerly known as Prince" (may he rest in peace!). See the examples below.

How to Solve Symbol Problems	Symbol Problem
Given this... *Don't get intimidated! Symbol Problems are easier than they look.*	$A \odot B = 6A - 5B$
Remember:	Match the numbers and corresponding variables using a left-for-left, right-for-right substitution. • The number you'll see on the left of the symbol is the value you substitute for the variable you'll see on the left of the symbol. • The number you'll see on the right of the symbol is the value you substitute for the variable you'll see on the right of the symbol.
Example question:	If $A \odot B = 6A - 5B$, What is $7 \odot 2$?
Using left-for-left substitution, we know A = 7 Using right-for-right substitution, we know B = 2 Plug in A = 7 and B = 2, then solve.	$7 \odot 2 = 6(7) - 5(2)$ $7 \odot 2 = 42 - 10$ $7 \odot 2 = 32$

All Your Word Problems Solved

How to Solve Symbol Problems	Symbol Problem
Given this... *Don't get intimidated! Symbol Problems are easier than they look.*	$$X \diamond Y = 3Y^2 - 4X$$
Remember:	Match the numbers and corresponding variables using a left-for-left, right-for-right substitution. • The number you'll see on the left of the symbol is the value you substitute for the variable you'll see on the left of the symbol. • The number you'll see on the right of the symbol is the value you substitute for the variable you'll see on the right of the symbol.
Example question:	If $X \diamond Y = 3Y^2 - 4X$, Evaluate $-2 \diamond 5$
Using left-for-left substitution, we know X = -2 Using right-for-right substitution, we know Y = 5 Plug in X = -2 and Y = 5, then solve. *Did you notice the trick in this problem? The Y variable comes first in the expression. So, you need to plug Y=5 into that first spot...not the -2!*	$$X \diamond Y = 3(5)^2 - 4(-2)$$ $$X \diamond Y = 3(25) + 8$$ $$X \diamond Y = 75 + 8$$ $$X \diamond Y = 83$$ **Common mistake – incorrect substitution.** Make sure you do not correctly execute the order of operations using the wrong variables!!! Pay close attention to the details! $$X \diamond Y = 3(-2)^2 - 4(5)$$ $$X \diamond Y = 3(4) - 20$$ $$X \diamond Y = 12 - 20$$ $$X \diamond Y = -8$$

MULTIPLE SYMBOL PROBLEMS, NESTED SYMBOL PROBLEMS & PEMDAS

What's a nested symbol problem? Well, it's just like a function-of-a-function, but it's a symbol-problem-of-a-symbol-problem. All the usual rules of the Order of Operations (PEMDAS) apply. Start solving the symbol problems "from the inside out" or "from the innermost parentheses" and work your way outward.

GENERAL SEQUENCE & SERIES NOTATION

You'll need to understand the basic notation for questions about sequences and series. It's helpful if you know not just how these are said aloud, but also what these variables and symbols logically represent.

Variable / Symbol	Said Aloud	What it Represents
a_1	"a sub 1"	The first term in the series
a_2	"a sub 2"	The second term in the series
a_3	"a sub 3"	The third term in the series
a_n	"a sub n"	The *n*th term in the series *N, here, is a variable. If you're asked to find the 13th term in a series, that means you must find a_{13}.*
a_{n-1}	"a sub n minus 1"	The *previous* term in the series
Σ	Sigma	The <u>sum</u> of the terms. Technically speaking, the term <u>sequence</u> refers to the set of terms, and <u>series</u> refers to the sum of the sequence. *Note: lowercase sigma σ, represents standard deviation. You won't see that one on sequences & series questions.*

All Your Word Problems Solved

WHAT KIND OF SEQUENCE IS IT?

When you approach a question about a sequence or series, you will need to determine whether it is arithmetic, geometric, or neither.

Type of Sequence / Series	Definition	Notation & Example
Arithmetic	To find the next term in an arithmetic series, you take the previous term and **add a constant**. *Think of subtraction as "adding a negative"*	Notation: a_1, a_2, a_3,...a_n Examples: 3, 7, 11, 15, 19... a_n First term a_1= 3, and you add a constant k= 4 to find the next term. 55, 50, 45, 40, 35... a_n First term a_1= 55, and you add a constant k= -5 to find the next term. With variables: 12, 16, 20, 24... a_n $a_2 = a_1 + 4$ $a_3 = a_2 + 4$ or $a_1 + 4*(2)$ $a_4 = a_3 + 4$ or $a_1 + 4*(3)$ Formula for the nth term: $a_n = a_1 + k * (n - 1)$ $n^{th}\ term = 1^{st}\ term + hop\ size * (\#\ hops)$

Type of Sequence / Series	Definition	Notation & Example
Geometric	To find the next term in a geometric series, you take the previous term and **multiply by a constant**. *Think of division as "multiplying by a fraction"*	<u>Notation</u>: a_1, a_2, a_3,…a_n <u>Examples</u>: 8, 16, 32, 64… a_n First term a_1= 8, and you multiply by a constant k= 2 to find the next term. 27, -9, 3, -1, 1/3, -1/9… a_n First term a_1= 27, and you multiply by a constant k= -1/3 to find the next term. <u>With variables</u>: 2, 10, 50, 250… a_n $a_2 = a_1 * 5$ $a_3 = a_2 * 5$ or $a_1 * 5^2$ $a_4 = a_3 * 5$ or $a_1 * 5^3$ <u>Formula for the *n*th term</u>: $a_n = a_1 * k^{(n-1)}$ $n^{th} term = 1^{st} term * hop\ size^{\#\ of\ hops}$ To help keep straight your formulas, you can also think about the geometric constant as <u>m</u> instead of <u>k</u>, where <u>m</u> stands for "multiple"

All Your Word Problems Solved

Type of Sequence / Series	Definition	Notation & Example
Neither of the above (this means you should <u>look for patterns</u>)	Use process of elimination to rule out the possibility that something is either arithmetic or geometric. If it's neither arithmetic nor geometric, look for patterns that simplify the required calculations.	<u>Examples</u>: Each term in series Q is defined such that $$a_n = a_{n-1} + \frac{1}{a_{n-1}}$$ Here, the formula indicates that each term is equal to the previous term, plus the fraction of 1 over the previous term. This is **not arithmetic**, because we're not adding a constant. It's also **not geometric**, because we're not multiplying by a constant. If the first term is 3, then the second term is: $$a_2 = a_1 + \frac{1}{a_1} = 3 + \frac{1}{3} = \frac{4}{3}$$ Then the third term will be: $$a_3 = a_2 + \frac{1}{a_2} = \frac{4}{3} + \frac{1}{\frac{4}{3}} = \frac{4}{3} + \frac{3}{4} = \frac{25}{12}$$

FINDING THE SUM OF AN ARITHMETIC SEQUENCE

To determine the sum of any **evenly spaced** sequence, use the following formula:

$$Sum\ of\ arithmetic\ sequence = (Average\ of\ the\ Terms) * (Number\ of\ Terms)$$

What do we mean by "evenly spaced"? An arithmetic sequence.

- Any sequence where you're adding a constant to one term to find the next term.
- Examples of evenly spaced sequences:
  - Consecutive integers (constant k = 1)
  - Consecutive even integers (constant k = 2)
  - Consecutive odd integers (constant k = 2)
  - Positive multiples of 6 (constant k = 6)

How do we find the **average of the terms**?

- Because the sequence is evenly spaced, the average of all the terms in the sequence is equal to the average of the largest and smallest terms.

$$(Average\ of\ the\ Terms) = \frac{(Largest\ +\ Smallest)}{2}$$

How do we find the **number of terms** in the sequence?

$$(Number\ of\ Terms) = \frac{(Largest\ -\ Smallest)}{Hop\ Size} + 1$$

- What's the **hop size**? That's a more memorable term for the constant, k, which you add to one term to find the value of the next term.

- *It's easier to retain and recall formulas quickly and accurately if you learn them in terms of what the variables logically represent, rather than in terms of generic variables. The formulas provided above are equivalent to:*

$$(Average\ of\ the\ Terms) = \frac{(a_n\ +\ a_1)}{2}$$

$$(Number\ of\ Terms) = \frac{(a_n\ -\ a_1)}{k} + 1$$

Using substitution, the complete formula for finding the sum of the terms is:

$$Sum\ of\ sequence = (Average\ of\ the\ Terms) * (Number\ of\ Terms)$$

$$Sum\ of\ sequence = \frac{(Largest\ +\ Smallest)}{2} * \left[\frac{(Largest\ -\ Smallest)}{Hop\ Size} + 1\right]$$

Example #1: Sum of the First N Terms

What is the sum of the first 20 terms of the following sequence? {4, 7, 10, 13...}

Start by finding the nth term (the 20th term):

- Find the first term. $a_1 = 4$
- Find the hop size, by subtracting a term from the one after it.
  - (7-4) = 3 and (10-7) = 3, so our hop size = +3
- We're adding a constant, so this is an arithmetic series.
- Find the 20th term:
  - $a_{20} = a_1 + k*(n\text{-}1)$
  - $a_{20} = 4 + 3*(20\text{-}1) = 4 + 3 * 19 = 61$

Now, use the formula for the sum of the arithmetic sequence:

$$Sum\ of\ sequence = (Average\ of\ the\ Terms) * (Number\ of\ Terms)$$

$$Sum\ of\ sequence = \frac{(Largest\ +\ Smallest)}{2} * \left[\frac{(Largest\ -\ Smallest)}{Hop\ Size} + 1\right]$$

$$Sum\ of\ sequence = \frac{(61\ +\ 4)}{2} * \left[\frac{(61\ -\ 4)}{3} + 1\right]$$

$$Sum\ of\ sequence = \frac{(65)}{2} * \left[\frac{(57)}{3} + 1\right]$$

$$Sum\ of\ sequence = \frac{65}{2} * [19 + 1] = \frac{65}{2} * 20 = \mathbf{650}$$

Example #2: Sum of the First N Terms

What is the sum of the first fifteen positive multiples of 3?

Start by finding the nth term (the 15th term):

- Find the first term. $a_1 = 3$
- The sequence will be {3, 6, 9, 12...}
- Find the hop size by subtracting a term from the one after it.
  - (6-3) = 3 and (9-6) = 3, so our hop size = +3
- We're adding a constant, so this is an arithmetic series.
- Find the 15th term:
  - $a_{15} = a_1 + k*(n-1)$
  - $a_{15} = 3 + 3*(15-1) = 3 + 3 * 14 = 45$

Now, use the formula for the sum of the arithmetic sequence:

$$Sum\ of\ sequence = (Average\ of\ the\ Terms) * (Number\ of\ Terms)$$

We already know the number of terms is 15, so substitute it into the equation:

$$Sum\ of\ sequence = \frac{(Largest\ +\ Smallest)}{2} * [15]$$

$$Sum\ of\ sequence = \frac{(45\ +\ 3)}{2} * [15]$$

$$Sum\ of\ sequence = \frac{(48)}{2} * [15] = 24 * 15 = \mathbf{360}$$

All Your Word Problems Solved

Example #3: Sum of All the Terms From X To Y

What is the sum of all the even integers from 42 to 96?

Start by finding the first term. $a_1 = 42$

- We're adding a constant, so this is an arithmetic series.
- The sequence will be {42, 44, 46…}
- Find the hop size. To find each even integer, you simply add 2 to each term.

Now, use the formula for the sum of the arithmetic sequence:

$$Sum\ of\ sequence = (Average\ of\ the\ Terms) * (Number\ of\ Terms)$$

$$Sum\ of\ sequence = \frac{(Largest\ +\ Smallest)}{2} * \left[\frac{(Largest\ -\ Smallest)}{Hop\ Size} + 1\right]$$

$$Sum\ of\ sequence = \frac{(96\ +\ 42)}{2} * \left[\frac{(96\ -\ 42)}{2} + 1\right]$$

$$Sum\ of\ sequence = \frac{(138)}{2} * \left[\frac{(54)}{2} + 1\right]$$

$$Sum\ of\ sequence = 69 * [27 + 1]$$

$$Sum\ of\ sequence = 69 * [28] = \mathbf{1932}$$

Example #4: How Many Terms Are There Between X and Y?

How many consecutive odd integers are there between 35 and 77?

This question is asking you about the sequence of odd integers from 35 to 77, but you're only asked to find the number of terms, not the sum of them. You can use the partial formula for the number of terms:

- We're adding a constant, so this is an arithmetic series.
- Find the hop size. To find each odd integer, you simply add 2 to each term.
- The largest term is given – 77
- The smallest term is given – 35

$$Number\ of\ Terms = \frac{(Largest\ -\ Smallest)}{Hop\ Size} + 1$$

$$Number\ of\ Terms = \frac{(77\ -\ 35)}{2} + 1 = \frac{42}{2} + 1 = 21 + 1 = \mathbf{22}$$

Example #5: Find the Nth term

What is the 6th term in the sequence? {5, -2, 4/5, -8/25...}

To find the nth term (the 6th term):

- Find the first term. $a_1 = 5$
- Determine what kind of sequence it is.
- It is geometric, because you can find each term by multiplying by a constant.
- Find the constant multiplier, by dividing the 2nd term by the 1st term. (You can pick any pair, dividing a term by the one which comes before it in the sequence).
    - -2 / 5 = -2/5, and 4/5 / -2 = -2/5, so our constant multiplier = -2/5

Find the 6th term:

$$n^{th} \ term = 1^{st} \ term * hop \ size^{\# \ of \ hops}$$

$$a_6 = 5 * \left[-\frac{2}{5}\right]^{(6-1)} = 5 * \left[-\frac{2}{5}\right]^5 = 5 * \frac{-32}{5^5} = \frac{-32}{5^4} = \frac{-32}{625}$$

Example #6: Find the Nth Term

What is the 8th term in the sequence? {9, 18, 36, 72...}

To find the nth term (the 8th term):

- Find the first term. $a_1 = 9$
- Determine what kind of sequence it is.
- It is geometric, because you can find each term by multiplying by a constant.
- Find the constant multiplier, by dividing the 2nd term by the 1st term. (You can pick any pair, dividing a term by the one which comes before it in the sequence).
    - 18/9 = 2, and 36/18 = 2, so our constant multiplier = 2

Find the 8th term:

$$n^{th} \ term = 1^{st} \ term * hop \ size^{\# \ of \ hops}$$

$$a_8 = 9 * [2]^{(8-1)} = 9 * [2]^7 = 9 * 128 = 1152$$

Example #7: Product of the First N Terms

What is the product of the first 12 terms of this sequence, defined for all integers n, such that: $a_n = \dfrac{n}{n+1}$?

First, determine what kind of sequence this is.

- This is <u>not</u> arithmetic, because we are not adding a constant.
- This is <u>not</u> geometric, because we are not multiplying by a constant.
- Because it is neither arithmetic nor geometric, there is most likely a **pattern** which you need to detect, which will simplify the process of calculating the product.

Start by outlining the first few terms, just enough until you detect a pattern:

$$a_1 = \frac{1}{1+1} = \frac{1}{2}$$

$$a_2 = \frac{2}{2+1} = \frac{2}{3}$$

$$a_3 = \frac{3}{3+1} = \frac{3}{4}$$

This continues until we arrive at the 12th term:

$$a_{12} = \frac{12}{12+1} = \frac{12}{13}$$

You've been asked to find the product:

$$\frac{1}{2} * \frac{2}{3} * \frac{3}{4} * \frac{4}{5} \ldots \ldots * \frac{12}{13}$$

Notice a **pattern**? Each numerator after the first one cancels out the denominator of the previous term. All that remains is the first numerator and the last denominator.

$$\frac{1}{\cancel{2}} * \frac{\cancel{2}}{\cancel{3}} * \frac{\cancel{3}}{4} * \frac{4}{\cancel{5}} \ldots \ldots * \frac{\cancel{12}}{13} = \frac{1}{13}$$

WORD PROBLEMS RELATED TO SEQUENCES & SERIES

When you encounter a word problem which gives you information which **describes a pattern**, and provides you another couple pieces of information, and you are asked to find:

- The number of something on the last day, in the last row of a theater, etc.
- The total of all the amounts on each day, in all the rows of a theater, etc.

Then this word problem requires you to apply your knowledge of **sequences & series**. *Cross-reference the sections on Sequences & Series, which discusses the concepts and formulas.*

You will need to use a little commonsense and logic to interpret:

- What is the question asking you to find?
    - The 1st term?
    - The Nth term?
    - The sum of the terms?
- Based on what is given, and what you need to find...
    - Which formula do you use? Then, write it in **Words First, Math Second**.
    - Where does each piece of info fit in the word problem? Then, place each piece of information in the right place in the equation.

Common types of word problems about sequences & series

Read the examples below, all of which are common ways that the major standardized tests ask questions which require students to apply their knowledge of sequences and series to solve for the unknown item. There are variations on each of these themes.

- **Seats in a Theater, Concert Hall, Auditorium, or Classroom**
    - A theater has a certain number of seats in the first row, and each row has (some number) of seats more than the one in front of it. If the last row has (some number) of seats, <u>how many rows of seats</u> are there in the theater? *Variation: Arithmetic Sequence, where you must find the <u>number of terms</u>.*
    - A concert hall has a certain number of seats in the first row, and each row has (some number) of seats more than the one in front of it. If the last row has (some number) of seats, <u>how many total seats</u> are there in the concert hall? *Variation: Arithmetic Sequence, where you must find the <u>sum of terms</u>.*
    - A classroom has a total capacity of (some number). If the last row has (some number) of seats, which is (some number) more than each row in front of it, <u>how many seats are in the front row</u>? *Variation: Arithmetic Sequence, where you must find the <u>first term</u>.*
- **Length of a Fence / Garden Path with pieces and gaps between each piece**

- A fence post is (some number) inches wide. Each fence post is placed (some number) of inches away from the previous fence post. If a fence is to be built in a straight line, what is the longest possible fence which can be made using (some number) of fence posts? *Variation: Arithmetic Sequence. Use the idea of the* <u>*number of hops*</u> *to remind yourself that the number of gaps is one less than the number of fence posts.*

- A garden path is made of square stepping stones, each placed (some number) of centimeters from the previous stepping stone. If each stepping stone is (some number) of centimeters wide, how many stepping stones are needed to construct a garden path which is (some number) of meters long? *Variation: Arithmetic Sequence. Use the idea of the* <u>*number of hops*</u> *to remind yourself that the number of gaps is one less than the number of fence posts. Note: This question also requires you to convert information to consistent units.* See the section on Dimensional Analysis.

- **Unconventional Payments or Rewards, which don't sound good at first**

  - Your boss promises to pay you one penny on your first day of work, two cents on your second day of work, four cents on your third day of work, and so on. How much will you be paid for the 30th day of work? *Variation: Geometric Sequence, because the payment doubles each time. This question asks you to* <u>*find the Nth term*</u>. *Hint: This is an extraordinarily lucrative deal and you should take this offer! Note: This question also requires you to be intentional about how you work with decimals.*

  - One grain of rice is placed on the first square of a checkerboard, which consists of 64 squares. Two grains of rice are placed on the second square. Three grains of rice are placed on the third square. How many grains of rice will there be on the entire checkerboard? *Variation: Arithmetic Sequence, because the number of grains of rice increases by one each time. This question asks you to* <u>*find the sum of terms*</u>.

- **Population growth or decline by a multiplier, a fraction or a percent**

  - A petting zoo acquired (some number) of rabbits. Each month, the number of rabbits doubled. How many rabbits will the petting zoo have at the end of (some number) of months? *Variation: Geometric Sequence, because the number of rabbits doubles each month.*

  - *Note: Think carefully about what to do when you see wording such as "at the* <u>*end of*</u>*...months" or "at the* <u>*start of*</u>*...months." The population at the* <u>*end of 6*</u> *months is the same as it will be at the* <u>*start of 7*</u> *months.*

  - *Note: You could also solve this type of question using the Exponential Growth formula or its simplified version, the Doubling Formula.* Cross-reference the section on Exponential Relationships.

What do the examples shown above have in common? Though the information is presented in a different way each time, these are <u>**all variations of the same thing**</u>.

- You will be presented information which **suggests a consistent pattern**, either adding/subtracting a constant (Arithmetic Sequence) or multiplying/dividing by a constant (Geometric Sequence).

- You will then get information for several of these parts: the **first term**, the **last term**, the **hop size**, and <u>either</u> the **number of terms** or the **number of hops**.

Example #1: Length of a Fence

A fence post is six inches wide. Each fence post is placed 20 inches away from the previous fence post. If a fence is to be built in a straight line, what is the longest possible fence which can be made using 60 fence posts?

Here, we are asked for the total length of the fence.

- **Use the Words First, Math Second approach to construct a simple formula**.

$$Length\ of\ Fence = Width\ of\ All\ Posts + Width\ of\ All\ Gaps$$

- Now, **drill down** to make the formula more detailed, one piece at a time.

    ○ The width of all the posts = the # of posts * the width of each post

    ○ The width of all the gaps = the # of gaps * the width of each gap

$$Length\ of\ Fence = (\#\ of\ Posts * Width\ of\ Each) + (\#\ of\ Gaps * Width\ of\ Each)$$

- Place each piece of information from the word problem into the formula, underneath its corresponding words.

$$Length\ of\ Fence = (60 * 6\ in.) + (\#\ of\ Gaps * 20\ in.)$$

- You're almost there! If we have 60 posts, going in a straight line, how many gaps are there?

    ○ Try working with a few <u>smaller, more manageable numbers</u> of posts to see if you can determine a rule using **patterns, logic, and reasoning**.

    ○ What if there were three posts? You would have two gaps.

    ○ What if there were four posts? You would have three gaps.

    ○ What if there were five posts? You would have four gaps.

    ○ What is the pattern described above? The number of gaps is always one fewer than the number of posts.

    ○ Thus, the number of gaps must be (60-1) = 59.

$$Length\ of\ Fence = (60 * 6\ in.) + (\mathbf{59} * 20\ in.)$$

- Solve for your final answer, obeying the order of operations.

$$Length\ of\ Fence = (360\ in.) + (1180\ in.)$$

$$Length\ of\ Fence = \mathbf{1540\ in.}$$

- Be sure you check if the question asks for your answer in inches or some other units. Use the **dimensional analysis approach** if needed, to convert your answer to feet, yards, or other unit of distance.

$$Length\ of\ Fence = 1540\ in. * \frac{1\ ft}{12\ in} = \mathbf{128.33\ ft} - OR - \mathbf{128\ ft.4\ in.}$$

Example #2: This Job Pays Just Pennies

Your boss promises to pay you one penny on your first day of work, two cents on your second day of work, four cents on your third day of work, and so on. How much will you be paid for your 16th day of work?

Look for a pattern, then determine what type of pattern it is.

- 1st day = 1 cent

- 2nd day = 2 cents

- 3rd day = 4 cents

- Is it an arithmetic pattern? Check if you are adding/subtracting a constant. Your payment grows by 1 cent from the 1st day to the 2nd day, and 2 cents from the 2nd day to the 3rd day. This is <u>not</u> an arithmetic sequence.

- Is it a geometric pattern? Check if you are multiplying/dividing by a constant. Your payment doubles from the 1st day to the 2nd day, and doubles again from the 2nd day to the 3rd day. This <u>is</u> a **geometric sequence**.

Now that you know the question is testing your knowledge of geometric sequences, determine whether you are supposed to find the Nth term or the sum of all the terms.

- The Nth term, in this type of word problem, represents your payment on a single day.

- The sum of the terms, in this type of word problem, represents your total income for N days.

- You are asked for your payment on the 16th day, so you just need to find the 16th term of this sequence. Use the appropriate formula for the **N[th] term of a geometric sequence**.

$$N^{th}\ term = 1st\ term * hop\ size^{\#\ of\ hops}$$

- Place each piece of information from the word problem into the formula, underneath its corresponding words. Remember, the number of hops is always <u>one less</u> than the number of terms.

$$16^{th}\ term = 1\ cent * 2^{(16-1)}$$

- Solve for your final answer, obeying the order of operations. Be mindful of the units!

$$16^{th}\ term = 1\ cent * 2^{(15)}$$

$$16^{th}\ term = 1\ cent * 32,768$$

$$16^{th}\ term = 32,768\ cents$$

- You will probably need to convert this to dollars to find an answer choice.

$$16^{th}\ term = 32,768\ cents * \frac{1\ dollar}{100\ cents} = \$327.68$$

Example #3: Seats in the Concert Hall

A concert hall has 14 seats in the first row, and each row has 2 more seats than the row in front of it. If the last row has 64 seats, how many total seats are there in the concert hall?

Look for a pattern, then determine what type of pattern it is.

- "Each row has <u>two more</u> seats than the row in front of it."

- Using the Words to Math approach, you can translate this to "add 2"

- So, the number of seats in each row = the number in the previous row + 2

- This is an **arithmetic sequence**. Our **hop size** is 2.

Now that you know the question is testing your knowledge of arithmetic sequences, determine whether you are supposed to find the Nth term or the sum of all the terms.

- "How many <u>total seats</u> are there in the concert hall?"

- This question is straightforward. "Total" and "sum" are synonymous. Therefore, you must find the **sum of the terms of an arithmetic sequence**.

Use the appropriate formula for the **sum of the terms of an arithmetic sequence**.

$$Sum\ of\ Terms = Average\ of\ terms * Number\ of\ Terms$$

Now, **drill down** to make the formula more detailed, one piece at a time.

$$Sum\ of\ Terms = \left(\frac{Big + Small}{2}\right) * \left(\frac{Big - Small}{Hop\ Size} + 1\right)$$

$$Sum\ of\ Terms = \left(\frac{\#Last + \#1st}{2}\right) * \left(\frac{\#Last - \#1st}{Hop\ Size} + 1\right)$$

- Place each piece of information from the word problem into the formula, underneath its corresponding words.

$$Sum\ of\ Terms = \left(\frac{64 + 14}{2}\right) * \left(\frac{64 - 14}{2} + 1\right)$$

- Solve for your final answer, obeying the order of operations.

$$Sum\ of\ Terms = \left(\frac{78}{2}\right) * \left(\frac{50}{2} + 1\right)$$

$$Sum\ of\ Terms = 39 * 26 = \textbf{1014 total seats}$$

All Your Word Problems Solved

Example #4: Seats in the Theater

A theater has 36 seats in the first row, and each row has 4 seats more than the one in front of it. If the last row has 200 seats, how many rows of seats are there in the theater?

Look for a pattern, then determine what type of pattern it is.

- "Each row has 4 more seats than the row in front of it."
- Using the Words to Math approach, you can translate this to "add 4"
- So, the number of seats in each row = the number in the previous row + 4
- This is an **arithmetic sequence**. Our **hop size** is 4.

Now that you know the question is testing your knowledge of arithmetic sequences, determine whether you are supposed to find the Nth term or the sum of all the terms.

- "How many rows of seats are there in the theater?"
- The question is not asking you to find the total number of seats, so you do not need to find the sum of the terms of an arithmetic sequence.
- The question gave you the first term and the last term, so we are not solving for the Nth term.
- Here, the question is asking you for the **number of terms**.

To find the number of terms, you can use a **partial formula** from the more complex formula for **sum of the terms of an arithmetic sequence**.

$$Sum\ of\ Terms = Average\ of\ terms * Number\ of\ Terms$$

All we need is the Number of Terms – so ignore the rest. Now, **drill down** to make the formula more detailed, one piece at a time.

$$Number\ of\ Rows = \left(\frac{Big - Small}{Hop\ Size} + 1\right)$$

$$Number\ of\ Rows = \left(\frac{\#Last - \#1st}{Hop\ Size} + 1\right)$$

- Place each piece of information from the word problem into the formula, underneath its corresponding words.

$$Number\ of\ Rows = \left(\frac{200 - 36}{4} + 1\right)$$

- Solve for your final answer, obeying the order of operations.

$$Number\ of\ Rows = \left(\frac{164}{4} + 1\right) = 41 + 1 = \textbf{42 rows}$$

Sometimes, you will encounter math questions on your standardized tests which are unlike anything you've ever seen or been taught to do before and you have no idea what formula to apply.

These "oddball" questions often fall into the category of **Patterns, Logic, and Reasoning**.

CLUES TO USE PATTERNS, LOGIC, AND REASONING

- Your calculator could not produce the desired result.

  o A number is raised to an exponent, and you are asked what the units digit of this would be. *The number and exponent are so ridiculously large that it would **break your calculator** (or give you something like 2.43e+55).*

  o You are given a fraction and its decimal equivalent, and you are asked what the Nth digit after the decimal would be. *That N is a large number like the 35th or 42nd digit. Most calculators do not show that many digits.*

- There are simply too many terms to be written out within the allotted time.

  o You are given an expression for a Sequence of numbers which you determine is neither an Arithmetic Sequence nor a Geometric Sequence. You are asked to find the sum of the first 15 terms or perhaps the product of the first 20 terms. **You clearly cannot be expected to write out all those terms,** *and then calculate an answer, can you?*

HOW CAN YOU APPROACH THESE QUESTIONS?

Choose one or a combination of these approaches:

- Analyze the question and carefully **translate Words to Math**, if relevant.

- **Draw a simple picture** if you believe that will help you visualize the information.

- **Write out the first few terms, to see if a pattern emerges.** Common patterns include:

  o In a sum, there are positives and negatives which will <u>cancel out to zero</u>. Only a few terms will remain, and those are what you need to find the answer.

  o In a product, there are numerators and denominators which will <u>cancel out to one</u>. Only a few terms will remain, and those are what you need to find the answer.

- **Extrapolate from the pattern** to the Nth position using **logic & reasoning**.

Example #1: Huge Exponents

What is the units digit of 17^{42}?

Analyze the question: You must find the **units digit**.

- That's a synonym for the ones place. All the other digits are therefore irrelevant.

- This would **break your calculator**, so this question is testing **patterns**, **logic**, **and reasoning**.

Write out the first few terms, to see if a pattern emerges. Remember, you only care about the **units digit**, so you can use a simple mark to indicate the tens/hundreds/thousands digits which are irrelevant.

- $7^1 = \_7$
- $7^2 = \_9$
- $7^3 = \_3$
- $7^4 = \_1$
- $7^5 = \_7$
- $7^6 = \_9$
- ...and so on.

- You can see the units digits follow a **pattern** of 7, 9, 3, 1; **repeating** every 4th term.

Now, you need to use logic and reasoning. If you were to go 42 places through something that repeated every multiple of 4, then you would go through the 7, 9, 3, 1 sequence 10 times for a total of 40 times, then go 2 more...which would land on the 9.

If this is not obvious to you yet, count off as you go through the list.

- You'll "land on" the 1 on the 4th, 8th, 12th, 16th (every multiple of 4) steps through the list.

- So the 40th power of 17 would have a units digit of 1.

- Thus the 42nd power of 17 means you would start back at the top, and go to the 2nd term in the list, with a units digit of 9.

The units digit of 17^{42} = 9.

Is there a faster way? Yes. This type of question is really a question that combines **patterns**, **logic**, **and reasoning** with **remainders**.

$$\frac{Position}{Length\ of\ Pattern\ Repeat} = Integer\ and\ \boldsymbol{Remainder} = \frac{42nd}{4} = 10\ \boldsymbol{remainder\ 2}$$

The integer tells you how many times the pattern is completed. But that's irrelevant.

The remainder is what matters! The remainder of 2 tells you that you'll choose the term which is 2nd from the start of the pattern. So, the 2nd term in the list has a units digit of 9.

Example #2: Spin the Wheel

A spinner is marked letters a through h, in order. If Joe flicks the spinner clockwise through 1347 tick marks, which letter will it land on?

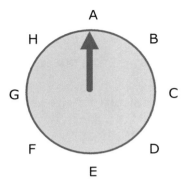

Analyze the question: The spinner needs to go clockwise (from A toward B, not A toward H). You might be thinking "what's a tick mark?" but then you see there are 8 letters marked on the spinner, and apply a little commonsense reasoning, to conclude that going from one letter to the next letter probably means going 1 "tick mark."

- The problem states that the spinner moves 1,347 tick marks in total.
- This is far **too many to count off by hand**, so this question is testing **patterns**.

Start counting off the tick marks to see if a pattern emerges.

- There are 8 letters representing 8 tick marks on the spinner.
- You can extrapolate a **pattern**, which is **repeating** every 8th tick mark.

Now, you need to use logic and reasoning. If you were to go 1347 places through something that repeated every multiple of 8, then you would go through the A through H sequence 168 times for a total of 1344 times, then go 3 more...which would land on the D.

The spinner will land on the letter D.

Is there a faster way? Yes. This type of question is really a question that combines **patterns**, **logic**, **and reasoning** with **remainders**.

$$\frac{Position}{Length\ of\ Pattern\ Repeat} = Integer\ and\ \textbf{Remainder}$$

$$\frac{1347th}{8} = 168.375 = 168\ \textbf{\textit{remainder 3}}$$

The integer tells you how many times the pattern is completed. But that's irrelevant.

The remainder is what matters! The remainder of 3 tells you that you'll choose the term which is the 3rd <u>move</u> from the start of the pattern. So, the 3rd term on the spinner is D.

Example #3: Nth Digit After the Decimal

If 3/7 = 0.4285714285... What is the 35th digit after the decimal equivalent of 3/7?

Analyze the question: You must find the **35th digit after the decimal**.

- After the decimal = toward the right of the decimal. The 1st digit after the decimal is 4, the 2nd digit after the decimal is 2, and so on.

- This would **break your calculator** (which probably only shows 8 to 12 digits total), so this question is testing **patterns, logic, and reasoning**.

Since the first few terms are already written out for you, say them to yourself to determine if a pattern emerges.

- 0.4285714285...

- This decimal appears to repeat again on that second "4285..."

- You can see the digits after the decimal follow a **pattern** of 4, 2, 8, 5, 7, 1; **repeating** every 6th term.

Now, you need to use logic and reasoning. If you wanted to find the 9th digit, then after 6 you would start again at the beginning of the list and go 3 more. If you wanted to find the 17th digit, then after 12 you would start again at the beginning of the list and go 5 more.

What does that <u>3 more</u> or <u>5 more</u> represent? **Remainders**, when you divide the Nth digit by the length of the pattern repeat. This is another form of problems involving remainders!

This type of question is really a question that combines **patterns, logic, and reasoning** with **remainders**.

$$\frac{Position}{Length\ of\ Pattern\ Repeat} = Integer\ and\ \textbf{Remainder}$$

$$\frac{35th}{6} = 5\ remainder\ \textbf{5}$$

The integer tells you how many times the pattern is completed. But that's irrelevant.

The remainder is what matters! The remainder of 5 tells you that you'll choose the term which is 5th from the start of the pattern. The 5th term in the list is 7, so the 35th digit after the decimal equivalent of 3/7 is **7**.

Example #4: Odd Kid Out

A kindergarten class has more than 20 but fewer than 35 students. When the teacher asks the kids to sit at tables with 4 kids per table, there is one table with only 2 kids sitting at it. When the teacher asks the kids to sit at tables with 5 kids per table, there is one table with only 4 kids sitting at it. If the teacher instead asks the kids to sit at tables with 6 kids per table, how many kids are at the table with fewer than 6 kids?

Analyze the question and carefully **translate Words to Math**, if relevant. You will need to break down each statement, one at a time.

- "A kindergarten class has <u>more than</u> 20 <u>but fewer than</u> 35 students."

    o The language "more than X, but fewer than Y" hints that you need a double-ended inequality.

    o Here, "students" and "kids" are synonymous. *Because the logical variable for students, S, often looks like a 5 when you are writing too quickly, you will use kids and the variable K to represent it in the rest of this problem.*

$$20 < Kids < 35$$

- "When the teacher asks the kids to sit at <u>tables with 4 kids per table</u>, there is <u>one table with only 2 kids</u> sitting at it."

    o Here, because the number of kids is divided into some unknown number of groups which are the same size (4 kids per table), you should immediately think about **either Factors/Multiples or Remainders**.

    o **Because exactly 1 table has a different size** (2 kids at this table), you can conclude this question is testing **Remainders**.

    o Let's write an expression to explain this. When you divide the kids into tables of 4, you will have some number of full 4-person tables and 1 table with just 2 kids sitting there.

$$\frac{Kids}{4} = Integer \ with \ Remainder \ 2$$

    - Here, the <u>integer</u> would represent the <u>number of **full tables**</u>
    - The <u>remainder</u> would represent the <u>number of **kids**</u> at the non-full table.

    o Because you are not given a value for the total number of kids, you must think about what values are possible. What are the possible values of K?

      - What if you had zero full tables?

0 full tables *4 kids per table + 2 kids at last table = 2 kids

      - What if you had one full table?

1 full tables *4 kids per table + 2 kids at last table = 6 kids

      - What if you had two full tables?

2 full tables *4 kids per table + 2 kids at last table = 10 kids

All Your Word Problems Solved

- o Let's see if you can extrapolate that pattern. The number of kids could be:
  - Kids could = {2, 6, 10...}
  - Since each term is 4 more than the last, just keep adding 4 to find all the values below 35 which fit the constraint in the statement you are breaking down. You'll then trim off any terms smaller than 20, because Kids must be greater than 20.
  - Kids could = {~~2, 6, 10, 14, 18,~~ **22, 26, 30, 34**}
- "When the teacher asks the kids to sit at <u>tables with 5 kids per table</u>, there is <u>one table with only 4 kids</u> sitting at it."
  - o You already know from the previous statement that this question deals with remainders.
  - o Let's write an expression to explain this. When you divide the kids into tables of 5, you will have some number of full 5-person tables and 1 table with just 4 kids sitting there.

$$\frac{Kids}{5} = Integer \; with \; Remainder \; 4$$

  - Here, the <u>integer</u> would represent the <u>number of **full tables**</u>
  - The <u>remainder</u> would represent the <u>number of **kids** at the non-full table</u>.
  - o Because you are not given a value for the total number of kids, you must think about what values are possible. What are the possible values of K?
    - What if you had zero full tables?

0 full tables *5 kids per table + 4 kids at last table = 4 kids

    - What if you had one full table?

1 full tables *5 kids per table + 4 kids at last table = 9 kids

    - What if you had two full tables?

2 full tables *5 kids per table + 4 kids at last table = 14 kids

  - o Let's see if you can extrapolate that pattern. The number of kids could be:
    - Kids could = {4, 9, 14...}
    - Since each term is 5 more than the last, just keep adding 5 to find all the values below 35 which fit the constraint in the statement you are breaking down. You'll then trim off any terms smaller than 20, because Kids must be greater than 20.
    - Kids could = {~~4, 9, 14, 19,~~ **24, 29, 34**}
- Let's pause for a minute and compare the two lists.
  - o Using the rule with 4 kids per table, Kids could = {**22, 26, 30, 34**}
  - o Using the rule with 5 kids per table, Kids could = {**24, 29, 34**}
  - o The only number which appears in both lists, and therefore meets both constraints, is **34**, so now you know for sure that **Kids = 34**.

- "If the teacher instead asks the kids to sit at tables with 6 kids per table, how many kids are at the table with fewer than 6 kids?"
  - You already know from the previous statements that this question deals with remainders.
  - Let's write an expression to explain this. When you divide the kids into tables of 6, you will have some number of full 6-person tables and 1 table with <u>an unknown number</u> kids sitting there. *Let's call that unknown number Q.*

$$\frac{Kids}{6} = Integer\ with\ Remainder\ Q$$

    - Here, the <u>integer</u> would represent the <u>number of **full tables**</u>
    - The <u>remainder</u> would represent the <u>number of **kids**</u> <u>at the non-full table</u>.
  - Plug in the total number of kids you found from the previous steps, Kids = 34, and find the remainder.

$$\frac{34\ Kids}{6} = 5\ with\ Remainder\ \mathbf{4}$$

  - The remainder = 4, so you know there will be 4 kids sitting at the non-full table.

Example #5: Inconsequential

What is the product of the first 40 terms of sequence J, if each term is defined by this expression? $a_n = \frac{n}{n+2}$

Analyze the question and carefully **translate Words to Math**, if relevant.

- What is the <u>product</u> of the 1st 40 terms of Sequence J... *Cross-reference the sections on Sequences & Series.*

- <u>Product</u> means multiply. So, you can write an expression:

$$Product\ of\ 1st\ 40\ terms = a_1 * a_2 * a_3 * a_4 * a_5 \dots \dots * a_{40}$$

You cannot possibly write out 40 terms in the time allotted, therefore write out the first few terms and **look for a pattern**!

- Since you know you must multiply the terms and there are fractions involved, look for pairs of numerators and denominators which cancel out to 1.

- $Product\ of\ 1st\ 40\ terms = \frac{1}{3} * \frac{2}{4} * \frac{3}{5} * \frac{4}{6} * \frac{5}{7} * \dots \dots * \frac{40}{42}$

Now, **extrapolate from the pattern**. Look for ways to simplify and solve.

- If you notice, the numerators start at 1 and go up to 40. The denominators start at 3 and go up to 42.

  - So, for every number between 3 and 40, there is both a numerator and a denominator which will cancel out.

  - Which numerators will remain, if you do all the easy cancelling? 1 and 2.

  - Which denominators will remain, if you do all the easy cancelling? 41 and 42.

  - Then, do additional cancelling if needed.

- $Product\ of\ 1st\ 40\ terms = \frac{1}{3} * \frac{2}{4} * \frac{3}{5} * \frac{4}{6} * \frac{5}{7} * \dots \dots * \frac{39}{41} * \frac{40}{42} = \frac{1*2}{41*42} = \frac{1*1}{41*21} = \frac{1}{861}$

Note, the test maker could offer the correct answer in the answer choices using either of two forms, the simplified expression or the final numeric answer. Make sure you check which form you need to find. Both of these are correct:

- $Product\ of\ 1st\ 40\ terms = \frac{1*2}{41*42}$

- $Product\ of\ 1st\ 40\ terms = \frac{1}{861}$

Example #6: Everybody High Five!

When 3 friends each high-five one another, there are a total of 3 high-fives. When 4 friends each high-five one another, there are a total of 6 high-fives. How many total high-fives are there if 5 friends each high-five one another?

Analyze the question. This is not *obviously* math-related, so there may be a pattern.

Drawing a picture might help you conceptualize what's happening. Using letters to "name" each of the friends can also help. Then draw lines to connect the letters to help visualize the "high-fives" and see that when A high-fives B, it's the same as when B high-fives A.

- 3 friends each high-five each other, and there are 3 high-fives (and 3 lines):

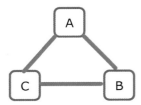

- 4 friends each high-five each other, and there are 6 high-fives (and 6 lines):

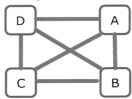

This word problem is really describing a **Combinatorics** scenario, where each high-five represents a pair of people chosen from the overall group. *Cross-reference the sections on Permutations & Combinations.*

- Because when A high-fives B, it's the same thing when B high-fives A, you can conclude that **order does not matter**, so you should use the **Combinations** formula. Here your number of options **N = 5**, and number chosen **K = 2**.

$$Total\ High-Fives = \quad _5C_2 = \frac{n!}{k!\,(n-k)!} = \frac{5!}{2!\,(5-2)!} = \frac{5*4*\cancel{3!}}{2*1*\cancel{3!}} = 10\ high-fives$$

- However, because the number of options involved is so small, it is possible to arrive at the right answer by drawing it. Use the same approach as the diagrams above, and make sure there is a line connecting each pair of letters, then count the lines which represent each high-five. Total lines = 10, so **total high-fives = 10**.

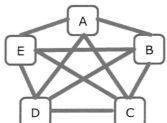

UNDERSTANDING THE TRIPLE VENN DIAGRAM

To understand how to solve questions using the Triple Venn Diagram on the GMAT, it's important to first get a background understanding of <u>why</u> certain relationships are true, and that requires establishing clarity on what certain terms mean, so that you can correctly **translate words-to-math.** *If you are not taking the GMAT, skip this section.*

Note: **This section is pretty dense and you may need to read it a few times to fully understand it**, because it's providing you with the <u>proof</u> for the two formulas found at the end of the section. Once you understand the "why" then you can know when to just use those two formulas at the end of the section.

Suppose there's a cool new burger restaurant in town. Before opening, the restaurant surveys 250 potential customers to find out how many of them like avocado, bacon, and/or cheddar on their burgers.

Let's also suppose you're given the following info, for your analysis. The number of customers who like each topping is as follows: Avocado = 50; Bacon = 120; Cheddar = 200

Of course, some customers will like all three of these; others will like two but not all three; and some will like either just one or none.

This means that the number of people who like avocado, 50, is really the sum of:

*   People who only like avocado, and do not like bacon or cheddar (A only)
*   People who like avocado and bacon, but not cheddar (AB)
*   People who like avocado and cheddar, but not bacon (AC)
*   People who like all three of these toppings (ABC)

This means that the number of people who like bacon, 120, is really the sum of:

*   People who only like bacon, and do not like avocado or cheddar (B only)
*   People who like avocado and bacon, but not cheddar (AB)
*   People who like bacon and cheddar, but not avocado (BC)
*   People who like all three of these toppings (ABC)

This means that the number of people who like cheddar, 200, is really the sum of:

*   People who only like cheddar, and do not like avocado or bacon (C)
*   People who like avocado and cheddar, but not bacon (AC)
*   People who like bacon and cheddar, but not avocado (BC)
*   People who like all three of these toppings (ABC)

Uh-oh! If you look at those lists, you will realize that if we simply find the sum of 50+120+200, then we'll **double-count the people who like exactly two** of the three ingredients, and we'll **triple-count the people who like all three**.

Let's explore that visually.

VISUALIZING THE TRIPLE VENN DIAGRAM

Section Descriptor	What It Includes
Green circle	Total number of people who like avocado
Purple circle	Total number of people who like bacon
Orange circle	Total number of people who like cheddar
A-only top portion of green circle	People who only like avocado, and do not like bacon or cheddar
B-only left portion of purple circle	People who only like bacon, and do not like avocado or cheddar
C-only right portion of orange circle	People who only like cheddar, and do not like avocado or bacon
AB	People who like avocado and bacon, but not cheddar
AC	People who like avocado and cheddar, but not bacon
BC	People who like bacon and cheddar, but not avocado
ABC Center section of diagram	People who like <u>all</u> three of these toppings
Outside the diagram	People who like <u>none</u> of these three toppings

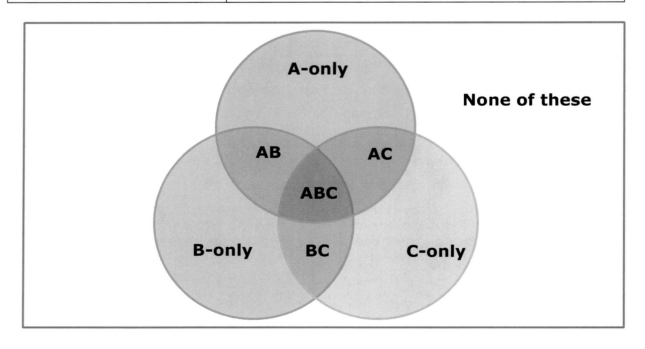

All Your Word Problems Solved

Remember, if we simply find the sum of 50+120+200, then we'll **double-count the people who like exactly two** of the three ingredients, and we'll **triple-count the people who like all three.**

- Sections AB, AC, and BC are all the "doubles" (people who like exactly 2 of the 3)
- Section ABC contains the "triples" (people who like all 3)

SOLVING THE TRIPLE VENN DIAGRAM

Now let's look at some formulas! You'll need to use two formulas, a bit of extra information, and then solve as a system of equations.

Here's one of the formulas. Note: The 3 rows in white address each of the 3 items individually. The rows highlighted in purple and green show how those rows sum up to a couple different ways of viewing the same information. The purple row shows the sum of each distinct column from the white rows; then, the green row restates what's in the purple row in simpler terms. For example, instead of **2AB+2BC+2AC**, we can restate this information as simply **2*Doubles**. *(like a proof – you don't need to do all this work on the test, but you need to understand why the 3-part Venn works the way it does).*

Given	=	Singles			+	Doubles			+	Triples
A	=	A only			+	AB		AC	+	ABC
B	=		B only		+	AB	BC		+	ABC
C	=			C only	+		BC	AC	+	ABC
A+B+C	=	A only +	B only +	C only	+	2AB +	2BC +	2AC	+	3ABC
A+B+C	=	1* Pop w/1 attribute -or- 1*Single			+	2*Pop w/2 attributes -or- 2*Double			+	3*Pop w/ 3 att. -or- 3*Triple

Here's the other formula you'll need.

Given	=	Singles	+	Doubles	+	Triples
Actual number of people	=	1* Pop w/1 attribute -or- 1*Single	+	1*Pop w/2 attributes -or- 1*Double	+	1*Pop w/ 3 att. -or- 1*Triple

Now, let's go back to the information given. We know that:

- Actual number of people = 250
- Avocado = 50
- Bacon = 120
- Cheddar = 200

Generally, then, the test maker will give you either:

- The total number of people who liked exactly 2 things (the "doubles", which is the sum of AB+BC+AC), or
- The number of people who liked all 3 things (the "triples")

If you're given the number of **doubles**, you'll be asked to solve for the triples. The reverse is also true. If you're given the number of **triples**, you'll be asked to solve for the doubles.

Be careful! Make sure you do not forget about the people who chose "**none of these**" and make sure to subtract them from the actual number of people. If the question tells you that "all survey respondents liked at least one of these toppings" then you know that the size of the population outside your triple Venn diagram will be zero.

Now, let's add this to the given info:

- All survey respondents liked at least one of the three toppings.
- 60 people liked exactly 2 of the 3 toppings.
- You're asked to solve for the number of people who like all 3 toppings.

We'll use the two formulas highlighted in green, from the tables above, and plug in the info we have.

Given	=	Singles	+	Doubles	+	Triples
A+B+C	=	1*Single	+	2*Double	+	3*Triple
Actual number of people	=	1*Single	+	1*Double	+	1*Triple

All Your Word Problems Solved

CHAPTER 32 CLOSING

Congratulations! You have finished the entire book and have learned quite a few new approaches for solving complex word problems along the way.

The next task at hand is to practice applying these approaches to a sufficient number of problems for your specific standardized test. As you gain experience applying the strategies in **All Your (Word) Problems, Solved** to solve different variations of questions about each of these topics, you will gain a tremendous amount of confidence in yourself and your math abilities!

The hardest problems you'll see on your test are those which combine multiple topics. Just remember, the difficulty comes in recognizing which topics are in play, outlining an approach, and working through a few more steps than usual. You may find, as many of my former students have, that this book has changed your relationship with math for the better and changed the way you think.

If you'd like to reach out to this book's author to share your success story or to engage her for additional one-on-one assistance, contact her at:

coachinginquiry@sparkadeptation.com

Given	=	Singles	+	Doubles	+	Triples
50+120+200	=	1*Single	+	2*60	+	3*Triple
250	=	1*Single	+	1*60	+	1*Triple

Using the order of operations, simplify and isolate the variables on one side, values on the other.

Given	=	Singles	+	Doubles	+	Triples
370	=	1*Single	+	120	+	3*Triple
250	=	1*Single	+	60	+	1*Triple

250	=	1*Single	+		+	3*Triple
190	=	1*Single	+		+	1*Triple

Now, you've only got just two variables and two equations, so you can solve as a system of equations. Take the first equation and subtract the second one.

250	=	1*Single	+		+	3*Triple
- 190	=	- 1*Single	+		+	-1*Triple
60	=					2*Triple

Now you know 60 = 2*Triple, so we arrive at our final answer:

Triple = 30